Greece: The Magic Spring

BOOKS BY JOHN A. CROW

Greece: The Magic Spring
Spain: The Root and the Flower
Italy: A Journey through Time
Mexico Today
The Epic of Latin America

Greece:
The Magic Spring

John A. Crow

1817

Harper & Row, Publishers
New York,
Evanston, and London

Grateful acknowledgment is made for permission to reprint excerpts from the following sources:

The Orestes Plays of Aeschylus, translated by Paul Roche. Copyright © 1963 by Paul Roche. Reprinted by permission of New American Library, Inc., New York.

Aristotle, Horace and Longinus, translated by T. S. Dorsch. Copyright © 1965 by T. S. Dorsch. By permission of the translator and Penguin Books, Middlesex, England.

Introduction by John Finley to *The Complete Writings of Thucydides.* New York, Modern Library, 1951. By permission of the author.

The Greek Ideal and Its Survival by Moses Hadas. Copyright © 1960 by Moses Hadas. By permission of Harper & Row, Publishers.

The Iliad of Homer, translated by Ennis Rees. Copyright © 1963 by Ennis Rees. Reprinted by permission of Random House, Inc. and the translator.

The Odyssey by Homer, translated by Robert Fitzgerald. Copyright © 1961 by Robert Fitzgerald. Reprinted by permission of Doubleday & Company, Inc.

The Odyssey of Homer, translated by Richmond Lattimore. Copyright © 1965, 1967 by Richmond Lattimore. By permission of Harper & Row, Publishers.

Greek Realities by Finley Hooper. Copyright © 1967 by Finley Hooper. Reprinted by permission of the author and the publishers, Charles Scribner's Sons, New York.

Report to Greco by Nikos Kazantzakis. Copyright © 1965 by Simon & Schuster, Inc. Reprinted by permission of the publishers.

The Greeks by H. D. F. Kitto, Copyright 1951 by H. D. F. Kitto. Reprinted by permission of the author.

Poems from the Greek Anthology by Kenneth Rexroth. Copyright © 1962 by the University of Michigan. Reprinted by permission of the University of Michigan Press, Ann Arbor.

FIRST EDITION

LIBRARY OF CONGRESS CATALOG CARD NUMBER: 73–88636

TO ROSE GORDEN

Contents

Prologue: A Journey Through Time   xi

I.   Aegean Dawn: The Dark Beginning   1

II.   The First Greeks Arrive   12

III.   Homer and the Age of Heroes   31

IV.   The Trojan War   42

V.   The World of Odysseus   58

VI.   The Flower of Youth: The Greeks Look Westward   73

VII.   Rise of the City-State   84

VIII.   The Burgeoning Vine: Athens and Sparta   102

IX.   The Persian and Peloponnesian Wars   118

X.   The Resurrected Gods: Religion and Literature   134

XI.   The Idealized Image: The Visual Arts   156

XII.   Greek Humanism   197

XIII.   The Universal State   219

XIV.   The Greek Renaissance   238

XV.   Greece Today: The Imprisoned Splendor   253

Appendix: Concerning Translations   279

Bibliography   283

Index   287

Illustrations

Stele of Hegeso   xvi
Santorini today   14
Entrance to Mycenaean beehive tomb   16
Beehive tomb at Mycenae   17
Bronze dagger   19
Gold cup from Vaphio   21
Second gold cup from Vaphio   21
Lion Gateway at Mycenae   25
Theater and columns of Temple of Apollo, Delphi   29
Temple at Segesta   97
Relief on base from Mantinea   111
Theater at Epidaurus   145
Orchestra and stage of theater at Epidaurus   145
Red-figured crater   160
Kouros from Sounion   167
Charioteer at Delphi   170
Head of charioteer   171
Bronze Poseidon   172
Head of Poseidon   173
Boy of Marathon   174
Young Greek man, sometimes called Paris   175
Apollo, Temple of Zeus at Olympia   176
Hermes with infant Dionysus   178
Funeral stele of Ctesileos and Theano   182
Temple of Hephaestus   185
Temple of Athena Nike on the Acropolis   187
The Mourning Athena   189
View of the Acropolis   190

The Parthenon   190
The Parthenon   191
Panathenaeic procession on Parthenon frieze   192
The Erechtheum   194
Temple of the Olympian Zeus, Athens   195

Note

Translations of poetic passages not otherwise identified are by the author.

See the note on translations in the Appendix.

Prologue:
A Journey Through Time

Pass me the sweet earthenware jug,
Made of the earth that bore me,
*The earth that someday I shall bear.**

Zonas

As the good ship *Renaissance* plowed through the blue Aegean we retraced man's lost steps in this fairest of all waters. We had come from Corfu, where legend says Odysseus landed after seventeen days on a raft at sea; we sailed then through the straits of Messina (Scylla and Charybdis) and visited in turn a dozen of the Grecian islands: Rhodes, beside whose harbor once rose the colossal Apollo of bronze; Thasos, the green island, dotted with pine trees and archaic ruins; Cos, under whose spreading plane tree Hippocrates asked his apprentices to take the medical oath still taken by doctors the world over; shining Mykonos, which today's tourists have made into the Greenwich Village of Greece; Delos, the sacred island of ancient Hellas, where Greeks from every *polis* came to worship at temples to Apollo and to Dionysus that symbolized the duality of the old pagan religion . . . the rocky shoals of Patmos . . . Santorini (the Thera of legend), whose volcano destroyed the fabulous Minoan palaces of Crete . . . Chios, where Homer was born . . . *Backward, ever backward turned the luminous wheel, as we were brought very near to the dark beginning. In this chapter we will remember only you, lone Patmos, whose breathing rock embodies so well the spirit of eternal Greece . . .*

Patmos, a scarred mountain that rises sharply from the sea, is one of the most beautiful of all Grecian islands. According to tradition the Apostle

* From *Poems from the Greek Anthology* translated by Kénneth Rexroth.

John was exiled to Patmos in the first century; he is reputed to have written the Book of Revelation in a grotto halfway up the mountain. The surrounding sea is incomparably blue and can be seen from any point on the island. On top of the highest point is the old monastery of St. John the Theologian; a recent earthquake has peeled off some plaster and revealed ancient twelfth-century frescoes underneath. The Greek who drove us up and down the mountain was singing all the way; it was a wild and almost unmelodious song. He was obviously compelled to sing, as Greek men are often compelled to rise and dance when the music stirs them, or to hurl their glassware against the tavern wall in a drinking bout.

At the monastery we met a young man from Birmingham, Alabama, who had come to Patmos to study for the Greek Orthodox priesthood. No acceptable training for this career exists in the United States. His young sad face contrasted abruptly with those of the black-robed, black-bearded priests who silently roamed about. We were given a folder which asked for contributions to the Patmos hospital whose construction was under way. The folder said: "The island of Patmos lacks even an elementary hospital in which it might be possible to administer first aid to those in need of immediate medical attention. The lack of transport facilities, the long distances and the inclement weather conditions put the health and life of the inhabitants of Patmos in continuous jeopardy, and as a result many of the islanders have failed to avoid an untimely and unnecessary death."

The simple statement concluded with these words: "The Committee in its wish to express its gratitude to donators of over 7,000 *drachmas* (about $230.00), has decided to inscribe their names with golden letters on a special plaque to be placed in the entrance of the Hospital." Precarious immortality for a handful of silver.

On the way down the mountain our driver stopped three times to exchange conversation with passing friends. This island was warm and friendly. My wife and I began to compare Patmos with Mykonos and Delos. We had just come from Delos, the sacred island, whose acres of ruins and unpopulated rock mark the very center of the Cyclades. Nearby Mykonos, with its gleaming windmills, houses and tiny Byzantine chapels emerging from the treeless earth, stood at the opposite pole. It is one of the most "in" of the Greek islands today and is thickly populated with tourists, foreign residents, hippies.

Halfway down the slope we got out of the car and walked toward the sacred grotto. The linked inlets below and the white houses shone in the bright sun. Patmos had a beauty all its own; even in the hills and in the water there was a resigned serenity. We stopped to take in the view; there was no sound except the voice of our driver who was still humming a song. The air was luminous and for a brief moment time had suspended its onward flow. Suddenly my wife began to sob. She took out her handkerchief and softly touched her face, but made no attempt to hide the tears.

"They came so close," she said. "They came so very close. They almost had the secret, but now it is all gone. I can feel the blood of these people coming up through the rocks and earth. I see them living, working, dying, never leaving Patmos. There is something terribly sad about all this."

I made no answer. What answer was there to make? Silently we descended the stairs over which grew an immense purple bougainvillaea, and entered the grotto. We saw where St. John was said to have rested his head in a hollow of the rock as he slept on the hard stone floor. Above where he used to lie the ceiling of the grotto was split into three clearly outlined enormous stones. "This cleavage was a sign of the holy trinity," we were told.

We examined with proper deference the icons on the grotto wall and then walked back to the waiting car. Our driver, who resembled a gnarled olive tree, greeted us with his imperturbable song. We looked at the sky, and it was unalloyed. The sun was the sun of Greece, blistering and bright. The red flowers seemed redder than before, and the mountains that were everywhere were floating across a sterility of blue. All of the colors breathed with light. We got into the car and drove down the hill and into the town. In the harbor our ship was waiting for us like a proud, white bird.

Greek literature does not stress either love or beauty. It is mainly tragic and sees man caught like a bird in the net of time. But occasionally, as in the poems of *The Greek Anthology,* a collection that spans several centuries, both love and beauty do appear, almost in flashes, as if the Greeks were afraid to linger on such emotions lest they be defiled. This repressed emotional tone gives to Greek love poetry the same serenity which is found in the finest Greek art.

> *Take off your clothes and lie down*
> *We are not going to last forever.**

This could easily be a folk couplet, springing from some age-old song; it catches the Greek attitude completely. The same urgency to live is embodied in these lines:

---

* This and the following three brief poems were translated by Kenneth Rexroth in *Poems from the Greek Anthology.*

Pass me the sweet earthenware jug,
Made of the earth that bore me,
The earth that someday I shall bear.

The Greeks had no use for anyone who wasted the precious gift of life. Greek sorrow was likewise never diluted, nor was it ever exaggerated in order to give balm to the living. On a gravestone at Corinth is this epitaph:

This little stone, dear Sabinos,
Is all the memorial
Of our great love. I miss you
Always, and I hope that you
Did not drink forgetfulness
Of me when you drank the waters
Of death with the new dead.

On an anonymous tomb appear the following lines, even more succinct than those above, and in the same sharp focus:

I grew from the earth.
I flourished in my day.
I am earth again.
My name was Aristokles,
The son of Menon,
A citizen of Piraeus.

Sappho of Lesbos, of whose poetry only a few scattered fragments remain, wrote most movingly about the pangs of love. Sappho lived in the sixth century B.C. and was the most loved of all Greek lyric poets.

My tongue is gone, I feel the tingling fire
Of love in all my veins, I cannot see;
The noise of roaring waves has deafened me.

Sappho also wrote the following epitaph for a girl she had known:

This is the dust of Timias
Who died unmarried,
And went into the Dark.

To mourn her death
The girls who were her friends
Cut off their lovely hair,
And laid it on her grave.

To cut off one's hair and place it on the grave was to leave a part of oneself with the person who had died, the only part which could be amputated and would in time grow back again. In such a manner did the ancient Greeks acknowledge the endless chain of life.

The Greek stelae, those upright slabs of stone which marked the early tombs, have caught and preserved this feeling in visual form for the succeeding centuries. Both in their inscriptions and in their simple carved reliefs they represent, perhaps to a more profound degree than any other Greek expression, that reserve and restraint of emotion which is so characteristic of Greek sculpture of the classical period. The inscriptions were never overwritten, as were so many of a later day, thus revealing more of the vanity and guilt of the survivors than of their grief. The Greek artist transubstantiated man's instinct for immortality into art.

The most common inscription was a simple Xáipe, or "farewell," and the most common relief was a simple parting scene, often of exquisite beauty. The sorrow was implicit, repressed. In the Archaic period these funeral reliefs were carved against a background of red; in the classical period the background became blue, the color of infinity. The Greeks felt a far deeper and more hopeless sorrow than any Christian sorrow.* But grief was passing; life and death went on unabated. Out of them man created his own nobility, which was his measurement and his value. The essence of the Greek attitude toward life was the Golden Mean, which was a Greek way of thinking long before it was Christian.

No one knew the weaknesses of this mortal clay better than Homer, who began Western literature. In the *Iliad* he puts it in these words:

Man was made to live in discontent, while the gods have no sorrow.
There are two urns beside the throne of Zeus: one urn of evils,
And one of blessings. If Zeus mingles these together,
And doles them out to a man, he wavers between good and bad fortune;
But if his deal comes wholly from the urn of sorrows,
That man is evil to the core, and a vile hunger drives him
Endlessly over the shining earth, where he is a wanderer
Honored by neither gods nor men.

There were popular undercurrents in Greece that strove to change this hardened view, but not until the time of Socrates and Plato did the educated Greek begin to believe that man had a measure of free will and a soul. And by this time Oriental mysticism had permeated the heart of

* This theme is expounded in J. P. Mahaffy's *Rambles and Studies in Greece.*

Harissiadis

*Stele of Hegeso, the seated lady who is dead. Her servant, wearing clothes that
indicate her station, has brought the lady's jewels so that she may dress well for
her departure. The serving girl is told not to weep. Date, circa 400 B.C.
Athens, National Museum.*

Greek philosophy, which was already on its way to becoming Christian four centuries before the birth of Christ.

When we think of Greece we must think of ourselves. There is a continuum in the history of mankind which goes back to one common root. In our Western culture that root is Hellenic. We will make an attempt to trace its growth, and to find something of ourselves in its growing.

I

Aegean Dawn: The Dark Beginning

> *There is a land called Crete,*
> *In the midst of the wine-dark sea,*
> *A fair, rich land surrounded by water,*
> *Inhabited by men and women without number,*
> *With ninety cities, and a confusion of languages.**
>
> Homer, *The Odyssey*

There is no place on earth more beautiful than where the hills of Greece emerge from the sun-swept waters of the Aegean suggesting the firmament of Genesis. It was on this land, bathed by the wine-dark sea, that mankind experienced his most glorious moment of creativity. Greece was the magic spring whose waters gave life to all the branches of Western civilization. The purpose of this book is to follow the main currents of that Greek story from its dark beginning, through its Archaic, Classic, Hellenistic, and Roman stages, on up to the imprisoned splendor that is Greece today.

There is hardly an institution or an idea in our civilization which was not Greek at its source. *Astronaut* is a Greek term, and so is *democracy*. *Politics* also is Greek, as are *psychology, economy, theology, history, cosmetics, marathon,* and *microbiology*. Greece gave us the two greatest epics in world literature, the *Iliad* and the *Odyssey,* which marked out paths followed ever since by the greatest Western writers. The Greeks also invented tragedy and comedy, and the Greek playwrights Aeschylus, Sophocles, Euripides, and Aristophanes produced a corpus of dramatic literature unique in the history of the world. Greek architects constructed great outdoor theaters with superlative acoustics for the performance of these works.

* Adapted from Butcher and Lang.

The Greeks also created the first academies, the physician's caduceus, the emblem of medicine, the Hippocratic oath, the Olympic Games, the principles of geometry, the gymnasium, and the mariner's astrolabe. They saw the necessity of catharsis for every man, and they developed to a high degree cosmetics for women. By combining mathematics with art they originated one of the most beautiful styles of architecture the world has ever known (Greek Classic), which our beautiful Lincoln Memorial has copied almost without change. They chiseled the finest sculpture, cast beautiful statues in bronze, painted admirable pictures, and of course the eternal myths which became the core of so much later religious, psychological, and literary thinking were all Greek.

The Greeks understood the harmony and fullness of human life perhaps more completely than any other people in history. They were pre-eminent in the creation of beauty and in the search for truth. They gave us the greatest philosophers and the world's most brilliant general, the father of medicine, and the father of history. The New Testament was written in Greek, and services of the early Christian Church were held in Greek. Roman culture emerged from the Hellenistic, and the Renaissance found its inspiration in these Greco-Roman roots. Our own constitution strongly reflects Greek political thinking. Many of us, from childhood on, are taught to "work like a Trojan," to take pride in a "Spartan" fortitude under adversity, to follow the "Socratic" method of teaching and inquiry, to be "skeptical" about new ideas, to acknowledge "erotic" and "platonic" love, to admire the "symmetry" of art, or to be long-range "idealists." In brief, whenever we act or think, create or feel, organize social forces or probe into the human "psyche," we follow a pattern established by the inimitable and omnipresent Greeks who were the fountainhead of our culture.

When and how did this culture begin? The written record of a civilization begins with a known focal point in history, but this is only the visible beginning. In nature strange roots, strong nutriment, and cross pollination all combine to produce a new flower. The civilizations of mankind follow a similar course, then appear suddenly out of nowhere, like the springtime of a year.

The beginnings of Greek civilization are lost in the preceding unwritten centuries. History had not yet been invented, but geography does not argue. The small Greek peninsula, with its hundreds of islands, stood at the crossroads of the Mediterranean world where from time immemorial it had absorbed wave after wave of migrant peoples. The Greece of 5000 B.C., with its unknown language (called Pelasgian, but undecipherable) and its primitive way of life, was about as un-Greek as Indian America in A.D. 1400 was unlike the present United States.

The arrival of the first Greek-speaking peoples in the peninsula around 2000 B.C. is one obvious starting point for Hellenic history, because without their glorious language there would have been no Classic Greece. But these first speakers of Greek were barbarians, and they might never have become civilized, or they might have become civilized in a very different way, if they had not confronted, fought, and mingled with the older inhabitants of the land, the very primitive Pelasgians and the already civilized Minoans, whose main centers were on the island of Crete.

The Minoans provide the second element in early Greek history. They occupied at least a part of Hellas before the Greeks, and before the Greeks they produced a culture which was the bedrock of everything that followed. The third component in Greek civilization was the dwelling place, the land itself, a land of beauty and sunlight, punctuated by mountains and rimmed by the sea, a hard and flinty land whose mild climate was propitious for supporting life, at first with wild honey, flocks and herds, and later more amply with fields of barley and wheat, the olive and the vine, and fish from the sea. Man, experience, and dwelling place mingled in a dynamic and harmonious mold; two different but adaptable peoples in confrontation, conflict, then spinning out their history in fertile lovemaking, intertwined, blended; in such a manner did this new culture and new way of life arise in history and march boldly toward the sun.

Climate and geography may not make a civilization, but they contribute strongly in the delineation of its nature. A mountain folk have never had the attitudes, the beliefs, the particular creative feelings of a seafaring race. A desert or a jungle people would be different from either. In the land of Hellas man could live outdoors most of the year and he was never far from the sea. His soil was a thin crust of earth from which the farmer could scarcely coax a living, while the shepherd could easily flourish. It was a land bedded with stones available in abundance for the construction of houses, fences, and temples. It was a land of high mountains and of shadowed islands, a natural dwelling place for the gods. No spot was more than ten miles from the mountains or more than fifty miles from the sea.

It was the sea that made Greek civilization possible. Civilization, indeed, came first to the islands, which like jewels star-scattered by the gods dotted the Aegean. "There is a land called Crete, in the midst of the wine-dark sea, a fair, rich land surrounded by water, inhabited by men and women without number, with ninety cities, and a confusion of languages." Thus sang Homer eight centuries before Christ. He was referring to a civilization about which he knew far less than we. To Homer it was simply a golden age when men were greater than they were in his own discordant times. A dream, perhaps, but the dream was true.

All this was a far cry from fifth-century Athens where the energies of more than two thousand years were finally focused to produce the miracle of Classic Greece. Athens itself was a sea power, and she defeated the Persians on the sea, thus saving Greece from Asiatic domination. The sea was the great highway in those days when roads were almost unknown; in fact, the Greek word for sea was *pontos,* which means "the road."

Both the *Iliad* and the *Odyssey* were told against a background of ships and of long sea voyages. The sea was an element in the religion and in the daily lives as well as in the literature of the people. "Here we sit like frogs around a pond," Plato wrote around 400 B.C. He knew these salt highways well and sailed on them to Syracuse in Sicily in order to help the ruler of that city establish a government controlled by the philosophers. Men being what they are, the venture failed.

The Greeks had a deep strong love for their native state, small and cramped as this inevitably was, for there was never a united Greek nation. Mycenae, Ithaca, Miletus, Athens, Sparta, Thebes, Corinth, Syracuse—and many, many more, each had its patriotism, its pantheon, its philosophy, and its art. Odysseus longed twenty years for his native land, the island of Ithaca. When Agamemnon returned to Mycenae from Troy "his heart rejoiced as he set foot again on his native soil, he touched the earth with his hand, and kissed it, and the hot tears streamed from his eyes." Oedipus, driven from Thebes, wandered like a grieving ghost until his dying day. Socrates found exile from Athens more bitter than death.

Our story begins on the island of Crete, in the epoch of prehistory, around 3000 B.C., for it was on this island that the land of Hellas produced its first bright glow: the Minoan culture. The name, of course, was given later, and was derived from that of the famous Cretan kings, called Minos. This word doubtless referred to the kingship rather than to any individual king, being the Cretan equivalent of Pharaoh or Emperor. Minoan (or early Aegean) culture was an extension of that of Asia Minor or Egypt, or both. Most likely it was an offshoot of a fairly generalized prehistoric culture of the early Mediterranean peoples. In Crete a nucleus of these people lived in peace, unmolested by invaders for the many centuries it took them to outdistance their neighbors. Their challenge was the sea; their response was the creation of an island culture amid the valleys and forest-clad Cretan hills, from whence it spread to the mainland of Greece.

The first inhabitants of Crete belonged to the early Mediterranean race; during the Stone Age they were the same folk who lived in Sicily and perhaps in faraway Spain. Around 3000 B.C. users of bronze arrived from Asia Minor and took control of the island. The mixture of these two stocks produced a short, swarthy people, with dark eyes, fine features, and extremely narrow waists, quite unlike the taller, fairer Greek-speaking invaders who poured into the peninsula from the north many centuries later.

Minoan culture, therefore, great as it was during its long heyday, was not Greek any more than the Etruscan culture of ancient Italy was Roman. The Minoans did not speak Greek; their language is still unidentified, but it was almost surely a Semitic (like Hebrew or Arabic) or a Hamitic (like ancient Egyptian, Berber, or Ethiopian) tongue. It belonged to a completely different family of languages than the Indo-European from which Greek as well as Persian, Latin, Russian, Sanskrit, and nearly all of the present-day European languages were derived. Minoan culture, with this undeciphered language at its heart, became something unique in the Mediterranean, and blossomed in beauty for almost two thousand years, making it among the longest lasting (as well as one of the oldest) cultures in the world. In Mycenae of the heroic age, in Classic Greece, in Rome in the Italian Renaissance, in modern Europe, and in the United States today there is more than one small gene of this Cretan legacy in the dark flow of what has been called "the collective unconscious." It took two billion years for Crete to flower; all of us now living in the Western world are hybrid fruit on the same gnarled tree.

For over three thousand years the Minoan culture was almost completely unknown, buried under tons of earth and stone, the location of its now famous monuments uncertain. It existed only as a whispered legend, like the story of Troy. Homer alluded obliquely to this culture in the *Odyssey,* but showed no real knowledge of what it was like. There were other references to Crete in the ancient myths, but no authority believed that any of them were true. The rest is silence.

The great German archaeologist Heinrich Schliemann, who had already excavated Troy and Mycenae, came to Crete in 1886 and located the site of Knossos, the ancient capital. It lies not far south of today's capital city, Heracleum. Schliemann haggled with the owner of the land over the price, decided it was too costly, and turned his back on what could have been the crowning achievement of his life.

In 1893 Sir Arthur Evans, a wealthy Englishman, who was also an amateur archaeologist, bought from some women in Athens a number of milkstone amulets with inscriptions on them in an unknown tongue. He found that the amulets had come from Crete, so he headed for that island and after protracted negotiations purchased the plot of land that Schliemann had turned down. By 1900 Evans had over a hundred men digging, and before long he had uncovered one of the greatest archaeological treasures of all time—the 5½-acre many-chambered palace of Minos, site of the fabled labyrinth in which lived the Minotaur. Legend tells us that this strange bloodthirsty creature, half-bull and half-man, demanded a tribute of seven Athenian young men and seven maidens every ninth year, whom it devoured alive.

Theseus, the original Athenian hero, came to Crete, and with the help of Ariadne, daughter of Minos, he slew the Minotaur, and freed Athens of this dreaded yoke. Perhaps the story is a symbolic way of saying that the sea power of Minos (the Minotaur) exacted its tribute from the Grecian mainland, even impressing young Greeks into the Cretan navy, until the emerging sea power of the peninsula, represented by Theseus, finally turned the tables. In any case, the ancient fable of Minos, the Labyrinth, Theseus, and the Minotaur linked the destiny of Crete with that of the mainland, and Greek history was ready to begin.

The palace of Minos was not the only discovery that Evans made at Knossos. He also unearthed hundreds of clay tablets bearing a strange script resembling that which he had seen on the amulets purchased in Athens many years previously. This script represented a shift from the older Minoan picture writing to phonetically represented syllables. At first it was assumed that all of the inscriptions were in the Minoan language, whatever that was, but a more careful examination revealed that the tablets contained two closely related but different kinds of writing. The similarity between them was so great that it soon became apparent that one was derived from the other.

Evans called the older basic script "Linear A," and the later derived script "Linear B." The term *linear* was used because the syllables were represented by arrangements of thin lines. They were not pictographs or wedge-made characters. Tablets with Linear A inscriptions turned up at several places in Crete, but Linear B existed only at the capital, Knossos. The approximate date of the tablets was 1450 B.C. No one could decipher the inscriptions; the mystery of Crete, now available in writing, still taunted the experts across the centuries.

In 1939 Professor Carl Blegen of the University of Cincinnati found additional Linear B tablets on the Greek mainland at Pylos, and a few years later similar tablets were discovered at Mycenae and at Thebes. This suggested that the inhabitants of the mainland, the Mycenaeans, might have captured Knossos where they adapted the Minoan script to their own language, later carrying it back with them to the peninsula. This supposition was verified by both historic and linguistic research, but the mystery of the language remained unsolved.

A brilliant young English architect with a classical education, Michael Ventris, provided the key in 1952. He was only thirty at the time; four years later he was killed in an automobile accident. The strange lines which had baffled the finest linguists and archaeologists for over fifty years became an obsession with Ventris. He agreed with his predecessors that the script was syllabic.

Ventris listed all of the syllables in their various positions and arrangements and on a complex series of grids worked out their patterns of behavior. One day something suddenly clicked in his mind and he realized that he was not examining an unknown linguistic pattern but one that was already familiar to him. The strange syllables were an ancient form of Greek. The Mycenaeans, therefore, spoke Greek, just as Homer had said they did. Having no written language of their own, their first written records were in the borrowed Minoan rebus script. This, of course, was nothing at all like the alphabet of Classic Greek which was taken over from the Phoenicians many centuries later (around 850 B.C.), only a few decades before Homer. This alphabet has remained almost unchanged from that day to this and is a perfect vehicle for one of the most melodious, most expressive, and most majestic languages ever invented by man.

The peak of Minoan culture was reached during the period from 1750 to 1450 B.C. When Homer in the eighth century sang of "the fair, rich land called Crete," he was going back in time several hundred years. Crete had already become a legend. It was, in fact, a kind of "Bronze Age England," an island where the dark Mediterraneans worked out their destiny alone until the invading Greeks or some geological catastrophe put an end to them.

Crete was a great maritime power, as the archaeological remains attest. Its hills were heavily forested with cypress and cedar and its fields were carefully tended by a large agricultural population. Its ships carried timber, wine, skins, olive oil, ivory, copper ingots, and many other items of trade to and fro across the Mediterranean as early as 2500 B.C. In this commerce the Minoans amassed considerable wealth, and the creation and acquisition of objects of beauty soon followed. It is a fair bet in history that culture and art will thrive where there is wealth.

Cretan artists made lovely paintings, pottery, and works of gold and bronze. They knew how to dash paint on wet plaster in the fresco manner, and thus decorated the walls of their palaces. They gaily held the mirror up to nature, and used bright colors to reproduce the figures of plants and animals which still breathe freshly where time has not completely destroyed them. Their graceful frescoes and pottery were decorated with lilies, tulips, narcissi, crocus flowers in delicate pink, blue, and orange, or with motifs of spirals, fish, helmets, octopus tentacles, and stylized figures of bulls.

One fresco shows a group of gaily dressed dancing girls in an olive grove; another is of nude priestesses spinning in a frenzied rite before a sacred tree. The figure of the double ax (called labrys) appeared often as a basic symbol sacred to their main goddess. Perhaps it signified power, perhaps it was a phallic symbol, perhaps it was both. From this motif came the name "palace labyrinth" or "palace of the double ax." The palace had many pillars which supported nothing except this omnipresent double ax. A symbolic representation of the male and female phalli seems inescapable.

The columns as well as the walls of the Minoan palaces were brightly painted. The murals contained many female figures, one of which has been called "La Parisienne" because of her stylish mien and dress. There were hunting scenes in which the hunters are accompanied by greyhounds and wildcats, frescoes of young men and girls grasping the horns and then catapulting over bulls, of dancing and athletic contests, paintings and statuettes of women in long skirts with tight waists and short-sleeved blouses which had delicate neckbands that left the breasts completely exposed. The goddesses were represented in the same manner. The Minoan topless style antedated our own by 4000 years and bore none of our prurient connotations.

The bull grappling of ancient Crete must have been a ritualization of primary human urges and hostilities, worked out in the arena. The athletes engaging in this rite were not armed. The bullfight (*corrida de toros*) survives as such in Spain today, but it is only in Portugal that groups of completely unarmed men still charge the bull and overcome him with their bare hands, throwing him to the ground but never killing him. This is the *forzada,* which, along with the fighting of the bull from the backs of beautifully trained thoroughbred horses, makes the Portuguese version of the bullring quite different from that of Spain and suggests at least an aesthetic parallel with the bull grappling of ancient Crete. Perhaps an even closer parallel is represented by the Mexican custom of vaulting over the bull on a long pole (*garrocha*). The taproot of history is often revealed in the survival of ritual and of games.

The original and primary religious symbol of the Minoans was the fertility goddess, of whom many representations have been found. She was at the opposite pole from the religious feeling of the Olympian Greeks to whom strong masculine gods with Zeus at their head symbolized the ruling forces of the universe. In the popular undercurrent of Greek religion, however, the two poles met and sometimes blended.

The Minoan, like so many other early Mediterranean cultures, worshiped the generative power found in the earth and they symbolized this in various forms. They called their main deity the Earth Mother, and to represent her they made little figures of a woman with large breasts and large buttocks which not only indicated her matronly function but which doubtless were also considered as her most beautiful adornments.

Oftentimes this fertility figure was crowned with a dove (later the sacred bird of Aphrodite) and had snakes in her hands as well as in her hair. This suggests that she was at least sometimes regarded as being capable of self-fertilization. The opposing masculine force was represented by the bull. It was the bull which had intercourse with the wife of Minos and thus brought forth the Minotaur. It was also the bull which was the central figure in the ritualistic games of the Minoans, and it was the bull pictograph that represented the first letter of so many early Semitic alphabets, later becoming the *alpha* of the Greeks.

The psychological expert could have a Freudian field day with all of these phallic symbols: the bull, snakes, the dove (the trembling female sex or breast), the sacred pillars, the double ax, the labyrinth. The Minoans based their beliefs on observed reality: awe-struck by the generative vitality of the earth and its creatures, they chose obvious symbols to represent it. They saw deity in this strange reproductive power and considered its worship vital to the continuance of life.

The Earth Mother was mysteriously responsible for bringing forth all living things, for giving birth to plants, animals, and men, and for the inevitable cyclic return of spring. She represented, therefore, man's victory over his archenemy, death. A similar idea of eternal regeneration is continued in the Greek Demeter, the Roman Ceres, and in the Catholic Virgin Mary. The earth has become womb and flower, without need of the masculine gods of the sky to fertilize it.

The early Greeks adopted the Earth Mother from the Cretans, but the more virile sky forces (Zeus, Apollo, i.e., thunder, lightning, sun, storm, rain) were their great gods. The deific force represented by these gods was masculinity incarnate and the later Greeks regarded this as the more important aspect of the generative process. The earth-bound religion of their predecessors was too restrictive for them. Hence, not only their religion but also their way of life glorified power and freedom, manliness, courage, strength, prowess in battle, and the superiority of man over woman. Even in Homer all kings are descended from Zeus, and in the drama of the Classic period woman is only the repository of the seed of life which proceeds from the father, who is the true creator.

There were no temples in Minoan Crete. Religious rites were either held in the palaces, where the king (who was also high priest) officiated, or before small private altars in the homes. The three great Cretan palaces were constructed about the same time (circa 1900 B.C.) at Knossos, Phaistos, and Mallia. Around 1700 these palaces were all destroyed, perhaps by an earthquake, perhaps by Grecian invaders, perhaps by both. After a 100-year hiatus a second series of palaces, much more impressive than the first, were raised on the ruins of the old (1600 B.C.).

The Cretan palaces were unfortified, as were the cities below them, thus indicating no fear of attack. Undoubtedly a strong Cretan navy discouraged potential invaders. The Minoans enjoyed several centuries of relatively peaceful coexistence with their neighbors during their own formative period, something of a record in the history of mankind. But brief or long, let any people find a way to peace and beauty and some other people will as surely seek to destroy them. Greed and envy go hand in hand with conquest as the great wheel of fortune turns a full circle that the cycle may begin anew. All civilizations follow the pattern of the changing earth. They come and they pass like the seasons; if they are not destroyed, they destroy themselves; they are born, they grow, and they die like every plant and creature. Love is the bridge. The love that blossomed four thousand years ago in Crete died yesterday in Texas.

The Minoans enjoyed their millennium of peace and worked out patterns of comfortable living. Their island home was dotted with fields and mansions, and a network of roads linked them all to Knossos. There was prosperity and a high degree of general culture. These people appear to have recaptured man's lost paradise. They did not have our feeling of shame about sex or nudity, and they regarded the body as a holy temple. They believed in rigorous cleanliness. One thing which immediately attracts attention at their palaces is the incredibly well-engineered water system. There are terra-cotta pipes that are so well preserved that they still function, and in some of the royal chambers were toilets that flushed, surely the earliest in history. Water was piped into these palaces, and the waste was piped out. The land was fruitful and at peace.

The aura of this Cretan paradise was still remembered when Homer sang his immortal songs. The poet concludes Book 18 of the *Iliad* with a description of a dancing floor on Achilles' shield:

Like the floor in wide Knossos that Daedalus made
So many years ago for Ariadne of the lovely hair.
There in the ring young men and seductive maidens
Held each other's wrists and danced. The girls were in
Soft linen gowns and wore garlands in their hair.
The men were dressed in fine tunics given a sheen
With olive oil, and had golden daggers hanging from
Silver belts. They all spun in the dance, their light feet
Twirling like a potter's wheel, then they formed long rows
And ran toward each other, intermingling, as a god-inspired
Bard strummed them a tune on his lyre. A large crowd
Watched the dance with great delight, and in their midst
A pair of acrobats, keeping time to the music, tumbled
In giant cartwheels.

It is a remembered idyll which has survived the depredations and ugliness of history. The Minoans were from all accounts a joyous, lusty people. They believed in merry games, in beauty, in sex, in life. They had no prudery about draping the most beautiful part of their women's bodies. They worshiped at the shrine of procreation, made love without fear of war, moved gaily through the dance of life, much like the Etruscans of Italy, who preceded the Romans. They were an earth people who like the tender grasses grew and multiplied abundantly among their island hills and valleys giving nutriment to all who followed.

II

The First Greeks Arrive

Earth Mother of us all, life-giving spring,
The oldest force man knows, to thee I sing:
All creatures of the land, the air and sea,
And every infant born or fruited tree,
Earth Mother, is your child, your progeny.

Hesiod, *Theogony*

The first Greek-speaking people entered the peninsula from the north, around 2000 B.C. Their thin wave of migrants did not get down to the southernmost tip of Greece until a century or two later. They belonged to the Aryan or Nordic race and spoke an Indo-European tongue; eventually people who spoke related Indo-European languages occupied all of the other countries of Europe. Their original homeland is unknown; according to some authorities it was probably somewhere along the boundary between Europe and Asia; according to others it was in Asia. The Greek tribes came to the Balkan areas from southern Russia and first occupied the Danube basin. Then, amoeba-like, they drifted southward as additional Greek tribes pushed in upon them from the east. At the time they reached Greece they had no written language. Neither did they have much of a culture; certainly, compared with the Cretans they were barbarians. But they did bring horses, and the horse changed the history, and even the religion, of Hellas.

It was the meeting and blending of these taller and fairer Greek-speaking invaders with the dark Mediterranean Pelasgians and Minoans which produced the Mycenaean (or Achaean) civilization about which Homer sang. Their fortress center, Mycenae, surrounded by cyclopean walls, occupied a hill about a hundred miles south of Athens, from where it can easily be reached today. Other well-known Mycenaean centers were at Pylos, Tiryns, Argos, Thebes; recent archaeological field work has pinpointed over three hundred others, as yet unexcavated.

The archaeologists call these people the Mycenaeans. In the *Iliad* and the *Odyssey* Homer refers to them as the Achaeans, Argives or Danaans. Their culture flourished in the Greek heroic age (1500–1150 B.C.), whose final stage produced the legendary heroes Agamemnon, King of Mycenae; Menelaus, King of Sparta; Odysseus (Ulysses), King of Ithaca; Achilles, sacker of cities; Ajax, Nestor, Diomedes, and many other kings and warriors who, according to Homeric legend, distinguished themselves at the siege of Troy. The beginning date of the Trojan War has recently been moved back from 1184 B.C. to circa 1250 B.C. There is now no doubt that it did take place, even if it did not follow precisely the course outlined in Homer.

The precise manner, dates, and nature of the important contacts between the Minoans of Crete and the Mycenaeans of the Greek mainland are not clear. During the crucial formative centuries of Hellenic civilization (2000–1100 B.C.) we are still in the earliest epoch of history, the Greek Bronze Age. Written documents are few, and most of these have not yet been deciphered. Every decision concerning chronology, human experience, or cultural development rests on tradition and archaeology. The man with the spade and the brush, digging and sifting the ancient remains, is our only reliable authority. Of course, there is always Homer, but what could literature have to say of an epoch remembered only vaguely in myth and story after the passage of four or five centuries? The specialists, therefore, examine what has been dug up and make their guesses.

The reader has a right to know what their guesses are, even if the experts have reversed their judgments with astonishing frequency in recent years. The guesses are these: the Mycenaeans (that is, the Greeks) reached Crete sometime between 1600 and 1450 B.C. The man with the spade has narrowed it down to that relatively brief span of 150 years. Whatever the precise date, we know that the Mycenaeans did occupy Crete and did take over a going concern as the Linear B tablets indicate. Like the Normans in England they displaced the native ruling caste but did not destroy or greatly disrupt the national life. The result is certain: two different linguistic groups, two different cultures opposed each other, then intermingled.

There is geological and archaeological evidence to support the thesis that the initial invasion took place between 1500 and 1450 B.C. Around 1500 some great catastrophe hit Crete, either a violent earthquake or a tremendous volcanic eruption (probably Santorini). Minoan society was shaken at its roots, and the Greeks were presented with an ideal opportunity to subjugate their wealthy neighbors. All of the great Minoan palaces were destroyed by the holocaust, but after the Greek occupation the one at Knossos was reconstructed, and it was here that the first of the invaluable

Santorini today, the ancient Thera, many believe the site of legendary Atlantis.
The huge volcanic crater down below is now filled with the sea. A Minoan city
larger than Pompeii and 1500 years older was recently discovered beneath a
heavy cover of ash on the island of Santorini.

Linear B tablets were found by Sir Arthur Evans in 1900. Examining the
archaeological remains Evans then went on to affirm that the rebuilt palace
at Knossos was again and *finally* destroyed and burned to the ground
around 1400 B.C. To Evans and his followers this was the end of Minoan
culture.

It was believed that around 1400 either (a) another earthquake or volcanic eruption took place or (b) the Greeks had a rebellion on their hands
and ruthlessly put Knossos to fire and sword. But this is not the end of the
story. Later archaeologists, with more accurate information at their fingertips, now affirm that the date of 1400 B.C. is off by a matter of two
centuries. Carl Blegen and others set the final destruction of Knossos at
circa 1200 B.C., at which time they believe the Dorians (the last and most
barbaric wave of Greeks) overcame, pillaged, and destroyed both the
Mycenaean strongholds on the mainland (Mycenae, Pylos, Tiryns) and
finally Knossos itself. After this the light went out in Hellas, and the
Greek Dark Age, a time of troubles, began.

Around the year A.D. 160 a Greek traveler named Pausanias, who was fascinated by the geography, history, architecture, and legend of his country, made an extensive tour of Greece and recorded his impressions among which were some pertinent paragraphs on Mycenae. In 1876 Heinrich Schliemann, fresh from his triumph at Troy, where he had proved Homer right about the existence of that city, determined to prove both Homer and Pausanias right about the importance and wealth of Mycenae. The site itself had never been lost to history, for the monolithic gateway of lions was forever visible above the forbidding hill which had swallowed up most of the great palace fortress. The name Mycenae was still attached to the place, although by classic times it had sunk to the level of a poor village. Later still the site became completely unpopulated and received a slow burial at the hands of nature.

In the *Iliad* Homer had described Mycenae briefly as a well-planned city of broad walks and colonnades where there was much gold, and he had given it literary immortality as the city of Agamemnon, leader of the Greeks before Troy. In the *Odyssey* he had spun the legend about the tragic fate of Agamemnon's family. The Greek dramatists of a later date took these same royal Mycenaeans and turned them into the symbolic characters of classic Greek literature: Agamemnon, the king; Clytemnestra, his adulterous wife; Aegisthus, her lover; Iphigenia, Orestes, and Electra, their children; Cassandra, the daughter of Priam, whom Agamemnon had brought back from conquered Troy. All of these characters enacted their legendary roles in the precincts of the mighty palace at Mycenae.

Schliemann took his crew and began to dig into the hill that rose in the midst of the fertile plains of Argos. The result is history. They uncovered an ancient citadel surrounded by cyclopean walls whose great stone gateway was crowned by two carved lionesses. This gateway still stands and is a marvel to behold. The figures of the headless beasts forever fixed in a rampant position astride the portal dumbly guard the gray and crumbled glory which was once proud Mycenae, the most famous city of pre-Homeric Greece.

This colossal gate was constructed in the thirteenth century B.C. and after this the lion became a main motif in Greek art. Lions appeared on vases attacking mules, bulls, and deer, and hunters were often shown pursuing the noble beast, sometimes with dogs. The lion became a symbol of majesty and of strength. There were wild lions in Macedonia until about 400 B.C., according to the best evidence of both history and art.* Lion hunting was

---

* Herodotus tells of wild lions coming out of the mountains of Thrace to attack the camels of Xerxes' army in 480 B.C. (VII, 125). Aristotle, Xenophon, and Pausanias confirm the presence of the lion in that area in the fifth century.

Crow

Entrance to Mycenaean beehive tomb. Note huge lintel stone above.

Beehive tomb at Mycenae, often called Treasury of Atreus because it was at first thought that Agamemnon's father, King Atreus, might have stored his gold here. The great vault is nearly 50 feet in diameter and 45 feet high. It is the most impressive monument of late Mycenaean times. Date, fifteenth century B.C.

perhaps the noblest sport of all, and surviving pictorial evidence indicates that several huntsmen with spears and large shields often formed these hunting parties, the front man casting his spear first, then dropping quickly under his shield, so that each successive hunter could do the same. The lion, pierced by several spears, was finally killed while hopefully the men were all still alive. A bronze dagger inlaid with gold figures (dated around 1550 B.C.) re-creates this hunting scene in a masterful fashion.

Within the walls of Mycenae were found several shaft graves dug out of solid rock which contained a precious treasure of objects of gold. Schliemann exultantly wired the king of Greece that he had uncovered the grave of Agamemnon! In hillocks below the citadel were also discovered a series of "beehive" tombs, constructed of finely joined stones, the largest of which was a vault 46 feet wide and 43 feet in height, the greatest such structure of early Greek history. The entrance lintel stone weighs 113 tons; green marble columns (now in the British Museum) lined the entrance. Schliemann called this vault the "Treasury of Atreus," although grave robbers had long since emptied it of all royal contents. Atreus was the father of Agamemnon. The finely cut and closely fitted stones of this tomb and of the entrance colonnade remind one of the best Incan stonework in Cuzco or Machu Picchu, Peru. There is, of course, no plausible connection between the two cultures. Man in his awkward thrust toward the stars may repeat himself in vastly separated times and places, driven by the same longing to create a beauty which will survive his passing. His hope is a palace built on sand.

The first cyclopean walls that surrounded Mycenae were put up around 1350 B.C.; they replaced earlier less impressive walls which had been destroyed. The acropolis of Mycenae had been continuously inhabited since neolithic days, but the earliest Mycenaean occupancy dates from about 1700 B.C. During the period 1500–1200 Mycenae was at its peak. The palace walls were decorated with frescoes of battle scenes and attractive colonnades led to the different parts of the citadel. As in Cretan Knossos, there were also "majestic flights of stairs." In the valley below were huddled the settlements of the supporting peasant population. Only ten miles away stood Tiryns, another Mycenaean citadel, whose walls were even more megalithic in size. Whether these two places were friends or enemies we do not know. The dust of centuries lies heavy on their scattered stones. They are friendly now, and uninhabited.

In any case, we do know that the Mycenaeans were a warrior people, not as refined as the Minoans, and every detail of their remaining monuments indicates that they regarded honor and courage in battle as man's noblest

Alison Frantz

*Bronze dagger with gold
panthers hunting ducks in a
papyrus swamp. Circa
1550 B.C. Middle period of
Mycenaean culture.*

traits, just as Homer has sung. When not engaged in fighting they reached for beauty, and every palace survival shows the touch of some ancient artist's hand: marble tablets embossed in gold, stools inlaid with ivory, ivory plaques (one with a lion killing a long-horned bull), an ebony chair inlaid with golden birds, artistic pieces of rock crystal, bronze weapons and utensils, a bronze dagger inlaid with golden figures, a considerable amount of gold jewelry, and the most famous find of all, two marvelous golden cups.

These cups were discovered in an untouched tomb at Vaphio, not far from Sparta, and are embellished with beautifully wrought figures of men capturing a bull with the aid of decoy cows. The muscular torsos of the two principal male figures and of the struggling bull caught in the net reveal the hand of a topflight artist. The date of these two cups (now in the National Archaeological Museum in Athens) is around 1500 B.C. They are reminiscent of other cups of gold mentioned with awe by Homer seven centuries later. The figures and the design are so Cretan that some experts have stated categorically that the cups were imports from Crete, while other authorities just as firmly attest that they are of Mycenaean workmanship. It does not matter greatly, for by 1500 the two cultures were already merging into one.

The game of snaring, taming, catapulting over and dancing around the sacred bull was so often depicted on Mycenaean rings and seals that it was surely almost as popular as in Crete. Mycenaean religion was thoroughly infused with Minoan rituals, motifs, beliefs. The cult of the Earth Mother, goddess of fertility, and her principal symbols: the double ax (labrys), the "sacred" pillar, and the "holy" dove, were all much in evidence. Small fertility figures were also often represented as a woman with large buttocks.

The fertility Earth Mother goddess, by way of further detail, was invariably associated with a young male deity, her son, with whom these symbolic relations originated. This incestuous phallic myth, transformed by time, creed, and distance, may have become the basis for the Oedipus legend of a later date in which the same relationship is regarded with horror by the Greeks of the Classic age. It is a well-known fact that Greek drama emerged from the riotous phallic festivals of an earlier day. Sex, of course, survives every desolation. The principle of life is not to be denied by the canons of religion or the mandarins of reason. There is a blind and reckless will in man which propels him toward the act of procreation, regardless of every taboo and limitation.

This phallic view of early Greek religion is partly conjecture, as is much of what has been written about the Mycenaeans themselves, who left

Gold cup from tomb at Vaphio near Sparta, Mycenaean workmanship. Scene shows man attempting to snare a wild bull. Note very modern handling of fallen man. Circa 1500 B.C.

Second of the pair of gold cups from Vaphio. Athens, National Museum.

nothing in writing except some tabulations. Everything must be surmised from the remains. The inventory is impressive, but let us not be led astray. After all is said and done so very little survives of those voiceless centuries: a few rare masterpieces in a handful of museums, hundreds of fragments of things which once were more beautiful, here and there on the scene frescoes gnawed away by time and the elements, innumerable pots and jars of every conceivable kind and description, and in architecture rows of trenches surmounted by gray stones that suggest only abandoned foundations rather than structures completed. Put all of these fragments together and we have but a faded glory.

Why do most cultures survive mainly in their pots? Molded clay is hardly the most durable form of art, but in survival it has been by far the most abundant. One palace, one pair of golden cups, but ten thousand pots. The scales are heavily weighted. The pots survive and become representative. But representative of what? We can fix dates with them, but it is difficult to tell much about the psyche and poetry of the people until at last the pot becomes a vase and a work of art in its own right.

Excavators always grasp for the proof of legend, for this popularizes their discoveries and encourages further subsidies. Schliemann, however, was incorrect in claiming that he had unearthed the tomb of Agamemnon and the treasury of Atreus. If Agamemnon lived at all, which is beginning to appear doubtful, his reign would have come a couple of centuries later than the date of his supposed tomb. But Schliemann did open a new window on the formative days of the ancient Greek world. The strong influence of Minoan art on the mainland was proved beyond any doubt. The meeting and initial merging of the Mycenaean and Minoan cultures was shown to be indisputable. After this it remained for the Mycenaeans to gather strength and momentum until their sea forces rivaled and finally surpassed those of Crete. When this was achieved they invaded and occupied the palace of Minos at Knossos, and the final stage of the Greek Bronze Age began. One thing dies and another rises to take its place. The old is always emptying itself into the new.

Why are these centuries (3000–1000 B.C.) of Minoan and Mycenaean civilization referred to as the "Greek Bronze Age"? First of all, before 3000 B.C. the natives of this land and these islands were a primitive neolithic people, that is, a people who used only implements of stone. They were fishers and hunters, with a few random flocks; they planted snatch crops, ate dandelions, and gathered wild honey. Shortly after 3000 B.C. a wave of immigrants arrived from Anatolia in Asia Minor who were users of bronze. These new arrivals quickly took over control of the native population which was unable to resist them. Bronze was the difference. Stone clubs and rocks were no match for shields and swords of metal whose sharp edges penetrated the human flesh with a minimum of effort, "robbing it of honey-sweet life," as Homer has sung.

Bronze is an alloy of copper and tin, and in order to make a hard bronze, the kind needed in warfare, at least 15 percent tin is needed in the mixture. Copper alone is much too soft a metal for effective use in battle. There was plenty of copper in the territory of Greece but precious little tin. Perhaps the Mycenaeans stumbled on a rare tin deposit and thus grew powerful and wealthy, but this is pure supposition. It is known that tin was generally imported, and that it was a scarce and essential commodity. Some tin actually came from as far away as Spain. This being the case, bronze was an extremely valuable alloy in Greece, and only the top echelons of soldiers could be provided with bronze weapons. These ruled the others, who could not effectively oppose them. An aristocratic society was the result, an age of warrior lords who held the strings of power, created the palaces, stacked up the inventories of products, made possible the initiative of artists, became the basis of a heroic literature in the Trojan War.

These Bronze Age warriors did not know how to smelt iron. Indeed, the rather frequent mention of iron in Homer's epics is one of the poet's fundamental historic errors. Iron *was* known in the heroic days, but it was not used for weapons, nor was it widely distributed. It was so scarce that jewelry was made of meteoric iron at both Knossos and Mycenae. A bit of iron was often set in the middle of a gold ring like a precious gem. But by the time Homer wrote, iron had become one of the staples of Greek civilization and, since five centuries separated the poet from the Trojan War, he simply could not conceive of a time when iron was not widely known. Herodotus made the same kind of mistake in his famous history; he thought that the pyramids of Egypt had been constructed with iron tools!

It is easy to imagine the heroic warriors of the late Bronze Age deriding the value of the first weapons of iron. These weapons must indeed have appeared ugly and puny compared with their brightly burnished broadswords and their gleaming bronze armor and shields. But what these warriors did not realize was the crucial abundance of iron. Once smelting was learned, *everybody* could possess an iron weapon, and this implied a real revolution in the concept of war. Before iron was smelted only a few choice soldiers took part in battle. Homer's poems emphasize this fact by invariably focusing attention on the engagement of individual soldiers, never on opposing contingents.

With iron great masses of soldiers could be armed, and the first tribe to be so equipped would overcome the rest. This is exactly what happened when the Dorians, a backward tribe of Greeks who invaded the peninsula around 1200 B.C., confronted the Mycenaean defenders and overcame them with vastly superior iron power. It was not the first time in history that a people with an inferior culture had won a telling victory over foes superior to them in every way but one—weaponry and numbers. Of course, wrong thinking also had much to do with the destruction of the Mycenaean centers. Their warriors were convinced that the old and known ways were best. They were unwilling to appropriate the discovery of their barbarous enemy, so they who had conquered with horses were defeated by a rabble with iron. By all odds they should have known better.

Greek statuary begins with the two rampant lions standing guard over the stone gateway at Mycenae, which were carved out of solid rock in the thirteenth century B.C. The animals are not complete, rounded figures, but emerge from the great block of stone much as do Michelangelo's incomplete statues in the Accademia at Florence. Despite the heavy load of time, they are still in high relief and give the impression of both size and strength. There was nothing like this in Minoan art. The Minoans, a race of small people, worked in figures of greatly reduced size, in statuettes and miniatures. Perhaps this was a kind of overcompensation for their small stature, paralleling that of the Mexicans of today, who will carve the immense pyramids of Teotihuacán on a peach kernel or make a miniature chess set so tiny that all the pieces can fit into a single walnut shell. In any case, there was nothing monumental about Minoan statuary.

The Mycenaeans, who girded their citadel with mighty walls of cyclopean stones, thought big in art as well as in fortifications, which the Minoans did not need. Perhaps one big thing led to another. Or perhaps being physically a larger and more warlike people, they needed no overcompensation in detail but boldly carved instead the most appropriate animal to symbolize their own strength. The great walls with their life-size lions were viewed by Greeks throughout the Classic and Roman periods with considerable awe, for Greek legend said that the Cyclopes themselves had borne the stones and erected the protective walls of Mycenae. These leonine figures, then, their sole adornment, represent the almost legendary origin of Greek sculpture.

When the Dorians overran the mainland of Greece (around 1150 B.C.) there was a great exodus of Mycenaeans (Aeolians and Ionians), who fled eastward and settled along the coast of Asia Minor and the coastal islands. Achaean (Mycenaean) culture went with them. The more important wing

Lion Gateway at Mycenae, circa 1250 B.C. From this gate King Agamemnon is reputed to have marched off to the Trojan War, and back through it he came to his death at the hands of his wife, Clytemnestra.

of this flight is known as the Ionian migration, and the region settled is known as Ionia. There the Achaean exiles established a series of colonies which for several centuries outshone the cities of the Greek mainland abandoned to the Dorians. Miletus, greatest of the twelve new centers of this transplanted Greece, preceded and outshone Athens in cultural importance for many centuries. Homer himself was almost certainly a Greek from Ionia, probably from Chios or Smyrna. What he wrote was an effort to recapture the great days of Achaean glory prior to the flight from Greece before the Dorian invaders.

Greek philosophy also was born in Ionia and from here was transported to the mainland for its further development. Ionia was the main refuge of all the accumulated centuries of civilization which Hellas had produced. There was, however, one other noteworthy haven, the city of Athens, whose citadel had withstood the Dorian assaults. Thucydides said that the Athenian defense was successful because Attica in those days was not worth bothering about and the Dorians never made a concerted attempt to take it. In any case, the torch on the Acropolis was never extinguished. Perhaps this is one reason why Athens was the center of the rebirth of Greek culture in the Classic age, with its blending of Dorian and Achaean elements. It also helps to explain the implacable conflict and rivalry between Athens and Sparta, for it was in this latter city that the Dorians established their greatest stronghold and developed to the fullest their highly regimented militaristic social order.

When the Greeks first came to the land that is now called Greece they brought new gods. The original inhabitants of the peninsula, the Pelasgians, worshiped primitive earth-bound deities, and so did the Minoans. A few of their gods dwelt in the sky, but most of them represented earth forces. The early Greeks, the Achaeans, and the later Dorians, deified these same earth forces, but their main gods represented the power of the sky. These two groups of gods, representing two religious attitudes, were known as (a) the Olympians (because Mount Olympus was where the sky-gods lived) and (b) the Chthonians, dwellers in the *chthon,* an ancient word for "earth."

The earlier earth-gods resembled more closely the kinds of deities worshiped by savages. In Greece they were taken over by both the Minoan and Mycenaean civilizations, and after these civilizations had been absorbed by the Dorian waves, the Chthonic gods continued to be worshiped in the outlying country regions of Hellas, while in the cities the new gods of the sky came into vogue. But the old earth-gods never completely died, and found their continuance in Demeter, Dionysus, Persephone, Asklepius, Orpheus, and others.

The primary symbols of the earth energy were the mother figure and the snake, for the snake never left the surface of the earth. The symbol of Asklepius, the healer, was also the snake, and from it is derived our medical emblem, the caduceus of snakes entwined about a staff. When sick people visited the great shrine of Asklepius at Epidaurus they were placed in a room to sleep with serpents (the original "snake pit"), for this reptile was believed to have great curative powers. As the years passed, the priests óf the temple learned more about how diseases behaved; they lost much of their faith in snakes and miracles and developed medicine and surgery. Hippocrates of Cos, the father of medicine, laid the basis for scientific medicine.

At Delphi an enormous Python epitomizing the earth energy (Ge) was believed to dwell in the innermost recesses of the earth. The Pythia or Pythoness (a young maiden) was the priestess of the Sacred Python, and it was she who spoke for the oracle of Delphi after a period of "incubation" or dreaming, during which she communicated with the goddess. Greeks believed that the center, or "omphalos," of the earth was located at Delphi, and the stone representing this still exists at the museum there today. Delphi, therefore, became a religious center of transcendent importance, and Greeks came from all parts of Hellas to consult the famous Delphic oracle; it even attracted "barbarians" from many lands.

As the centuries went by, ancient Delphi disappeared beneath a thick layer of earth on which rose a small Greek village. The French bought the entire village in 1891, moved it to its present location, and excavated the famous monuments that we are able to see today. The wild setting of the place among soaring mountains and immemorial olive groves is one of fitting majesty.

The second phase in the history of Delphi began with the arrival of Apollo. Apollo came from the island of Delos (the Cretans say from the island of Crete) on a dolphin and he slew the sacred Python with his arrows. Apollo represented the sun, and his arrows were the sun's rays or, symbolically, "the light and purity of truth." The earth (Ge) was thus vanquished by the sky and Greek religion moved into a higher sphere. The dead Python sank into a fissure in the earth and lay there letting off a deific stench. Inhaling this odor was supposed to induce in the Delphic priestesses the trance necessary for an answer to the questions asked the oracle, but the officiants probably intoxicated themselves by chewing laurel leaves. These priestesses were now married women of over fifty who dressed themselves as young maidens.

All questions had to be presented to the oracle in writing. Before answering the priestess placed herself on the sacred tripod (now in Istanbul) and the holy men or priests of Delphi read her the questions. Answers from the drugged priestess were given in a kind of unintelligible gibberish, which the holy men interpreted. They used a peculiar kind of double-talk, summarizing what they had to say in verse, and almost always allowed for more than a single interpretation. When Philip of Macedon asked the oracle if his war against Persia would succeed, the answer was: "The ready victim crowned for death before his altar stands." Philip thought the victim would be the king of Persia, but it was Philip himself. The over-all influence of the oracle at Delphi was one of moderation and restraint. A more sophisticated religion had with the arrival of Apollo supplanted the earlier primitive view of life.

Apollo became one of the greatest and most Greek-like of all the gods. He symbolized not only the sun; he was also lord of the pastures and herdsmen, god of light, truth, of music and art. He was spirit essence. He was probably originally from the Near East, for he was non-Greek at birth, but he became so widely loved in the Greco-Roman world that the Romans later took him into their own pantheon with his name unchanged. In a way he was a fusion of both earth and sky like the deific union symbolized by the plumed serpent of ancient Mexico.

Apollo was also the aloof and withdrawn god; he stood for *sophrosyne,* "self-control," which meant moderation, and in the *Iliad* he warns Achilles not to indulge his excessive wrath. Any excess was repulsive to Apollo. Of all the gods he represented best the "Golden Mean." When the English lady Jane Harrison first grasped this truth in her study of the Greeks she went about the house for several days feeling as if a new door to freedom had suddenly opened to her. The import of this teaching was: "Do whatever you wish in life, but *nothing to excess,* for only the excess is contrary to nature." To make certain that spirit would not obliterate body force the Greeks believed that Dionysus took Apollo's place at Delphi for three months out of the year.

Apollo greeted the visitors to his temple at Delphi with the famous phrase: "Know thyself." As Homer says in the *Iliad,* Apollo believed that "men are as leaves who feed on what the earth gives, then fade away and die." Human life was the shadow of a dream, no more than that. But when God gives His brightness to this dream, life is honey-sweet. Apollo's advice

*Theater and columns of Temple of Apollo, Delphi. Mount Parnassus is on
the left.*

to know oneself did not mean to the Greeks what it means to us today. It
originally meant "know what man is, know how different are the gods
from men, see the great distance that separates them. Know the limitations
of being human."

Apollo's symbols were both the bow and the lyre. The bow symbolizes

distance and silent power. The lyre means music. But both instruments are
made of wood and are strung with animal sinews. When a man makes or
holds either of them he becomes an attuned trinity of vegetable-animal-
human. Moreover, the lyre and indeed all stringed musical instruments
were most likely derived from the original hunter's bow. Often in Homer
appears a passage in which the bow of a warrior twangs and sings aloud.
When Odysseus strings his bow his great skill and strength enable him to
put it in place as easily as if "he had been stretching the string on his lyre."
When he tests the bow it sings under his touch "like the song of a swallow." Wood and animal guts gave man both his first long-distance weapon
and his first real musical instrument of quality. Death and beauty—are
they not a harmony of opposites? A symmetry of one? Man's ultimate
measure?

Mount Parnassus still keeps its lonely vigil at Delphi's side and the
sacred spring, hidden among the rocks, still flows. Broken columns, sustain-
ing nothing, reach toward the sky, and there is a sad wind blowing through
the olive trees. The last utterance of the Delphic oracle has put it well:

> *Go tell the King:*
> *The great walls have fallen,*
> *Apollo has no sanctuary,*
> *No prophetic laurel, no*
> *Speaking spring. The garrulous*
> *Water has dried up at last.**

---

* Last three lines of poem translated by Kenneth Rexroth, *Poems from the Greek
Anthology.*

III

Homer and the Age of Heroes

*Homer was divinely inspired beyond all other poets. Of his two
poems the one, the* Iliad, *is simple in structure and a story of suffering; the other, the* Odyssey, *is complex (for it has discovery scenes
throughout) and turns on character; moreover, they surpass all other
poems in diction and in quality of thought.**

Aristotle, *Essay on Epic Poetry*

Classical Greek civilization began with Homer, who was its fountainhead,
its greatest and best-loved poet, its symbol of brotherhood, its historian, its
mythmaker, its teacher, its high priest, its unimpeachable Bible. No other
poet in history comes even near to rivaling this position in the history of his
country. When we say "Homer" we mean the author or authors of the
Homeric epics, the *Iliad* and the *Odyssey,* which are the earliest and
greatest epics in Western literature. Greek drama, several centuries later,
takes the Homeric heroes and re-creates their tragic lives following the
Homeric pattern.

The poems of Homer retold stories which were reputed to have happened in the final year of the Trojan War and in the decade following.
This would place the events themselves around 1250 B.C. in time. Were
these supposed happenings real or were they simply the embroidery of
some poet's, or series of poets', gifted imagination? The Greeks thought
they were real, and (with a few notable exceptions) believed in them with
the same fervor that Christians believe in the Scriptures. However, later
historians came to regard the Homeric tales as pure legend, and before
Heinrich Schliemann unearthed the ruins of ancient Troy, precisely where
Homer had said it was, their view prevailed. Excavations at Troy, Mycenae,
Pylos, Tiryns, and Knossos changed all that. Now we know that the world

* From *Aristotle, Horace, Longinus: Classical Literary Criticism,* translated by T. S. Dorsch.

Homer described did indeed exist and that at least some of the events he tells about took place.

Who was Homer and when did he live? Some modern scholars believe that there were at least two poets involved in the *final authorship* of the Homeric epics, one of the *Iliad* and another for the *Odyssey*.* The language, subject matter, and general tone of these two poems are so different that they must have been organized and edited by two separate persons. The time of final composition (or editing) was between 750 and 650 B.C., somewhat later than was believed a few years ago.

The *Iliad* was put together first, probably by a bard who lived in Asia Minor or on one of the nearby islands. The *Odyssey* was composed several decades later, possibly by a younger relative or by a disciple of the author of the *Iliad*. No mention is made of the *Iliad* in the *Odyssey*, yet there is frequent reference to the events which are described in it. From the general outlook of the *Odyssey* it is clear that its author knew a great deal about ships, shipbuilding, and navigation. He was a man familiar with the sea, and he may have been born (or reared) on the Greek mainland or on an island off the coast.

Unlike the composer of the *Iliad*, who tells mainly of the exploits of war, the author of the *Odyssey* weaves a tale of adventure, travel, fantasy, romance, and final reunion of the hero with his family. In the *Iliad* "purple death," to use the Homeric phrase, walks starkly and bloodily on almost every page. In the *Odyssey*, until the shockingly bloody end, there is very little fighting, and much wandering, fairy-tale adventuring, and searching. It almost seems that two different worlds are being described.

Such, however, is not really the case. What we have are two aspects of the same world, a world that had existed five hundred years before the time of these poems which described it. There was no written history in those days, so what survived was oral tradition. The Homeric bards were re-creating and in a way idealizing a world that had been dead for four or five centuries. They saw this world with the eyes of a poet viewing it with pride, wonder and nostalgia. They may have altered this world to suit the tone of their poems or because they did not know the facts, but they did not deliberately distort history.

When they described a way of life they did it as accurately as they could. They mentioned the foods that were eaten, the furniture in the dwellings, the herds that were kept and the way of tending them, the fruit trees and the farm crops; they described the dances, the religious sacrifices, the attitudes toward the gods, the code of conduct, the weapons, the armor, the

---

* Samuel Butler and Robert Graves hold the theory that the author of the *Odyssey* was a woman.

ships, and even the palaces (which they had never seen) in terms they thought were accurate, and frequently, but not always, they were right. Later excavations have proved the degree of their accuracy and the degree of their distortion in history. The fact is that today we know much more about those heroic days than did the first Greeks who wrote about them.

The Homeric bards were describing an age during which an old society (the Mycenaean) was being broken up, an age of invasions, of displacements, of wanderings, and of changes, an age that was ending. It has been referred to as "The Greek Heroic Age"; there are parallel epochs in many other countries and centuries. These occur when "an established civilization is in the process of being broken up by barbarian conquerors."

Homer himself was probably a descendant of one of the families which had fled from the Greek mainland to Ionia around 1150 B.C., after the Dorian conquest. Indeed, the entire group of Homeric bards might well belong in this category, and thus would have strong emotional roots that reached back into the lost glorious past from which history had torn them, like children from the umbilical cord. They and their peoples would have more than just cause to exalt the past since the present was so clearly inferior.

This Heroic Age was followed by four centuries of "darkness" during which the old society that had disappeared was remembered fondly but vaguely, its main concrete achievements having been destroyed. Even its form of writing had disappeared, and it was not until the ninth century B.C. that the Greeks again began to use writing, this time with a new alphabet. During these dark centuries of no writing oral tradition flourished, and slowly the folk bards built up their tales and preserved them for Homer's use later.

The core of the Homeric epics was thus growing in the womb of these transition centuries. The relative "darkness" of this epoch is due to the breakup of the old order, the migrations and impoverishment of the people, the disappearance of monuments and of writing, but the new order was already clearly in genesis, and Homer brought it into the light. The *Iliad* and the *Odyssey*, therefore, come at the end and not at the beginning of a poetic tradition. They idealize and glorify a past, the youthful flower of a culture, holding it up for the admiration of all mankind. The characters, the episodes, many of the set poetic phrases, entire paragraphs of material had been so often used by previous folk bards that they had already become a part of the common literary storehouse. Several bards had obviously participated in composing these heroic tales, which gradually assumed a set and preferred form as the centuries passed.

Greek tradition said simply that Homer was the author of both epics.

Seven cities claimed to be his birthplace: Smyrna, Rhodes, Colophon, Salamis, Chios, Argos, and Athens, and obviously he could not have been born in all of them. However, there could easily have been seven cities in which the Homeric poetry, and the even more ancient lays which led up to it, were so deeply rooted that each of the seven considered this literature as its own creation.* Certainly the original Homer, who in every story of his life is reputed to be blind, did not sit down and make up the *Iliad* and the *Odyssey* in the way that a modern poet might compose a long poem today. He had an abundant accumulation of ancient lays to use as a base. What he did do was to take these materials and select from them, organize them, give them form and perspective, iron out discrepancies, elaborate details, link them together in a unified and artistic whole.

Then almost immediately the second part of the process began. Rhapsodists (in Greek the word means "stitcher of songs") began to recite the new epics just as they had recited the older lays, and as they recited they inevitably altered or took away verses that did not appeal to them and interpolated other verses which suited their fancy. The two epics that we now have are the end result of this long process of accumulation, oral recitation, sifting and resifting until a more or less final form was produced (around 700 B.C.). In this form the poems were widely recited, known, and loved all over Greece. Despite political fragmentation they were a bond of union that held the culture together.

The Greeks of those centuries attributed an entire corpus of ancient poetry to Homer, not only the *Iliad* and the *Odyssey* but dozens of other poems including seven epics of the "Trojan cycle." They were following the same practice as the Hebrews of the Old Testament who credited Solomon with authorship of the biblical Proverbs and David with the Psalms, when clearly these two kings were responsible for collecting and editing these books of the Bible but not for writing them. As time passed, the other poems Homer was supposed to have written were no longer attributed to him, and finally only the *Iliad* and the *Odyssey* (and a few "Homeric hymns") still bore his name. Epics that have disappeared told of "The Creation of the Gods," "The Death of Odysseus," "The Marriage of Telemachus," "The Life of Achilles," etc.

A whole school of professional bards grew up which carried on the Homeric tradition, reciting before eager crowds and entertaining them just as they are seen to do in the *Odyssey*. These bards probably used for

* A couplet by Thomas Heywood, 1635, based on an old epigram of Aulus Gellius says:
Seven cities warred for Homer being dead,
Who living had no roof to shroud his head.

accompaniment a gittern harp, an instrument without a very good sounding box, but they did not attempt to play or sing in our sense of those terms. Against a background of simple monodic strumming they presented the poems in a kind of singsong chant or incantation and could go on for hours depending exclusively on their memories. Such performances were for centuries one of the basic entertainments of the ancient Greeks.

The manner in which the rhapsodist recited Homer was fixed by tradition. He did not simply declaim the lines. He occupied a raised podium and so stood above the multitude who would hear him. He wore a flowing robe of white which had a winglike swirl under the right shoulder as its upper portion circled up and over the left shoulder. The shoulder on the right was bare, the left one fully covered. The right arm was extended as far out as he could reach, almost parallel with the earth, and in the right hand was the rhapsodist's staff, a long branch of oak knotted up and down whose bottom end rested on the podium beside the rhapsodist's right foot. The staff thus was the hypotenuse of a large open triangle composed of the body, the outstretched arm, and the staff. The rhapsodist held his head proudly high, and on one ancient vase he is shown as wearing a black beard which extends from the ears to about six or eight inches in front of the chin. The beard is parallel to the extended arm.

The pose of the rhapsodist is not accidental. He was performing one of the most important, perhaps *the* most important, public ritual of ancient Greece. He symbolized religion, power, majesty, and poetry rolled into one. Such a pose and such performances of folk poetry were not limited to Hellas, they were common throughout the Mediterranean area. Later we find similar professional bards in the other parts of Europe and even in Spanish America. The minstrel of Spain or Latin America would often take his stand in much the same fashion and commence his performance with ritualistic words like: "Here I take my place to sing, and all the verses that I speak will flow like waters from a spring." Then the story proper would begin. The whole performance was dramatic, symbolic, ritualistic, and every one of those present felt that he was participating in the act.

In 1934 Professor Milman Parry, a specialist in epic poetry, proved that a well-trained rhapsodist could do the same thing today. In Serbia he encountered a sixty-year-old bard who could neither read nor write, but who did recite for him a poem as long as the *Odyssey*. The recitation took two weeks with the bard performing for two hours in the morning and for another two in the afternoon. He "composed" most of the poem as he went along, but depended strongly on formulaic expressions and lines. Not once did he break the meter. Something like this must have taken place in the early days of Greek epic singers. In both the *Iliad* and the *Odyssey* approximately one third of the poetry consists of formulaic phrasings, lines, or blocks of lines which occur more than once. With this linguistic aid to facilitate the retelling of stories which were already well known the ancient Greek bards paved the way for Homer, who put the finishing touches on what had gone before.

Homer makes very artful use of the repeated formula but even a casual reader would be struck by some of the recurrent lines and phrases: the Greek soldiers are always "the well-greaved Achaeans" or "the long-haired Achaeans"; dawn always comes and "stretches out her fingertips of rose"; gods appear in battle "bearing the awesome tasselled aegis"; when a soldier is killed "purple death comes down on his eyes and powerful fate embraces him"; Achilles is the "sacker of cities" who is "fleet-footed" and invariably speaks "winged words"; Odysseus is "the man of many devices" or "resourceful Odysseus" or "teller of tales"; the Mediterranean is "the wine-dark sea" or "the fish-cold sea" or "the salt-immortal sea"; serving maids in the palaces "tip water for the hands of the men from a golden pitcher into a silver bowl" or "cover the handsome chairs for them with clean white fleeces"; in sacrificing an animal to the gods the officiant performing the rite would "sprinkle the earth with barley, draw back the head of the victim, cut its throat, and slice out the thigh pieces." He "wrapped this in layers of fat, and placed it on the burning wood, sprinkling the meat with sparkling wine."* There were set formulas for combat, for storms at sea, for prayers, for storytelling, for night to fall, for feasting, for greeting and farewell, for the appearance of the gods, for almost anything and everything. The Homeric epics are not composed in words but "in sequences of ready-made phrases; in 28,000 lines there are 25,000 repeated phrases, large and small," writes Denys Page of Cambridge University. The curious thing is that when literature is oral its appeal is widespread, long-lasting, of profound impact and influence. When it is passed on in writing among a widely literate people it becomes mostly an empty vehicle for promptly forgotten characters and ideas.

HOMERIC TEXTS

How did the *Iliad* and the *Odyssey* manage to survive for twenty-nine centuries and come down to us intact? Do we actually have the original manuscripts or at least some portion of them? The answers to these questions are a history in themselves. First of all, we do not have even a single

* These translations are from *The Iliad of Homer,* translated by Ennis Rees.

line of the original manuscript of either epic. What we do have are copies of copies. And the main reason that these great works survived at all when so many hundreds of other works disappeared in the destructive whirlpool of history is that they were so *extremely* popular for so many centuries. Literally hundreds of copies of them were made by different commissions and scholar scribes at different epochs in ancient and medieval times, so the law of averages prevented the destruction of every single copy of a copy of a copy of Homer's epics.

The texts of the *Iliad* and the *Odyssey* went through the following stages before they became established: (a) folk composition in separate lays, (b) stitching together by the bard Homer, (c) oral transmission and further editing, (d) original written form, (e) continued oral retelling and more carefully edited copies, (f) copies made of these copies until we finally get what we have today.

It is probable that the first written manuscripts of the poems were made as early as 650 B.C., but we have no proof of this. We do know that around 550 B.C. the tyrant of Athens, Peisistratus, appointed a group of specialists to edit the poems and *to restore their original unity* so that they might be recited in this form at the Panathenaeic Festival. The Peisistratus commission carefully examined the various versions of the poems, threw out what they considered to be obvious interpolations, but added interpolations of their own, and trimmed the epics to much the same length and form in which they have survived. Even though not one line of any of these 550 B.C. editions has come down to us in the *original manuscript,* quotations of several passages from each poem do appear in the works of Plato, Aristotle, Herodotus, and other Greek writers of the Classic period (490–325 B.C.). There are also fragments of both epics on pieces of papyrus which have been found in Egypt, some of them reaching back to 300 B.C. In the main these fragments from both Greece and Egypt agree substantially with the epics as we know them today. There are, however, sufficient variations (Aristotle, for example, quotes some passages which are otherwise totally unknown to us) to indicate that the texts of the "authorized" editions of 550 B.C. were not by any means definitive, and that other versions were still circulating in the Classic period.

This was how things stood in 150 B.C. when the scholars of Alexandria under their leader Aristarchus of Samothrace, head of the Alexandria library, decided to re-edit and reissue the poems in definitive scholarly editions. These experts in Egypt went through much the ·same process of copyreading, collating, adjusting, and rejecting materials as the commission of Peisistratus had followed four centuries previously. The scholars of

Alexandria, of course, had access to the famous library in their city which contained the greatest collection of ancient manuscripts ever assembled. (All of Plato's great library passed on to Alexandria.) Aristarchus and his assistants not only re-edited the Homeric manuscripts but added numerous marginal notes of interpretation. Aristarchus had a wonderful knowledge of the Homeric language and without his comments many passages would have been unreadable to later scholars. These editions of Aristarchus, like those of Peisistratus before him, have all been lost. Alexandria was captured by the Arabs in A.D. 640, and what remained of the famous library there was consumed in flames. It had previously been broken up and partly destroyed when Aurelian burned the Royal Quarter in A.D. 272.

Copies of these Alexandrian manuscripts certainly reached Europe (especially Constantinople), but there is a thousand-year hiatus before the next clear step in the Homeric story. The earliest complete manuscript that we have today dates from the tenth century (circa A.D. 950), sixteen centuries after Homer. There are several other medieval manuscripts of both epics, and from these came the Renaissance and our own present-day versions. The splendid folio edition of the *Iliad* and *Odyssey* (plus the lesser works of Homer), which was published in 1488 in Florence by Chalcondylas, is noteworthy because it is one of the best. An earlier manuscript, the Marcian index of the *Iliad,* of the eleventh century, was found in San Marco in Venice by Villoison and first published in 1788. Without these medieval manuscripts we would not have either the *Iliad* or the *Odyssey* today except in fragments.

It is not known which specific manuscripts the medieval scribes used to make their copies, how they got hold of these manuscripts, or what has happened to them since. It is known that copies were brought from Alexandria before 640, that others came into Europe from Constantinople before that city fell to the Turks in 1453, and that still others were brought to Europe by the Arabs whose flourishing culture in Spain and Sicily in medieval times reintroduced many Classic Greek writers to the Western world. Perhaps, too, there still existed in Greece even more ancient manuscripts of the *Iliad* and the *Odyssey* which have since been lost. It is barely possible that one of these priceless relics may yet be discovered in one of the many religious libraries of Europe or Africa where great piles of uncatalogued and uncritically examined manuscripts still lie in darkness.

As M. I. Finley, one of the most distinguished contemporary scholars of Greek history, has pointed out, Homer was without a rival in the struggle for literary survival among the lost Egyptian manuscripts. Papyrus fragments containing scraps of 1,233 books (not separate titles) have survived. Of these, 555 contain passages from the *Iliad* or the *Odyssey* or commentaries on them. The *Iliad* is the more numerous of the two, being represented by 380 papyri to 113 for the *Odyssey*. Demosthenes comes next with 74 papyri, then Euripides with 54, Hesiod with 40, Plato with 36, and Aristotle with only 6. It is obvious that the *Iliad* and the *Odyssey* got around almost as much as all the other Greek writings combined.

HOMER AS A HISTORIAN

How accurate was Homer as a historian? He was supposedly describing the life of the Achaeans (archaeologists would say Mycenaeans) at the time of the Trojan War, circa 1250 B.C. When Schliemann, inspired by Homer, unearthed first Troy and then Mycenae, he believed he had proved once and for all that Homer was a good historian as well as a wonderful poet. The Trojan War had taken place, just as Homer said; the Achaeans spoke Greek, as he had also said; and Mycenae was a rich and powerful city, worthy of being Agamemnon's citadel. Therefore, all that Homer wrote about the battles, dress, palaces, armor, customs, et cetera, of the Achaeans, and about their kings, Diomedes, Nestor, Menelaus, Odysseus, and Agamemnon, their great commander, must also be factual. It is a big "therefore," which does not logically follow. Even Schliemann had to admit that he was mistaken in calling the shaft grave of 1500 B.C. at Mycenae Agamemnon's tomb. Later historians have expressed serious doubts that Agamemnon ever existed at all, and no authority now believes that he was the King of Kings who led the combined forces of the Greeks at Troy.

Other errors in Homer's history have been pointed out by modern historians. Iron was often mentioned in the poems, but it was scarcely known to the Achaeans except as a rare meteorite substance. There was no smelting of iron in Greece until about 1100 B.C. Homer has his dead heroes burned on great funeral pyres, but the Achaeans buried their dead in well-constructed tombs of stone. The Homeric armor and weapons are either later interpolations or resemble those which are remembered in tradition helped out by actual relics; they were not the war gear which has been unearthed in Mycenaean ruins: figure-of-eight shields, inlaid swords, long rapiers, and so on. Homer dresses both men and women (in the versions we have) in the old-fashioned Attic style, not in the Mycenaean bathing drawers and flounces. Warriors are dressed in the bronze panoply of an age much later than that of Mycenae. The gods in Homer had temples, where the Mycenaeans erected no temples but carried on their religious rites in the open air or in homes and palaces. Homer had no idea how chariots were used in warfare. His heroes jump into their chariots, race toward the scene of battle only a short distance away, and there dismount and fight.

Homer, however, was careful never to mention the Dorian invasion which overran the Mycenaean citadels. He did his best to make the society in his poems appear to be pre-Dorian. He did describe in some detail Mycenaean utensils of gold (cups, pitchers, basins) like those which have later been found, and palaces with elaborate bathrooms similar to those which have since been excavated. Even the mural decoration of lapis lazuli which he attributed to the palace of Alcinous on the island of Phaecia (probably Corfu) has been found in one of the Mycenaean palaces, not, however, on a Greek island. In Homer's own day such palaces were unknown, and golden cups were certainly not in use. But the poet could have seen such cups, and he could have seen the ruins of such palaces or heard about them from others who had. This, and a fragile kernel of Mycenaean lore about war and sailing the seas, was all he did know about the history of the epoch and people described in his poems. He mixed together customs from remotest Greek antiquity (primitive cult rituals, excessive cruelty, human sacrifices) and these idealized Mycenaean memories.

The other colorful details with which Homer sprinkled his poems belong to a period much later than that of the Trojan War and only a century or so before his own time, that is, to the period 900–800 B.C. With no written history to guide him, it is easy for us to understand how the poet confused the centuries. It was as if someone today were to attempt to describe the American Revolutionary War without benefit of historic records. He would start with a few relics of that war, or an even later one, and would then expand the story by combining and elaborating the two. For example, he might be able to recall many details and episodes of the Civil War told to him as a child by those who had fought in it, and he might simply repeat these details in his presentation of the Revolutionary War, considering them to be ancient enough to apply to that time as well.

But, the Homer enthusiast may object, there *was* a Trojan War, and for years no one believed this either. And Troy *was* found where Homer placed it. Homer also affirmed that the Mycenaeans spoke Greek, and no one believed that until the Linear B tablets were deciphered in 1952. (No one, that is, except the astute Englishman Sir William Ridgeway, who stated so in 1901.) The only reasonable answer here is that Homer's accurate statements certainly do not prove his dubious statements and obviously cannot prove statements which we now know to be false.

There was, indeed, a Trojan War; or rather, there were a great many Trojan wars. Possibly (but not probably) one of them was triggered by the abducting of an honored queen. More likely the Troy referred to in the Homeric epics was sacked by a horde of barbarians. In any case, for the Mycenaeans to have got together an armed armada consisting of 1,186 ships (Homer's total) carrying at least 60,000 soldiers is inconceivable. No such combination of forces was possible at that stage in Greek history. And for the war to have lasted for ten years is also inconceivable. It might have lasted for ten weeks, which would have been a very long time in those days, and later these ten weeks might have become ten years. War in Mycenaean times was for booty, and there were no long-sustained campaigns. It would not have been possible to supply a large force with the necessities of daily life for anything like ten years on the plains before Troy.

The whole fabrication reminds us of a much later epic, *The Song of Roland,* which was composed (circa A.D. 1050) less than three centuries after the events described in it were supposed to have taken place. These events were exaggerated out of all verisimilitude for the purposes of heroic literature. There certainly was a battle on the border between Spain and France (circa A.D. 778) in which several French soldiers who composed the rear guard of Charlemagne's army were slain, probably by the Spanish Basques. In this rear-guard action Roland, or Roland's prototype, was one of those killed. But the poet takes this border skirmish and builds it up into a mighty battle between 400,000 Spanish Saracens who overpower 20,000 Frenchmen. In this case we know absolutely how ridiculous those figures are; we also have written documents of the time to disprove them.

The same kind of exaggeration is repeated five centuries later when the Spaniards under Cortes overcome Montezuma and his Aztec warriors; the latter become as numerous as the leaves in the forest. The priest Bartolomé de Las Casas estimated that twenty million Indians were slain by the Spanish conquistadores, a figure somewhat larger than the total pre-Columbian population of the New World. In such a manner does poetic license operate throughout history. We do not need to go back three thousand years to find parallels equally absurd, equally heroic. Indeed, does it not take an element of the absurd to constitute a basis for the heroic? Myths have always moved men more deeply than facts, and so myths have been created constantly out of the episodes of daily life in order to ennoble the dead and to impassion the living. Homer was privileged to stand at the beginning of this poetization of history.*

* English translations of Homer and Greek drama are discussed in the Appendix.

IV

The Trojan War—
The Ethos of Ancient Greece:
Religion, Morals, Values

The lives of men are like the leaves that flourish
And feed upon the earth, then fade away and die . . .

Homer, *The Iliad*

The *Iliad* and the *Odyssey* were both composed in order to be recited before aristocrats by wandering professional bards. This is undoubtedly one reason for making kings and queens the principal characters. The society depicted in these poems was strictly an aristocratic one in which the lower classes enjoyed little power and less social status. Within this frame Homer almost instinctively looks down his nose at the ordinary people and exalts the heroes.

The Achaean royalty traced its descent directly from the gods and all the epic heroes had at least one parent or ancestor who was a god. This placed them very literally in a category far above the masses. Achilles' mother was Thetis, the sea nymph, and his father, Peleus, was the grandson of Zeus. Aeneas was the son of Aphrodite; Odysseus, son of Laertes, was "of the seed of Zeus"; Helen was the daughter of Zeus, who had raped Leda in the form of a swan. Agamemnon and Menelaus were both great-great-grandsons of Zeus, and Agamemnon carried a staff which Hephaestus (Vulcan) the god-smith, had made for Zeus.

This god-descent was believed implicitly; it was no empty symbolism meaning simply "divinely inspired" or "divinely good" or "given divine strength," interpretations which a later social order might give to such a genealogy.

The only patent of respectability and honor in any Greek house or city of those early centuries was foundation by a hero or by the direct descendant of a hero. As sons or grandsons of the gods these heroes were the source from which all Greek nobility was derived. Many royal houses were considered to be directly descended from Zeus or Hercules. The line of royal and aristocratic power was both divine and unbroken, and not to be challenged by lesser folk. The Romans themselves, when they first came into contact with Greek culture, felt a sense of cultural inferiority when confronted with these beliefs and at once accepted the story invented for them by some unknown but wily Greek that they themselves (the Romans) were a colony of Trojans led by Aeneas, who after the Trojan War made their way to Italy where they gave birth to the Roman race. Vergil based his great Roman epic on this legendary event. His poem begins with the words:

> *Arms I sing, and the hero, who first,*
> *exiled by fate,*
> *Came from the coast of Troy to Italy . . .*

In Book 2 of the *Iliad* Homer's bias is made plain. There is an Assembly at which Agamemnon harangues the Greeks before Troy and tells them that after nine years of stalemate it is time to go home. The soldiers, wearied of the war, are eager to follow his advice, but Hera intervenes and sends Athena as a special messenger to prevent their departure. Athena takes Odysseus aside and persuades him that such a flight would be ignominious. Odysseus then successfully undertakes to reverse the decision, and here is where Homer's aristocratic point of view appears most strongly. Whenever Odysseus addresses a king or an aristocrat he uses soft words and a gentle manner of persuasion, but on encountering "a man of the people who was raising his voice he would strike him with his staff and shout at him: Be quiet, and show deference to your betters!"

One commoner, Thersites, was unwilling to be quiet. Homer gives a very unpleasant description of him, saying he was "wordy, disorderly, and vain, and surely the ugliest man on the plains of Troy. He was bandy-legged and lame, with his shoulders all hunched over his chest, and his skull went up to a point where it was covered by sparse woolly hair." This man berates Agamemnon for having taken the lion's share of gold and of beautiful women captives, and he urges the soldiers to go home, as they had spontaneously decided. Odysseus rushes up to Thersites and shouts: "You have no right to open your mouth and argue with kings . . . If you do it again I will drive you out of the Assembly and send you scurrying back to the ships." So saying, he cracks Thersites over the back with his scepter, raising a bloody welt. Thersites, frightened, sits down in tears. Then Homer adds that the men looked at each other and said: "Odysseus has done many great things for the Achaeans giving good counsel and heading men in battle, but this is much the best thing that he ever did, throwing this upstart out of the Assembly. Never again will he be rash enough to rail at kings!" The poet concludes, *"So spoke the crowd."* (Translated by Rees.)

Not only does Homer's sympathy lie with the aristocrats; he clearly demeans the ordinary soldier, and he implies that the crowd itself favored this point of view. "They all like it the way it is," in other words. In Book 9 of the *Iliad* there is another Assembly and Diomedes rises to accuse Agamemnon of cowardice and folly. He adds that he dares make these statements "in the Assembly where speech is respected" (Rees). Obviously, this respect extended only to the aristocrats. In the *Odyssey* when Odysseus returns to Ithaca and meets his old swineherd, the same paternalistic viewpoint is again expressed. The swineherd cannot praise his master enough. It is almost "Massa Odysseus, what a wonderful, kind and understanding man he was."

The Homeric religion was strictly anthropomorphic, that is, Homer made his gods like men. He also made his men like gods. The Homeric gods lived on Mount Olympus in a kind of superkingdom of their own. Long before Homer's day Zeus himself had killed his own father in order to snatch the godhead, as did many a prince in order to occupy his father's throne. All the Olympian gods act like exalted Greeks; they are powerful and cruel, vengeful and conceited. With the exception of Athena (and on occasion Apollo and Hera) they are not at all likable. They are absurdly proud, they fornicate shamelessly with each other and also with human beings, they quarrel among themselves incessantly, they take sides in every battle between men, and find ingenious ways to protect their favorites. Frequently a god will appear on the battlefield for the sole purpose of deflecting a weapon from its course, or to stanch a wound, or in order magically to spirit a helpless favorite out of the reach of certain death.

The gods also mingle with the soldiers in human form in order to participate in the fighting. The difference is merely one of degree. They can be wounded, though real red blood does not flow from their veins. Diomedes (egged on by Athena) spears Ares (Mars) in the stomach and Aphrodite in the hand, when she is caught in an unguarded moment not making full use of her godly powers. As his spear struck the goddess,

Diomedes shouted: "Stay out of the battle, daughter of Zeus! Is it not enough that you are able to infatuate and overpower feeble women?" Homer says that the spear "slashed through her ambrosial robe and pierced her tender palm, and from this wound the goddess's immortal blood began to flow, that is, the ichor that runs in such blessed beings, because they eat no food and drink no wine, and so are both bloodless and immortal." Athena also urged Diomedes to strike her brother Ares, whom she called "that raving double-dealer, that curse made only for evil!" (Rees.) She hated Ares not because he represented war itself, but because he was on the wrong side, fighting for the Trojans.

Even the gods were not above the rule of fate. They were wounded, manacled, seduced, punished, ridiculed and beaten by each other, and occasionally by mortals. They suffered the pangs of uncontrollable jealousy. In Book 21 Hera calls Artemis a "brazen bitch" and boxes her ears, scattering her arrows about, and Athena strikes Aphrodite a terrible blow on the breasts. Zeus struts around enjoying all of this uproariously.

In only two basic ways were the gods different from human beings: they were immortal and they were eternally young. Zeus is often referred to as "all powerful," the "hurler of thunder and lightning," the "cloud-gatherer," but Homer inserts these phrases just to keep the record straight. Zeus is simply a tremendously powerful and immortal king, and let no one forget it. He boasts outrageously of his various feminine conquests in front of his wife, apparently to impress her with his virility. He is often referred to as "crooked in counsel," for he is as devious as he is almighty. He also has homosexual proclivities, as the episode of Ganymede indicates. There is seldom any feeling of reverence toward him or toward any of the gods; neither are they pictured as loving or merciful. They are a cut above the Carthaginian Baal, who demanded the sacrifice of babies on his fiery altar, but they are a cut below the stormy Jehovah of the Hebrews.

In Homer's pantheon of Olympic gods the reckless masculine force very clearly prevails. It is a driving and relentless energy. The older Earth Mother, the fertility principle of Crete and Mycenae, has by now taken a second place. Demeter, goddess of spring, is mentioned half a dozen times, but Homer gives her very little importance. Athena, the outstanding goddess of the poems, had no mother, but emerged full grown and in battle gear from the mind of her father, Zeus. She is a sexless abstraction. Her affinity for Odysseus is because of his gift for cunning, deceit, craftiness, which reflects her own. There is no love among the gods, but there is plenty of sex play, which is always a game, a snare. Hera pretties herself and arouses Zeus in order to give him sex pleasure followed by sleep, so that he will not help the Trojans. Aphrodite cavorts shamelessly, using her body to entice both gods and men, and Zeus calls on his magical powers to the same prurient end.

The Homeric picture of Olympus, therefore, shows us a society freed from the restraints of religion. The poet was dealing a death blow (no doubt unconsciously) to the Olympic religion with his scenes of sin and crime among the gods. These gods enjoy great power and dominion, but they are hardly to be admired and certainly not to be loved. Love of faction (and for no sensible reason) overpowers all other considerations and justifies every violence and deceit. The gods have no compassion, no tenderness; with few exceptions they are pitiless, unscrupulous, cold. Homeric religion was of a simple contractual sort; there was little room in it for reverence.

The gods were directly responsible for the Trojan War. It was not a man-made struggle. In order to cause trouble on Mount Olympus, Eris, goddess of discord, tossed a golden apple among the goddesses. The inscription on the apple read: "To the Fairest." Finally, the choice was narrowed down to three: Hera, wife of Zeus; Aphrodite, goddess of love and beauty; and Athena, goddess of wisdom. The goddesses asked Zeus to decide to which of them the apple should go, but Zeus had no wish to become embroiled in their quarrel and suggested that they ask Prince Paris of Troy to be their judge, as he was most knowledgeable in matters of beautiful women. The goddesses found Paris tending sheep in a field near Troy and explained their dilemma. Each goddess promised him a special reward if he would choose her. Hera promised him the lordship of Europe and Asia, Athena promised him a great victory over the Greeks, and Aphrodite promised him the most beautiful woman in the world. It was to her that he gave the apple. The woman desired was Helen, wife of King Menelaus of Sparta.

Paris abducted the goddess-smitten and helpless Helen and took her back to Troy with him. Agamemnon, the king of Mycenae, brother of Helen's husband, Menelaus, assembled a great host of Greeks and sailed for Troy, which they besieged for ten years before its final destruction when the Greeks swarmed out of the wooden horse that had been pulled inside the walls and opened the gates, thus letting in their companions. The episode of the horse, however, is nowhere mentioned in the *Iliad*. It appears only briefly in a flashback in the *Odyssey*. The human beings involved in the Trojan War, therefore, were powerless to avert it. This war was fated by the gods. Paris could not help making his choice, Helen could not prevent her adultery, Agamemnon and Menelaus could not let the insult to their kingships go unanswered.

Paris, in fact, feels only a carnal lust for Helen; his is no profound romantic love like that of Tristram for Iseult. The Homeric Greeks did not know such love. And poor Helen despises her new husband, Paris, because he is "wavering and gutless." Her feelings of blame and guilt are equally strong. She refers to herself as "bitch-hearted me," wishing that she were dead, "but since the gods ordained these horrors, I also wish I had been the wife of a better man" (Rees).

One version of the story stated that Helen never reached Troy at all but was left in Egypt when a storm blew Paris off his course and forced him to land near the mouth of the Nile. Here the attendants of Paris deserted him and reported what he had done to Proteus, the king, who was greatly angered by the insult to Menelaus. Proteus allowed Paris to depart but kept Helen until her true husband could come for her. Herodotus relates this version in considerable detail, and agrees with the Egyptian priests who had assured him of its truth. According to Herodotus, if the Trojans had had Helen inside their walls they would simply have turned her over to the Greeks when the tide turned against them and thus ended the war. But Helen was held in Egypt, says Herodotus. Euripides makes use of this version in his play *Helen,* and one of his most moving scenes shows Menelaus and Helen meeting in Egypt after the fall of Troy.

The *Iliad* describes only a few weeks of fighting in the tenth year of the Trojan War. It does not even carry the story to the end of the war, although the eventual destruction of Troy is mentioned several times in the poem as something which is bound to occur. The *Iliad* "begins with a quarrel and ends with a funeral," as Finley Hooper puts it. The quarrel is between Agamemnon and Achilles, because Agamemnon had absconded with the girl Briseis, one of the pretty captives who had fallen to Achilles' lot. Achilles felt that his honor had been wronged. He sulks in his tent throughout most of the poem, refusing to bear arms for the Greeks, who without his power are unable to subdue the Trojans. But finally Achilles arms and sends his dearest friend Patroclus to fight in his place.

Hector slays Patroclus and keeps as a trophy the armor of Achilles which he is wearing. Achilles piteously bemoans the death of his friend, and then in a fury he puts on new armor especially forged for him by Hephaestus, and so attired he challenges Hector to combat. Hector sees the sunburst which casts a halo around Achilles' body and is seized with an uncontrollable trembling; three times Achilles chases him clear around the walls of Troy. But at last Hector turns and fights, knowing that he is fated to die. After Hector is slain the poem describes in great detail the funeral games held for Patroclus, and it ends with the funeral of Hector, "tamer of horses."

The *Iliad* was only one of several epics telling about the Trojan War; it survived because it was the best of the lot. The story of the war itself was so well known in oral tradition that few details of Homer's were new to the hearers of these poems. But we must remember that the poems themselves were transmitted orally after they were composed, and were recited at place after place by traveling rhapsodists, who could hardly resist manipulating them for their own purposes.

It is not difficult to spot some of these manipulations which came to stay. The passages describing the exploits of Diomedes of Argos were undoubtedly expanded when the poem was recited at Argos, Nestor surely became a much wiser old king when the recitations took place at Pylos, and Hector was certainly made to appear like a second-rate Greek hero when the poem was recited in any of the cities of Greece that identified themselves with the Achaeans, which would be most of them.

The truth almost certainly was that in the original *Iliad* Hector was a great hero, second only to Achilles. But his reputation was gradually hacked away in successive recitations until he became the confusing character that he is in the poem as we have it today, a warrior who is twice defeated in combat and is twice whisked away and saved by the gods. Homer repeatedly describes him as "tall, bright-helmeted Hector," "peerless Hector," "noble and shining Hector," but the phrases hardly seem to fit the character before us, who is most active when he is "hectoring" the minor Greeks opposite him in the fray.

The Trojan War should have ended after Menelaus defeated Paris in single combat before the two armies. This was what had been agreed upon by both sides. But Hera and Athena were still too vindictive toward Paris for having chosen Aphrodite as the most beautiful goddess, and refused to let the issue rest. When Menelaus knocked Paris down and began to drag him across the field by his helmet, Aphrodite broke the strap that was choking him and Menelaus "shot forward with an empty helmet." He quickly turned and charged again with his spear poised but Aphrodite "whirled Paris away with the ease of deity working," enclosed him in a cloud, and set him down in "his high-vaulted and perfumed bedroom" (Rees). The weak, effeminate character of Paris is clearly suggested by these words.

Homer individualizes every engagement of the Greeks and Trojans. Although thousands of men were supposedly taking part in these battles, the poet never once· describes any real mass action. He concentrates on the combats between individual warriors, each of whom is named and briefly characterized as the combat takes place. A few such descriptive phrases are "battle-roaring Menelaus," "flame-hearted Ajax," "flawless

Bellephon," "gutless Paris," "tall brave Acamas," etc. (Rees). Occasionally a couple of the warriors will pause long enough before fighting to give a rundown on their family trees. In Book 6 of the *Iliad* Diomedes catches sight of a huge Trojan who stands in his way, and he shouts: "Who are you, big man, who among mortals?" (Rees.) His foe, Glaucus, at this point delivers a two-page speech on his ancestry which reveals that there are many mutual friends in the two family trees. Diomedes is so impressed that he jumps from his chariot with Glaucus quickly following suit. The two men embrace and exchange armor as a pledge of permanent friendship and promise thenceforth to avoid each other carefully, no matter how thick the battle.

The *Iliad* is clearly a glorification of war, for it is only in battle that men face the moment of truth and reveal their true worth. And symbolically, of course, life itself is a battle which no man can escape. The entire poem is masculine oriented, as was the society it depicts. Helen inspires only a vulgar passion in Paris. Achilles and Agamemnon wrangle over a captive maiden like two angry schoolboys while men are dying by the dozen on the field of battle. Hector's wife Andromache does show a note of tenderness, and Hector reciprocates, but this is brief and it is exceptional. Also it comes along with the knowledge that Hector's death is already fated. It is not so difficult to show tenderness in the face of death; what is difficult is to be tender during the long hours of toil and tedium of life's daily routine. Only in the *Odyssey* do we get a glimpse of this aspect of married affection.

Homer takes a naturalistic delight in describing how the warriors die. One will be pierced in the chest exactly above or below the right or left nipple, another will take the sword in his belly and his guts will drop out, yet another dies as the spear "struck him in the right buttock, glanced around the bone, and pierced the bladder beneath." Agamemnon chased one Trojan and "thrust his spear into the man's back between the shoulders, and drove it out the chest on the other side. He crashed to the earth with his armor clattering on top of him." Another warrior slashed at his foe and "lopped his heavy arm off; streaming blood it fell to the ground, and purple death came down on his eyes." (Rees.)

Diomedes, who is really the best warrior among the Greeks if we judge from what actually takes place on the battlefield, at one point kills seven men in about half a page. The first of these dies as Diomedes "slashed off his shoulder in a single great blow, shearing it from the neck and back." Odysseus slays another seven Trojans in less than a third of a page. The *Iliad* is filled with slaughter from start to finish. Even the mighty Achilles grows weary of the war and cries out: "I am here in a land of strangers, fighting on horrible Helen's account with men of Troy." (Rees.) It is a man's world, and it is not romanticized. Goethe caught the spirit of the poem when he said: "An inch beneath the *Iliad* is hell."

When life is gone, nothing remains but the aura; there is no hope for a better life to come. Men's souls in Hades are only pallid shades wandering helplessly over the fields of asphodel, enjoying nothing. This is made clear in the *Odyssey* when Odysseus visits Hades and sees the ghosts there lapping up blood in a throwback to earlier and more primitive religious beliefs. In Hades he meets Achilles, who says to him: "I would rather be the meanest slave on earth than king here among these shadows."

Since the gods brought on the Trojan War, it is but a short step to viewing the whole ten years of slaughter before Troy as a kind of blood festival or game of the gods in which they take a demonic delight. But perhaps this would be doing Homeric religion an injustice, for in truth it was the Greek and Trojan soldiers who alternately reveled and panicked in the midst of battle which tried men's souls. The gods were there not only to take sides and so oppose each other but also by their presence to help men to fight their best.

When two men met in mortal combat and one was killed the victor immediately stopped fighting and tore off the armor of his foe. This was the concrete proof of his triumph, his trophy, his fruit of victory. Armor snatching was a close second to killing in this clash between Greeks and Trojans. The armor always took on a special value if it had a long history. Some of the prestige of its former owners, and of its maker, was passed on to the armor itself. The same thing was true of gifts which warriors frequently exchanged as tokens of hospitality, friendship, or reconciliation. Men and the possessions of men formed a kind of unity; the circle was closed when something passed from one hand into another.* Despite Homer's imagined palaces and cups and pitchers of gold and silver, the Homeric world was intrinsically poor and in it material objects took on great symbolic value.

The code that emerged from all this carnage was that man must always be at his best when in mortal combat. He had to prove himself before his peers and he had to prove himself before the gods. This did not mean that he never panicked. On one occasion we see Odysseus fleeing as fast as his

---

* In Book 23 two Greeks give a mare back and forth, each insisting that it belongs to the other. This is typical Mediterranean overgenerosity, that is, it is not generosity at all but is done in order to make the giver feel good even if the recipient is made to feel uncomfortable.

feet will carry him. Diomedes shouts to him: "Seed of the gods and son of Laertes, resourceful Odysseus, where are you going in such a hurry with your back to the battle like a coward? Have a care or some warrior will ram a spear between your shoulders as you run away. But stop, and help me fend off this fierce Trojan from old king Nestor." Homer then adds, "But long-suffering, noble Odysseus heard him not as he flew by on his way to the hollow ships." There was nothing really disgraceful in such conduct, because Odysseus on a better day would stand in the forefront and exchange blows with the best of them. But if possessed by panic, which came from the god Pan, he was compelled to run, just as on another day when encouraged by some other god or fulfilling his own reality he would fight like a lion and a hero heedless of death.

All the basic values in this world were predetermined by a man's birth. He was expected to fulfill his role in life just as he was certain to meet his preordained fate. Nothing could alter that. There is no such thing as a rational discussion in the *Iliad,* as Moses Hadas has pointed out. The pros and cons of possible courses of action are never weighed so that an intelligent decision might be taken. Decisions are foregone conclusions and arise out of the basic value system, which left no room for debate. Honor was perhaps the intrinsic basis of everything else; when honor collapsed the moral existence of the dishonored man collapsed with it.

This explains Achilles' long sulk in his tent and his refusal to bear arms among the Greeks until his honor has been salvaged. The captive girl Briseis seized from him by Agamemnon was worth very little, she was only a chattel, one girl among hundreds, but in this particular case she was of great symbolic importance because she was the repository of the honor of Achilles, something that belonged to him and of which he must not be dispossessed. Therefore, until Agamemnon made proper restitution, Achilles would not fight. According to the Greek code he was right; according to present-day values he was simply acting like a spoiled, self-centered adolescent. Agamemnon does make restitution with a series of symbolic gifts of great value, for the honor of Achilles was something of great value. But even after this Achilles does not enter the battle until his dear friend Patroclus is slain by Hector; then all of a sudden he becomes a veritable fury.

First, however, he weeps and wails like a person possessed; he throws himself down wallowing in the dust, he tears at his hair, and he pours ashes over his head. His lamentation goes on for hours. He acts exactly like an Asiatic woman who has lost her man or, as the line in the *Iliad* states, "like a wailing lioness who has lost her cub." This was supposed to suggest the close tie and loyalty of true friendship, but it also suggests homosexual overtones. The Greeks took homosexuality in stride. It was one of the facts of life and in no way impaired their potency with or desire for intercourse with women. Both kinds of sexual outlet were practiced and taken for granted. Prudery, indeed, was regarded as a form of avarice. What was *not* sanctioned was a homosexual relationship which ruled out intercourse with a woman, thus ruling out children. The Greeks looked askance at any such "unnatural" custom, for it would have meant the death of the race. In that world of constant war every single child was a chance for survival.

At the end of Book 18 of the *Iliad* there is a description of Greek home life highlighted in just the way that an absent soldier might call it to mind. The poet becomes suddenly lyrical and paints some very idyllic scenes of the bountiful harvest season on an Achaean farm. He does this by having these rural scenes embossed on the new shield of Achilles, which came to him as a gift from the gods. Achilles had given his old armor to Patroclus, who was slain by Hector, and Hector of course took off the dead man's armor and left Patroclus lying naked on the field. Achilles was thus left without arms, so his mother persuaded Hephaestus to make him a new all-shining shield and suit of armor. Hephaestus (and Homer) lavished great care in decorating the shield with typical scenes of Greek daily life.

The earth, the sky, the sea, and the moon were there, and many of the constellations too. Homer names them all, from Orion to the Pleiades. There was a bridal procession led by torchbearers, there were young men whirling about in a dance to the accompaniment of flutes and lyres, there was also a typical court scene where a case was being tried before the judge. There were plowmen guiding their teams down the furrows, there were reapers mowing the wheat, women were sprinkling meat for a feast with abundant white barley, and in a vineyard clusters of grapes were supported by silver poles. Two lions had pulled down a lowing bull as dogs attempted to drive them away. There were flocks of sheep and herds of cattle, and done in great detail was the etching of a famous dance scene in wide Knossos on Crete. To round out the picture there was also a city besieged by shining hosts of bronze-armored men; wives, small children, and old men were guarding the walls, while the soldiers went forth behind Ares and Athena, whose figures were embossed in gold and wearing golden armor.

On Achilles' shield Hephaestus, the ambidextrous god of crafts, re-capitulated Greek daily life, both in war and in peace, in the same manner that Ghiberti's gilded doors on the Baptistery at Florence recapitulate biblical scenes. As Homer describes the making of the shield he is filled with nostalgia and idealizes even the most tragic scenes. Life in battle was pictured only briefly and much as the poet had described it dozens of times in other parts of the *Iliad*. But life at home was for the most part bountiful and serene, though subject to the assault of wild lions and bandits. Everything was pictured on the shield in miniature: white sheep and cattle tended by their herders, farmers tilling the soil or drinking wine, rich fields of grain, golden sheaves, grapes on the vine, barley, roasting meat, music, dancing girls in sheer gowns, even the gods themselves, the earth, the sky and moon and constellations above. It was an Achaean idyll, a paean to life. The beautiful shield of Achilles was an artistic microcosm of the Greek world, as in later days man's mind was regarded as the microcosm of the universe. Man the measure was the bedrock of the Greek humanistic ideal, which was passed on to the Renaissance and from the Renaissance to all of Western civilization.

Book 23 of the *Iliad* describes in detail "The Funeral Games for Patroclus," the companion of Achilles killed by Hector. This book begins with Achilles befouling the body of Hector, flopping it face down in the dirt. Several times he takes cruel vengeance on the dead body as if it were still alive. He delights in dragging Hector's corpse around Patroclus' burial barrow, hoping thus to disfigure it in the most repulsive manner, but Apollo intervenes to prevent any scar, and Achilles continues in his fury. He refuses to honor Hector by burning his body, but lets it lie in the open hoping the dogs will devour his flesh.

Book 23 is the only place in Homer's poems where human sacrifices take place, representing a throwback to an even more primitive age. Achilles slits the throats of twelve valiant young Trojan men beside the pyre of Patroclus, but the poet is careful to point out that this was "an evil act he had planned in his heart" (Rees). Even Achilles, who was himself half-god, had no right to sacrifice human lives.

The games themselves give us a detailed rundown of Greek athletic contests many centuries before the First Olympiad, whose legendary date is 776 B.C. Such games may not have taken place in 1250 B.C., the actual time of the Trojan War, but they obviously were already thought of as being very ancient by the time Homer wrote. The poet begins the games with a chariot race on which he spends several pages. King Nestor tells his son how to manage his team in the race, how to guide them close around the turnpost, how to tilt his body most effectively, and he makes it clear that skill, not strength, will win the day "just as skill makes the fine woodcutter and enables the pilot to keep a straight course on the stormy, wine-dark sea." The chariot race is followed by a boxing match in which the hands of the fighters are bound with leather thongs. One Achaean knocks another flat on his back with blood spurting from his mouth. The third game is a wrestling match between Ajax and Odysseus, and when these two lock arms it is "like heavy timbers that hold up a roof." Neither man can throw the other, and the spectators become bored. The wrestlers decide to take turns lifting each other off the ground; in this manner each man wins one fall, and at this point Achilles calls off the match, judging it a tie.

The fourth game is a foot race, with a mixing bowl of silver as the prize. This bowl had a long and famous history, having belonged to several kings, which gave it a unique value. Here again Ajax (the *other* Ajax)* and Odysseus tangle, but Ajax slips and falls in a pile of bull excrement left on the track where Achilles had sacrificed several bulls. With this filth all over him, even in his eyes and nose, Ajax became a spectacle of gleeful laughter. He excuses his loss by saying that "Athena made me lose the race; I slipped because of her. She is standing always at the side of Odysseus mothering him about."

The fourth contest is between two fully armed warriors. This time Ajax takes on Diomedes, and the fight is called a tie when it appears that Diomedes might be able to reach over Ajax's shield and spear him in the throat. Then come the discus throw, the archery contest, and finally the javelin throw. In the archery contest the target is a dove at the end of a cord tied to the mast of a ship. The first archer cuts the cord, and the second grabs the bow and hits the dove in mid-air. In the discus contest the discus itself is of pig iron (writes Homer anachronistically), and the prize is "all the iron a man can use for five years." When the final game, the javelin contest, is about ready to get under way Achilles simply announces that everybody knows that the high king, great Agamemnon, was the finest javelin thrower of all the Achaeans, so he was awarded first prize with no contest.

It is obvious from this portion of the *Iliad* that the Greeks took great pride in their athletic prowess, which went hand in hand with their prowess in war. The one quality esteemed above all others was manliness. This quality could best be proved in a contest, which might take the form of combat with its single moment of truth, or it might be an athletic contest in which the superior athlete won, or in the *Odyssey* it might be man pitting himself against the elements. But the element of contest was necessary and prerequisite to the element of measure. When the chips were

* Homer frequently refers to "the two Ajaxes," great warriors from two different Greek cities. They generally fight side by side.

down the true man revealed himself. A series of contests or trials, therefore, became the measure of the degree of manliness. A Greek man could honorably shed copious and frequent tears, but he must never be cowardly "like a woman." Hector's fear before Achilles is prepared for by the poet first presenting Achilles fleeing madly to escape from the river Xanthos, which chased him in a very human fashion across the fields before Troy. Neither hero was a coward because when the moment of truth arrived each man turned and faced it bravely. But the poet was telling us that even the heroes were not perfect.

The lamentations of Achilles over the death of Patroclus and his consequent defiling of Hector's body are repeated several times toward the end of the *Iliad,* so many times that they must have palled on a sizable number of the early listeners. The keynote of the soul of Classic Greece was moderation, harmony, order, and even as far back as the time of Homer this ideal was evident. There must be a reasonable length of time for grief and a rapid end to senseless defilement of the enemy dead.

Apollo speaks the mind of all who shared this feeling when he says at the beginning of Book 24: "Achilles has lost all sense of pity, and his heart is shameless. Many a man has grieved one closer to him than this, perhaps a brother from the same womb, perhaps a son. But after he has wept and mourned him properly, there is an end to his grief, for the gods have given a tough and enduring soul to man. Achilles, having killed Hector, now insists on dragging his body daily around his comrade's barrow. Nothing good can come of this. Let him take care lest we gods grow angry with him, great as he is, for now in his rage he is defiling the senseless clay!"

Zeus suggests that Priam, Hector's father, send fitting gifts to Achilles, in return asking for his son's body. He also lets Achilles know the gods are angry with him and orders him to accept Priam's ransom for the body, which is indeed a kingly treasure: twelve beautiful robes, twelve cloaks and as many blankets, mantles, and tunics, ten talents of gold, two shining tripods, four bowls, and an exquisite goblet from Thrace, one of the king's rarest treasures. Achilles accepts the gifts, and Priam is led by Hermes into the Achaean camp to meet with him. Priam pleads his case, and Achilles, impressed by the old king's calm dignity, at last allays his own fury. "Come, and sit here beside me," he says. "We will let our sorrows lie quiet in our hearts, for though our pain is great, grim lamentations will avail us nothing. This is the lot that the sorrowless gods have spun for wretched men: that pain should be inseparable from life." Priam then is permitted to take the body of his dead son back with him into the city of Troy. His gifts have made justice possible.

Achilles does not die in the *Iliad,* nor does Troy fall into Achaean hands before the poem ends. But Hector is dead, and just as he had cried out before his death, "My fate has found me!" so also is it certain that Achilles soon must die, shot in the heel by weak and gutless Paris. There is no need to detail the obvious. The *Iliad* begins with the wrath of Achilles, which Agamemnon attempts to assuage with gifts of great value; then the poem proceeds to the death of Patroclus, followed by the death of Hector, and finally to the ransom of Hector's body. In order to make Achilles the great hero that he was to all Greeks, Homer could not end the story with him still in a fury at dead Hector's clay. He had to rise above that before his own fate found him so that he could go out in a blaze of glory. So the poem concludes with a forgiving Achilles, who speaks generous words to old Priam of Troy.

Achilles is the first tragic hero in literature. Early in life he was given a choice: either he could have a long and very ordinary life or he could have a brief but glorious one. He made the *right* choice, knowing that it would lead to his death. He made his own fate inescapable. To the Greeks there could be no real tragedy unless the life of a great man was at stake. The ordinary man who suffers a tragic lot in life could not have been the basis of a Greek tragedy. This was not conceivable in terms of the Greek value system, for the ordinary man's death was a thing of little importance. The same thing applied to honor: there could be no honor if honor was a quality shared by every soldier. It was a very special quality limited to the great heroes and bestowed by the gods. Tragedy and honor went hand in hand in the *Iliad,* as they did in early Greek life. The dead hero is a glorious hero, and the ever-struggling energy of men in misfortune gives life nobility. As Simone Weil wrote, "Only he who has measured the dominion of force, and knows how not to respect it, is capable of love and justice."

To the present-day reader Achilles may not appear as a great hero. He sulks far too long, even his victory over Hector is aided by the gods, who deflect Hector's weapon, and his vindictiveness over Hector's body and his womanlike grief over dead Patroclus would hardly endear him to those of us who read of his exploits in the twentieth century. But times and customs have changed fundamentally; neither is our Lord the Jehovah of the Old Testament, though indeed at times our actions, private and national, do still appear to manifest themselves after his violent and vengeful nature. Achilles is the epitome of the great Greek warrior, the strongest of the strong, the very spirit of the Achaean hosts before Troy. Without him they could not win. With his aid victory would come, but the victory itself, like

Achilles' death, would be tragic, for many noble Trojans (men, women, and children) would perish.

All the inhabitants of Troy thus become tragic heroes on a grand scale, just as centuries later the Persians, who had been defeated by the Athenians and their allies, became tragic heroes in classic Greek drama. The Greeks were merciless with their enemies. They slew the men they had beaten and took their women as captives into slavery. But they did not despoil their enemies of glory. Even though Hector's stature has undoubtedly been diminished by manipulations within the *Iliad,* the Trojans en masse still emerge as tragic heroes. Priam of the good ashen spear, Andromache,* Hector's tender wife, their little child Astyanax, whose future days are stark and cruel now that his father is dead—all these and many others besides, but most especially the hapless child, epitomize the tragedy of the Trojan race. Much of this feeling has come down through Western literature, and even today we instinctively regard the epithet "Trojan" as one of great praise and dignity, while being called "Greek" is often not a synonym for one's esteem. Such is the fate of the brilliant but confusing flowers in the garden of history.

* Euripides ennobles the Trojan suffering in his plays *Andromache* and *The Trojan Women.*

V

The World of Odysseus

*There are only two remedies for the suffering
of the soul: hope and patience.*

Pythagoras

The *Odyssey* may be regarded as a continuation of the *Iliad*. It takes one
Greek warrior, Odysseus, who had fought ten years before Troy, and
records what happens to him on his long journey home, which lasts another
ten years. In the meantime Telemachus, the old warrior's son, has set out in
search of his father.

Odysseus relates his adventures in a flashback before the assembled
courtiers of King Alcinous of Phaecia, his last stop on the way home. The
king gives the hero a ship and many costly gifts and bids him godspeed.
Odysseus safely reaches Ithaca, where he was king, but he is not recognized. He finds his palace occupied by a group of gluttonous and importu-
nate suitors for the hand of his wife, Penelope. Odysseus' identity is
gradually revealed, he overcomes the suitors, is recognized by Penelope,
and all ends well.

In both the *Iliad* and the *Odyssey* men are superior to the gods, if not in
power at least in dignity, and of all Homeric heroes the Odysseus of the
Odyssey is most clearly dignity incarnate. He foreshadows both the magic
and the reality of the incomparable heyday of Greece. Until he (epitomizing the Greeks in general) had conquered the elements there could arise no
firmly rooted culture in Hellas. The *Odyssey* is also a very realistic story of
blows given and blows received, with the hero, who deals and takes, never
going under.

But there is another part of the story that is not realistic at all, in which
the poet takes special delight as he weaves a fairy tale of fantasy. There is
much more of this kind of magic in the *Odyssey* than in the *Iliad:* the

winds being shut up in a small bag, Odysseus' men setting them loose, Circe turning his men into swine, Hermes giving Odysseus a magic herb to turn them back into men again, Polyphemus grabbing a mountaintop to hurl at the departing ship, another ship being turned to stone, the many times when Athena conceals Odysseus by surrounding his body with a sudden mist, and of course the frequent occasions when the goddess herself appears in a form other than her own. She is a small child, a young shepherd, a Phaecian courtier, a male or female companion, as the case demands.

Athena is not only Odysseus' protector among the gods. She and he represent essentially the same thing. Eventually the two merge symbolically into one as the new value system is proclaimed. Athena also looks out for Telemachus, and is anxious throughout the story to see father and son reunited, the hangers-on at the palace at Ithaca challenged and killed, and Odysseus restored to his position as king. She is more of a mother to Telemachus than Penelope has been, and her sheltering tenderness is often quite obvious, as for example early in the poem when she speeds him on his way saying, "Some immortal one who cares for you will make a fair wind blow."* At the end of the poem she even stops time by holding back the dawn, she also turns Odysseus' rags to royal tunics with a touch of her wand, and finally she rejuvenates both Odysseus and his father, Laertes. Nothing is too wonderful for those who are under her protection.

Among the Homeric characters Odysseus is the one who most clearly grows as the two epics progress. He is, in fact, the only person who is a main character in both poems, and his full stature is not revealed until the end of the *Odyssey*. In the *Iliad* Odysseus is hardly the ideal hero, despite the poet's frequent reference to him as one of the greatest. He lies frequently, he kills after having promised safe-conduct, he shows fear in battle and does not hesitate to turn tail and run. Then in the next episode, bolstered by Athena, he will face about and hold at bay an entire army of Trojans. But in the *Odyssey* he is a different man. He is still called "resourceful Odysseus," "the man of many devices," "the great tactician," but he does not in fact depend on deception or dissimulation in order to control events. He does use them to mask his identity, but most of all he feels a compulsion to re-create himself in his actions.

In Book 13 of the *Odyssey,* when after all his adventures he is finally left on the shores of Ithaca by the Phaecians, the old warrior does not recognize the place. Athena appears to him in the form of a young

* From Homer: *The Odyssey,* translated by Robert Fitzgerald.

shepherd and tells him where he is. Odysseus promptly fabricates a tale for him, saying he has just arrived from Crete, where he had killed a man who robbed him of his rightful spoils of war. Athena then changes her form to that of a beautiful young lady, and stroking his hand, she says softly to Odysseus:

> No one can get the edge on you unless he's sharp
> And crafty as they come; even a god is no more
> Knowledgeable in guile and stratagem.
> You are a master of deceit, a man so devious
> That even here at Ithaca you pull the same old trick.
> It is your nature to dissimulate. Let's waste no words,
> You and I, cut of the same cloth we are!
> Among the gods my forte is common sense,
> But I am a great deceiver, too, Odysseus,
> Not even you could guess my real identity.
> I am Pallas Athena, daughter of Zeus,
> In times of crisis always at your side.

Athena thus occupies a very special place in the *Odyssey.* There is nothing comparable in the *Iliad,* where the gods line up and take sides, with no particular one of them playing a unique role. But in the *Odyssey* Athena's role is not only unique, it is a kind of divine constant measuring out the life by values epitomized in Odysseus. The goddess is truly at his side through every test and trial, adding that extra quotient which ensures victory.

She begins the book by pleading for Odysseus before the throne of Zeus and ends it as peacemaker between the opposing factions in Ithaca. There is no doubt that Odysseus is her very special charge, and that through her no harm can come to him. In fact she "accompanies him everywhere like a mother," just as Ajax had said when Odysseus defeated him in the foot race before the walls of Troy. When she first pleads for him before Zeus, her father, Zeus replies that he will never forget that godlike man "who is beyond all other men in mind and who beyond all others has given sacrifice to the gods."* Hearing these words Athena puts on the golden sandals which transport her magically across the sea to Ithaca where she starts Telemachus, the son of Odysseus, on his search for his father. With this stroke the action begins.

It is not coincidence that both Athena and Odysseus symbolize mind over matter, wisdom and resourcefulness over brute force. The *Odyssey*

---

* From Homer: *The Odyssey of Homer,* translated by Richmond Lattimore.

might also be regarded as an extension of the legendary struggle on the Acropolis between Poseidon and Athena for the city of Athens. Poseidon had struck a rock and sea water gushed forth, signifying great sea power for the city if it chose him. Athena struck a rock and an olive tree sprouted from it. Her gift was food, light, and wisdom if the city should choose her. The men all voted for Poseidon, and the women for Athena, and as the women outnumbered the men by one, Athena was chosen goddess of Athens. The corollary was that Poseidon in a rage flooded the city, and the men, holding the women responsible, denied them equal rights and made them second-class citizens.

In the *Odyssey,* in a parallel struggle, Odysseus overcomes Poseidon by surviving his fiercest storms until his final landfall on Ithaca. Odysseus is also the prophetic forerunner of Athenian sea power and of the Athenian aristocrat, strong mind in strong body. Athena, for her part, is patroness of the city in which intelligence reigned supreme. Together they represent the new Greek culture emerging awkwardly from the Mycenaean-Dorian mold, as a butterfly emerges from its ugly and misshapen chrysalis.

The *Odyssey* tells of the wandering and homecoming of an old warrior who is anxious to return to his wife. He is strong and steadfast, and she is faithful. This basic story of Odysseus and Penelope, with its happy ending, unfolds against the background of the frequently mentioned tragic fate of Agamemnon and Clytemnestra. A parallel is drawn in the first few lines of the poem, which tell of Agamemnon's homecoming and murder at the hands of his adulterous wife and her lover. Odysseus recalls Agamemnon's fate on several occasions with new elements being added each time. In Book 11 the ghost of Agamemnon tells the story from his own point of view, and he warns Odysseus not to make the same mistake that he made, trusting his wife, "so put your ship to land secretly at Ithaca, and slip unknown into your country." He cruelly adds: *"The day of faithful wives is gone forever."* (Fitzgerald.)

However, in Book 13 Athena takes the edge off this warning by inform- ing Odysseus that Penelope *is* still faithful to him and longs for his return. Odysseus is profoundly grateful to learn that the conditions which pre- vailed in Agamemnon's Mycenae do not prevail in Ithaca. But he begs Athena to give him courage to see things through, and he promises to take on 300 fighting men if only she will brace him. Athena promises that she will, and as they sit under "an old gray olive tree," she plans with him the strategy; in a most unladylike speech she prophesies victory and sees the blood and brains of Penelope's suitors "splattered all over the floor" of Odysseus' palace in Ithaca.

The basic element of suspense is thus taken away from the story, because the auditor-reader now knows what the outcome will be. But the poet does not give up his advantage that easily; he draws on the living corpus of tradition for a highly complex series of adventures which will maintain steady interest. How will Odysseus reach Ithaca? Will he really sneak in and check up on Penelope? How will he reveal himself to her and to the suitors? What will their reactions be? How will he and his son meet, and what will take place at this encounter? What will the final struggle to the death between the two groups be like? Homer's bag of tricks is still far from exhausted, and the resources of his poetic creativity will keep the stir of life moving rapidly forward as answers are given to all these and many more questions.

Basically the poet is interested in values and judgments rather than in the drama of action for its own sake. Perhaps unconsciously, but nonetheless deliberately, he is laying down a definition of the Greek ideal of man against which all later men, both real and fictional, are to be measured. The *Odyssey* represents the New Testament of the ancient Greeks, much as the *Iliad* represents the Old. Without the strong religious overtones of Hebraic scripture, these two epics taken together are in a very real sense the Bible of Hellas.

This judgmental quality of the *Odyssey* is made clear from the very first lines of the epic, which introduce Odysseus "the man of many ways who was driven on far journeys" (Lattimore). In line 7, to be precise, mention is made of the destruction of his companions *"who were destroyed by their own wild recklessness* for devouring the sacred cattle of the Sun God, Helios"* (Lattimore). Then the poet describes the gathering of the gods on Mount Olympus where they recall the sad fate of Agamemnon after his homecoming. Zeus speaks to the assembled gods (lines 32–34):

> It is a great shame that mortal men blame us,
> The gods, for every evil that befalls them,
> When it is truly they, who by their own folly
> Increase their sorrows far beyond what we have
>   Ordained.

Later, in Book 18, Odysseus states man's point of view before the assembled suitors in his palace:

> Listen to what I have to tell you, and understand:
> Of all the creatures on the face of this earth
> There is none weaker or more helpless than man.
> It never occurs to him to think of future misfortune

As long as his heart has courage and his knees
    are strong.
But when, against his will, the blessed gods send
    grief
He must endure it with a steadfast heart.
For the spirit of men upon this earth is as their
    day
Which comes to them from the father of gods and
    men.

In other words, man is subject to the laws of the gods but within these limits he is condemned to a freedom of choice by which he may either double his sorrow or improve his reputation. The gods are just, but they are not merciful. Mercy is a quality that is not known in Homer. The Darwinian struggle for existence prevailed centuries before Darwin. Man must use his unique quality of manliness within the limits imposed on it. When he exceeds these limits he is hurt severely. But he is not "punished" because he has committed a "sin"; he is hurt because he has tried to manipulate the clearly defined laws of life for his own selfish purposes. The overtones of "guilt" are scarcely evident.

THE REALITIES OF GREEK LIFE

In addition to being a poem of adventure with symbolic overtones which could not possibly have been apparent to its early auditor-readers, the *Odyssey* contains many details of Greek reality, just as did the *Iliad* before it. First of all, it presents a wide panorama of Mediterranean geography. Homer not only knew the sailing routes and the stars, he also knew many lands that shored upon that salt immortal sea. Odysseus speaks familiarly of Troy in Asia Minor; of Egypt, where he claims to have lived for several years; of Crete, which he also appeared to know intimately; of Libya, land of the Lotus Eaters; of Malta (perhaps Calypso's Island); of Italy (the Circe episode) and of Sicily (Scylla and Charybdis); of Corfu (the Paradise of the Phaecians); of Ithaca, his home; perhaps of Corsica; and certainly of many other islands, some identifiable, others not, in the Mediterranean.*

The poet also tells about Telemachus at Pylos and at Sparta on the Greek

---

* Ernle Bradford in *Ulysses Found* (New York: Harcourt, Brace, 1964), traces what he thinks was the actual route of Odysseus. Bradford, convinced of the geographic authenticity of the *Odyssey,* sailed in the wake of the great traveler for many months, Homer in hand. He notes all landfalls, and makes an interesting case. His findings are summarized in the National Geographic's *Greece and Rome,* 1968, a beautifully illustrated book.

mainland, and he mentions many other cities scattered throughout the Greek world of 1250 B.C.—Mycenae, Argos, Knossos, Athens, Thebes, and others. Many mountains, bays, rivers, and valleys also are mentioned, and some of them are described with brief but telling effect. The *Odyssey*, indeed, is a compendium of Greek geography of the Homeric and pre-Homeric periods.

In Book 15 the poet speaks of the traders who then plied the sea. These were mostly Phoenicians who traveled from place to place exchanging jewelry and gauds for products of the land. Sometimes they remained for a year or more before leaving for the next destination on their journey. Odysseus' swineherd remembers a lovely golden chain all strung with amber which one of these traders offered for sale. Gold is mentioned frequently but only once as a currency, when it became the passage fee for a trip on the sea. Cargoes of cattle were often shipped by the traders from one point to another, indicating that there was a considerable commerce in heavy goods. The Phoenicians are presented as the shrewd traders of a later date; they are stereotypes of the sharp dealer even in this area where haggling is an old custom.

Family life in the *Odyssey* is more suggested than described. But the family is clearly the symbolic unit of man's social instincts. Telemachus, Odysseus' son, is "sweeter to him than sunlight," and Penelope, "shining among women" (Fitzgerald), is very cautious in acknowledging her husband until he has revealed himself with all the secrets of their long-lost life together in their prime. After this revelation she is convinced, and as he reaches out for her his faithful wife moves into his arms. He longs for her embrace "as a spent swimmer longs for the warm and welcoming shore." Their lovemaking is mentioned tenderly, but is not described. The poet gives verisimilitude to Penelope's inability to recognize her husband by having Athena change his appearance radically—shriveling his skin, sinking his eyes, changing the color and fiber of his hair.

Sex is a constant in the *Odyssey*, but there is not a single word which might be called titillating. Odysseus has sexual relations with several women, among them the nymphs or goddesses Circe and Calypso; the adulterous relations between Aphrodite and Ares are also described in some detail. Divine coitus rather than sex between ordinary men and women is the rule in the *Odyssey*, but the sexual theme is very unimportant in the epic as a whole. The modern reader will be surprised at the unconcerned manner in which young and beautiful women prepare hot baths, bathe the bodies of men, then rub them down with perfumed oil. Both Telemachus and Odysseus are bathed in this fashion, and the poet very briefly describes the bath in the most matter-of-fact tone. The element of sexual stimulation is completely absent from these passages, which makes one wonder if the intervening centuries have indeed altered the focus of our erotic impulses and the manner of their expression.

As we read the *Odyssey* we see the Greek countryside of hills and valleys, with its stone or mud houses, its fences of piled stones (much as today), its herds of cattle, sheep, goats, pigs, its olive trees and vineyards, its apple, fig, pomegranate, and pear trees, its currants drying in the sun, and near the grapevines the long rows of vegetables. In Book 7 fruit trees and vines are irrigated by ditches that flow from a great fountain. Of course, this irrigated garden is the Paradise of the Phaecians; it hardly represents the ordinary farmer's field or orchard. There are woods of alder, pine, black poplar, cedar and frequent cypress, tall vines with clusters of purple flowers, beds of violets and parsley, brightly colored birds, owls, hawks, doves, thrushes, larks, geese, cormorants, bats, sea gulls, and nightingales. Horses and mules draw carts along shaded lanes, and the carts on Phaecia have brightly painted wheels. Lions, wolves, and dogs are frequently a part of the background of the story.

Food is good and apparently it is abundant, at least in the favored places where the wanderings of Odysseus take him. There are beef, pork, mutton, cheese, and milk; meat of all kinds is prepared on spits and heaped on great platters; wine flows freely; there is bread and honey and fruit. The butchering of a pig is described minutely, first the hard blow on the head, then the knife at its throat, followed by the immediate quartering. Pieces of fat are dipped in barley meal and thrown in the fire as offerings to the gods, while the rest goes on the spit to be eaten at once. There are also goat stomachs filled with blood puddings, broiled tripe, fish for the poor, and olives aplenty; there are generally no spoons or forks; people eat with their hands, using a knife to cut a piece of meat or else picking it up directly from the platter along with a hunk of bread, which is baked not as a thick loaf but in pancake dimensions.

As most of the eating takes place in palaces, there are many mentions of golden pitchers and silver bowls for washing the hands and of golden drinking cups with two handles. In one of the palaces there are even silver bathtubs. There is also a silver basket with wheels on it and a golden distaff. These are the imagined utensils of Mycenaean royalty. Some of them did exist but they were certainly not as common as Homer makes out. Less pretentious utensils were goblets or bowls of ivy wood or of pottery and tripods and caldrons of bronze.

Every dwelling is guarded by watchdogs, and Odysseus himself almost gets badly bitten by "four dogs like wild beasts" when he returns home incognito and takes up with his old swineherd. Later at the palace in Ithaca he sees his old dog Argos, covered with flies and fleas, lying in a pile of filth near the doorway. Argos recognizes his master despite an absence of twenty years, lays his ears back, and becomes so excited that he dies. Argos must have been at least twenty-one years old, something of a record for the dogs of history, and incredible for a dog which had been so poorly fed and meanly treated.

Odysseus is careful when he goes to sleep at night to keep a sharp spear at his side to protect him from the wild dogs which might attack him in the dark. There are wild dogs roving the countryside in bands which often attack the sheep and cattle. When the boar hunt is described the poet tells of hounds tracking and cornering the beast, but no detailed description is given of the appearance of these ancient Greek dogs. Pictures of them on Greek pottery indicate that the most common canine variety resembled a Great Dane or a large greyhound but thicker and heavier than the ones we have today.

There were hound-like dogs in Egypt centuries earlier than this. Dogs have been with man since prehistory; the earliest drawings of them in caves go back almost fifty thousand years. These animals are shown hunting with men. The only question is: Were they true dogs or were they tamed wolves or foxes? Perhaps what we know as the dog grew out of a crossing among other canine species or perhaps it was a species in its own right. History is not sure on this point.

Homeric furniture was of wood, often ornately carved, and on occasion inlaid with ivory, gold, or silver. Diners sat in chairs along the walls and ate at small tables placed between them. Chairs and stools were not unlike our own, but legs were usually curved outward like the fingers of a hand placed firmly against the flat surface. Chairs were invariably covered with heavy fleeces, and often in the *Odyssey* maids are placing clean ones of crimson or white in position for the guests.

Beds were generally of piles of fleeces, with another fleece or a woven blanket as a covering. When the bed was made outdoors a cured oxhide was placed beneath the fleeces to insulate the body from the ground. In more rustic surroundings heaped fir tips or brushwood made a soft base on top of which the bedding was laid.

Odysseus forced Penelope to recognize him (and to sleep with him instead of putting him out in the open as she had intended) by describing the bed which he had made for them twenty-odd years previously. He had built their bedroom of stone around the cut-off trunk of an old olive tree, and had allowed just enough of the trunk to remain to serve as a bedpost. He trimmed and planed the trunk to size and then bored holes in it. After planing his other posts in the same manner he drilled them all, inlaid them with ivory, silver, and gold, and strung crimson thongs of hide between them to serve as a flexible mattress. Hearing him describe this bed, Penelope knows that he is her long-lost spouse.

In the so-called palaces fleeces and woven rugs covered the earth or stone floors. There was a columned porch and entrance-way and a columned main hall with the hearth in the center. Around its sacred fire the family and guests gathered to feel the spark of contact, to keep warm, and to discuss the vagaries of fate and the vicissitudes of life. There were no windows in the walls as we have them today, but there were skylights and also clerestories or openings just beneath the ceiling where the gently sloping roofs of reeds and clay met the wall. At night torches mounted on tall stands along the walls gave off a shimmering but uncertain light. The quarters of the women were rigorously separated from those of the men, and in Odysseus' palace in Ithaca the women's quarters were securely locked at night.

Garments were ordinarily of a single large rectangular cloth draped on the body across the shoulders, fastened with a pin, and reaching almost to the knees. Princes sometimes wore embroidered cloaks or tunics and princesses on occasion dressed in embroidered and richly woven gowns. Helen gave Telemachus an elaborately wrought robe which she had made herself that "shone like a star." Both sexes wore jewelry, and necklaces and earrings of gold and amber were especially desired. Pins and brooches of gold, silver, and bronze also were used. Hide sandals were worn out of doors, but indoors the custom was to go barefoot. If the weather was cold a sheep or goatskin cap or coat was often added to the other garments to keep the wearer warm.

Homer's royal characters, despite having plenty of servants and slaves, took pride in performing manual labor. Odysseus worked as a stonemason and carpenter to construct his own house and furniture, Helen made beautiful robes by hand, Queen Arete of the Phaecians and Penelope both wove cloth on their looms, and Princess Nausicaa washed clothes at the river with her handmaidens, stamped on the laundry with her feet, spread out the clean wash on the rocks to dry, and then played ball with the girls in the grass. There is no loss in dignity when the Homeric aristocrat uses his hands; on the contrary, he is proud to surpass others in manual labor as in other activities of Achaean life. Such will not be the case when we reach the fifth century and Classic Greece.

THE "AUTHORIZED" HOMER

The *Odyssey* is a well-told story of adventure, wandering, search, romance, and homecoming, but its conclusion is hurried and reaches a gory climax. With Athena's aid Odysseus, Telemachus, and two servants (the oxherd and the swineherd) rapidly dispatch five times as many well-armed suitors and the palace floor turns crimson. Odysseus, "like a lion splashed with mire and blood" (Fitzgerald), stands over the dead bodies like Achilles over Hector. Then the maidservants who have been sleeping with the suitors are dragged out and forced to clean up the carnage, after which (at the behest of Telemachus) they are all strung up on ship's ropes and hanged, "their feet fluttering like the wings of birds, but not for very long." Melanthios, the goatherd, who had passed over to the side of the suitors, is not only slain but his nose, ears, and private parts are sliced off and fed to the dogs.

This savage climax hardly seems to belong to what had been a romance of high adventure and homecoming, but it must have been such a well-known episode in the ancient lays that no rhapsodist dared alter it. Either this, or some rhapsodist deliberately imitated the parallel scene in the *Iliad* where Achilles repeatedly defiles Hector's dead body and then demands a human sacrifice of twelve young Trojans to avenge the death of Patroclus. In the *Odyssey* human sacrifice at least becomes the "execution of traitors," a custom which has not yet entirely disappeared from civilization.

Many other shocking episodes in both poems have been altered or glossed over in the versions which have survived. For example, from early commentaries made on the poems we know that in the original version of the *Iliad* Hector is cruelly tortured while he is still alive, but in the version we have this is turned into a defilement of his corpse. Many other episodes of cruelty or abusive language are similarly deleted or softened. Also, King Alcinous and Queen Arete of Phaecia were originally brother and sister, but a marriage between siblings was not acceptable to the Greeks of a later date. Plato himself in his *Republic* reveals that there were passages in the poems which caused revulsion in his generation "and we must beg Homer not to be angry if we delete them."

The Greeks of Athens, who were responsible for the final form which these epics took, were reluctant to represent their idealized ancestors as savages, but the few surviving unaltered (or very slightly altered) passages indicate the pre-Homeric origin of the poems and recapitulate an age when human sacrifice was common and human vengeance took the most brutal form. This Athenian editing of Homer may also explain Hector's resembling a second-rate hero rather than being the resplendent Hector that he most certainly was in the ancient lays and also in the lost epic about Thebes. The historic Hector was said to be a heroic defender of Thebes, not Troy, and his grave was for many centuries pointed out to those who visited that city. The Athenians could not endure a great Theban hero, even if he was later turned into a Trojan and his deeds transported to Troy.

Athena plays with rare skill her dual role as guardian angel of Odysseus and as the particular goddess and protector of the city of Athens. At one point in the middle of the poem she suddenly takes leave of Odysseus and returns to the Erechtheum on the Athenian Acropolis and at another point a procession carries the *peplos* (large shawl) to her in the same manner that it was borne in the Panathenaean celebration many centuries later. In the end Athens was victorious over Homer just as Athena had been victorious over Poseidon in their contest for the lordship of Athens. This may not necessarily be a bad thing; perhaps the Athenians improved the ancient poems with their polishing, removing an excess of gore. Who can be sure?

After the battle in the palace hall and the death of the suitors Odysseus reveals himself to Penelope, and they go to bed together sharing bodies and memories. Penelope laments that they have irretrievably lost "their young and flowering years" and must now try to make them up. Athena even holds back the dawn so that this memorable night may last longer than the usual allotted span. Odysseus then visits the shades of the dead suitors, a quite unnecessary episode, and finally goes to the farm of his father, Laertes, makes himself known, and tells what he has done at the palace. The kinsmen of the suitors soon arrive on the scene demanding revenge, and the opposing groups again confront each other, but this time Zeus angrily hurls down a smoky thunderbolt and Athena intervenes as peacemaker, after which she quickly disappears and the poem comes to an end. The conclusion is not as satisfying as the rest of the story, and the rhapsodists who are responsible simply did not "stitch their songs together" as well as they might have in these final lines.

The city of Athens placed its indelible mark on both the *Iliad* and the *Odyssey* around 550 B.C., when the tyrant Peisistratus "restored" the ancient order of the Homeric epics.* This same tyrant also elaborated the celebrated Panathenaea, a series of festivities "of all Athenians" held every four years. There were three important parts to the Panathenaea: first, the

---

* In the *Odyssey* one of Nestor's sons who helps Telemachus is named Peisistratus. This may be more than coincidence.

recitation of the works of Homer "and no other poet" by professional rhapsodists; second, a series of games held in order to rival the Olympiads; and third, the Panathenaeic procession in which the newly woven *peplos* and many other gifts were borne to Athena, whose statue in full armor stood on the Acropolis.

The "Works of Homer" recited at the Panathenaea were the *Iliad* and the *Odyssey;* other so-called Homeric poems were not included. The rhapsodists observed a fixed order of recitation, and followed each other by taking a cue, so that each man knew exactly where to stop or where to begin. A single rhapsodist's turn lasted for about two hours, and the recitation of the two poems, of course, took several days.

The other ritualistic part of the Panathenaea was the procession of the *peplos.* This was a saffron-colored shawl-like cloak newly woven for the occasion by the women of Athens, which was richly embroidered with scenes of the battle between the gods and the giants. After being borne along the sacred way it was received by a priest and draped on the shoulders of Athena's statue. The procession was one of especial splendor and consisted of hundreds of people of all ages, many of whom carried gifts. Athletes and men on horseback also formed a part of the procession, as did all the animals which were to be sacrificed.

The Parthenon Ionic frieze depicts the formation of this procession wondrously in stone. There were originally 525 feet of this continuous frieze, which once circled the enclosed portion of the temple, but only 420 feet survive. Phidias probably sculptured the finest sections, most of which are now in the British Museum. A few sections still remain in place on the west and south sides but the viewer must stand inside the columns and look upward at an uncomfortable angle in order to see them.

The Peisistratus edition of the *Iliad* and the *Odyssey* recited at the Panathenaea certainly embodied many interpolations and omissions which reflect the aesthetic, moral, and martial customs and attitudes of the city of Athens. This even carries over into such relatively unimportant matters as manner of dress, armor, and fighting in battle. The heavy bronze suits of armor so frequently described in the *Iliad* belonged in fact to a much later date and closely resemble those of the Athenians. The method of hoplite (full armor) fighting was also not Mycenaean but later Greek. So was the dress of the Homeric heroes, which resembled the Attic style rather than the short kilt-like garments of the Mycenaeans. In Book 2 of the *Iliad* the Catalogue of Ships (probably based on an ancient document listing the ships mustering at Aulis, rather than those moored off Troy) mentions every city of consequence in Hellas except Thebes, Aegina, and Megara, which were the enemies of Athens. Only the Athenians could have had reasons for these suppressions.

The story of a wanderer who returns home after a long absence and is not recognized by his wife is one that is common to all folklore. Nature's own wanderer, the Wind (Aeolus in Greek mythology), may have been its source. Aeolus was the grandfather of Jason, the sea-roving Argonaut, whose exploits in search of the Golden Fleece rivaled the siege of Troy in popularity among the heroic tales. In the *Odyssey*, when Odysseus reached the realm of Aeolus on his errant homeward voyage (Book 10), he was received like a son, and Aeolus handed over to him the bag of caged "contrary" winds. Other mythical wanderers whose homecoming followed years of trial and long voyages were Hercules, Dionysus, Orpheus, and Sinbad, the sailor. More recent parallel figures are Robinson Crusoe, Rip Van Winkle and Enoch Arden. The story is as old as history, and undoubtedly predates the events narrated in the *Iliad*. But the treatment given the adventures of Odysseus has a more human cast than does the tale of Troy, and the story is more appealing to modern readers. The *Iliad*, on the other hand, was the favorite of ancient Greece.

The *Odyssey* also suggests the wide orbiting and conjunction of astral bodies. The twenty years (twenty fingers and toes) that the hero is gone from home coincide with the twenty-year cycle in ancient astronomy, after which there is a legendary meeting of the sun and the moon. In the poem Odysseus and Penelope do indeed meet after twenty years on *the exact day* when this union of the two heavenly bodies was supposed to take place. The poem also tells us that Odysseus had 360 boars, one of which died each night; obviously, this was inspired by the ancient riddle about the days of the year.

Helen of Troy, who was first Helen of Sparta, was in history a marriage-goddess in Sparta, and in that city the marriage ceremony concluded with the carrying off of the bride. Consequently, Helen is "carried off" many times and to many different places in Spartan legend. In some versions only her insubstantial image is transported to Troy, while the real Helen is hidden away safely by one of the gods. This, of course, saves her reputation and makes her a more suitable wife when Menelaus brings her back from Troy. It also makes Spartan women in general look more honorable. Euripides uses this version of the story in his drama *Helen*. None of these correlations is basic to one's enjoyment of the Homeric epics, but they do indicate how ancient were the sources from which this heroic poetry emerged. The *Iliad* and the *Odyssey* are a brilliant tapestry which recapitulates a thousand years of Hellenic culture. No other civilization in the history of the world can boast as much. Even so, they were only the begin-ning; Greece's most splendid flower was yet unborn.

The *Iliad* and the *Odyssey* were by no means the only early Greek poems which told of the Trojan War and of the homecomings of the Achaeans, among them Odysseus. There was an entire post-Homeric epic cycle of several poems which supplied the details lacking in the two great epics attributed to Homer. These poems have not survived, but summaries of them have come down to us, and a few random lines have been preserved in the words of later writers. These cyclic poems tell of Paris and the golden apple, the death of Achilles, the suicide of Ajax, who goes mad when Odysseus is awarded Achilles' armor, the episode of the wooden horse and the taking of Troy, the death of Odysseus, the marriage of Telemachus, the sacrifice of Iphigenia at Aulis by her father, Agamemnon, in order to appease the goddess Artemis, whose sacred stag he had slain, and so on. Many episodes related in this post-Homeric cycle clarify and make more understandable things that take place in classic Greek drama. For example, the sacrifice of Iphigenia, who is not mentioned in the *Iliad,* makes the consequent murder of Agamemnon by his wife spring at least in part from a mother's natural passion.

The post-Homeric epic cycle of poems, however, is not comparable in aesthetic value to the *Iliad* and the *Odyssey,* and the conclusions which they present of the deaths of the heroes (Achilles, Ajax, Odysseus, and others) diminishes the nobility of their characters. Literary history has since so mingled what Homer sang with the post-Homeric follow-ups that only a fresh reading of the *Iliad* and the *Odyssey* will keep clear the line of demarcation between them.

In any case, literature is singularly fortunate to have the two finest epics of man's struggle in complete form, while the poorer poems of the epic cycle have become the basis for so much of the classic Greek drama which, along with Homer, is still the wonder of Western letters. Freud without Greek drama is almost inconceivable, as is the mythology of our culture without Homer. Humanity has lost so many of its treasures through hatred, neglect, and ignorance that we should be ever grateful that both the Bible of our religion and the Bible of our literature have been saved from the holocausts of history, whose sad recording shows that when one man creates a thing of beauty another man will try his level best to smash it into the earth. Human energy is, outside of nature, the only source of beauty in a constantly changing universe. Despite every adversity, man's creative roots find nutriment and struggle to flower as the world struggles to flower in beings that are human.

VI

The Flower of Youth:
The Greeks Look Westward

There is no happier day for any man
Than to sit in a great hall at a table
Filled with bread and meat, hearing a bard perform
As a steward passes about filling each cup with wine,
And fellowship spreads joy throughout the land.
This is the finest thing in life!

Homer, *The Odyssey*

The *Iliad* alone gives only a partial picture of ancient Greek life. It shows
the Greek aristocrats at war, which was their glory and, according to this
epic, almost their sole profession. But the *Iliad* and the *Odyssey* must be
taken together to comprise the full duality of the Hellenic ideal of the
heroic age. Achilles was the ideal Mycenaean or Achaean (as Homer saw
the Achaeans); he was the perfect warrior, the strong, passionate, and
avenging friend, the tragic hero, the ideal champion. Achilles represented
the Hellenic past, a Mycenae which had already been dead for at least four
centuries when Homer wrote. He also represented in many ways the Asiatic
hero, at least the hero of the Asiatic (Ionian) part of Greece in Asia
Minor. The entire Trojan War takes place in Asia Minor, near the
Dardanelles, of which it is the fortress. Hence, the *Iliad* is oriented eastward in geography and backward in history.

The *Odyssey*, on the other hand, is oriented westward in geography and
forward in time. Greek civilization now moves from Asia Minor out onto
the open Mediterranean and to the western Greek islands; it extends to
Egypt and to Sicily, to Italy, to Corsica, and perhaps to Spain. Odysseus is
the great seaman, the great navigator, the great explorer, the new Greek
spirit, which, while striving to find its home again, discovers new paths

and creates new destinies. The spirit of Odysseus is reproduced in the age of the great discoveries when the argosies of Portugal and Spain cross the dark Atlantic and bring a new world into the European orbit.

But Odysseus in the poem is more than this; he is also the just and merciful patriarch, the kind ruler, the restorer of justice, the man who "had no evil thoughts, but was kind as a father to his people" (Fitzgerald). When he returns to his home he reinstitutes the rule of justice, the rule of law, the reign of the just and kindly king. Prior to this final confrontation Odysseus verbalizes the noble ideal that he embodies in his conversation with Penelope. He has not yet revealed his identity to her when he expresses great praise for her and for himself by saying that she is like the sweet honor of "some blameless king, who in fear of the gods rules among men many and strong, and upholds righteous judgments; to him the black earth bears wheat and barley, the trees are heavy with fruit, the flocks bring forth without fail and the sea provides fish, because of his good leading; and the people prosper under him." *

Odysseus is not the violent and tempestuous hero that Achilles is; he does not blaze like a falling star, as did Achilles; rather, he is a man of many resources, of many devices, of many experiences, who brings all this to bear on the determination of his own individual fortune and on the governing of his people. Odysseus does not depend on his reputation to save him, for throughout a good part of the *Odyssey* he presents himself as a stranger, unknown to his many hosts. But in each instance, in each "trial," he proves himself out of his inner resources, his interior self.

The ancient Greek rhapsodists often dramatized the *peira,* or trial, "by which a man established his quality." Odysseus survives trials by (a) terror, the *cannibalistic Cyclops, the monster Scylla,* etc.; by (b) force, *the storms sent by Zeus and Poseidon;* and by (c) temptation, *the bag of winds, the lure of the Sirens, the desire to remain forever with the Lotus Eaters, with Circe, Calypso, or Nausicaa.* The allegorical implications of these trials exist only in the mind of the modern reader. To Homer's listeners they simply represented heightened adventures to test the mettle of a well-known, valiant, resourceful, and much-enduring hero. Odysseus passed them all by exercising to the fullest his qualities of manliness: "physical strength and courage; ingenuity where these might fail; restraint, patience, tact and self-control; and the *will* for home" (Lattimore). In later centuries Odysseus has acquired dimensions that Homer never intended for him. He is the absolute man who passes through every trial and affliction to a state of spiritual restoration, which is almost a resurrection,

* From Homer: *The Odyssey,* 19.111. Adapted from Butcher and Lang.

for his homecoming was the return of a man long considered dead. A further extension of this symbolism would lead to religious implications.

Although Odysseus is proud of his fame as a warrior who had been mighty in battle, he conceals these exploits in the *Odyssey* and chooses to rely instead on his cunning and his intelligence. He is modern man confronting his problems with the resources of his own spirit; he is the epitome of his culture and of its future, not of its history. In a way Odysseus, through his travels and his trials, is actually writing the history of the future. He is the first example of the Classic Greek spirit on the stage of Hellas. He represents also the cosmic restlessness of modern man, who reaches always for the utmost star. When he muses outside his own subverted palace, "Be steady, my heart, we have endured far worse than this," he speaks for every man.

The *Odyssey* not only faces westward and embodies the Western spirit, but the travels and travails of Odysseus are symbolic and universal regardless of whether or not Homer intended it this way. They parallel man's journey through life. Later literature (James Joyce, et al.) has drawn further parallels, which, while not precisely accurate, may easily be suggested by what takes place in the *Odyssey,* that is, the son's search for his father, who is to be his rod, his staff, his measure. This can be carried further still and become every man's search for his father, which is the quest of all life after birth. In the womb there is a security that is warm and dark and unseeing. After the umbilical cord is cut all of life is a quest to recapture that lost security. The search for the father represents that quest. Ideally one's father should be this symbol of security, but so very often he is not, so the quest becomes a search for a way of life, an importance, a religion, a god, and so on, which may bring security. There is also in later literature the parallel search of the father for a son to continue him, to be his growing seed, to give him immortality.

But these ideas are mainly Joyce's, not Homer's. Homer, however, does have his hero succeed from scratch. Unconsciously, as often happens in great literature, he universalized his hero, just as Cervantes did his Don Quixote. Thomas Wolfe used the phrase "naked and alone we came into our exile," but the phrase fits Odysseus like a glove. He was thrown up naked, alone, and half dead on the beach of the Phaecians, the princess Nausicaa found him and took him for a god, and it was in the palace of King Alcinous of Phaecia that like an ancient minstrel he recounted his famous adventures. He re-created himself in this story of his life, basing most of the narrative on very realistic adventures, but fancy takes over when the moment and mood call for it.

Odysseus is a dualistic adventurer, for in his life what has happened and what might have happened merge to such an extent that they become inseparable. This mixing of imagination and reality is the patrimony of every intelligent man who possesses one iota of imagination. Odysseus epitomizes the dream of all men for adventure, travel, dangerous exploits, beautiful women, a faithful wife, the continuance of high station, a loving son, a gift for making friends, victory over one's enemies, the absolute proof of manliness, and the triumph of a full life.

If Achilles was almighty, Odysseus was intelligent and resourceful. If Achilles represented body over mind, Odysseus represented mind over body. Achilles was the Mycenaean hero; Odysseus was the Hellenic ideal. Achilles was also the tragic hero, whereas Odysseus suggests the romantic ideal. The theme of love is quite different in the two poems. Achilles feels great love only for his friend, Patroclus; women to him are merely instruments or possessions. Odysseus, on the other hand, relates much more fully with women. He enjoys sexual love with goddesses on flawless beds, and the beautiful princess Nausicaa adores him with a romantic soul; meanwhile, his faithful wife waits patiently twenty years for his return.

The contrast here with Clytemnestra, wife of Agamemnon, who took an adulterous lover while her husband was at Troy and then with that lover's help slew him the day of his homecoming, all of which is made quite clear in the *Odyssey,* gives to the husband-wife relationship between Penelope and Odysseus a special significance and brings it nearer to the Judeo-Christian (Western) ideal. Odysseus, throughout the *Odyssey,* longs only to return to the bosom of his loyal and loving family, and with his homecoming to restore order and legitimacy among his people and to complete the adventurous circle of life.

At the crucial point in the poem, when after twenty years he does return to Ithaca incognito, Odysseus feels that he must test the loyalty of his old swineherd, he must test his old nurse, he must test even his son and his wife; but finding them all loyal and faithful, he is able to proceed to the final stage of his adventures, which is to smash the mandarins of subversion in his own household, the greedy suitors for the hand of his wife. This done, the romance is ended and all is well. Everything remains just as it had begun: the family is happy, the kingdom is at peace, justice is restored, the enemy is vanquished. The only point of difference is that everyone is older by twenty years.

But nothing has really altered, nothing has been able to conquer the human spirit which in the *Odyssey* endures and outlives every adversity. Tennyson said it well in his poem on Ulysses: "To follow knowledge like a sinking star, beyond the utmost bound of human thought . . . Old age hath yet his honor and his toil . . . To strive, to seek, to find, and not to

yield." There is no conscience in the *Odyssey* in our sense: man is a thinking reed, a sensuous animal, intense, meteoric, noble. He is without guilt
and he is without neuroses. He is untrammeled human intelligence bound
in a body of indomitable courage and strength. He is human energy incarnate, creating the first myth of a Golden Age in history.

No bards appear in the *Iliad,* although Achilles himself is singing the
deeds of great heroes to the accompaniment of his lyre when Agamemnon's
peacemakers reach his tent, but in the *Odyssey* the reciting of poetry occupies a position of high honor. In fact, it is closely linked with "the voice of
the gods," who exult in the nobility of man. In Book 1 Phemios, the
minstrel at Odysseus' palace in Ithaca, regales the suitors by singing of the
sad homecoming of the Achaeans from Troy. Penelope, overcome with
grief, begs him to change the subject. Telemachus says to her rather tartly:

> Why, my mother, do you begrudge this excellent singer
> his pleasing himself as the thought drives him? It is not the singers
> who are to blame, it must be Zeus is to blame, who gives out
> to men who eat bread, to each and all, the way he wills it.
> There is nothing wrong in singing the sad return of the Danaans . . .
> Go therefore back in the house, and take up your work,
> the loom and the distaff, and see to it that your handmaidens
> ply their work also; but the men must see to discussion,
> all men, but I most of all. For mine is the power in this household.
>   [Lattimore]

After this command to his mother Telemachus turns to the suitors and
adds:

> You suitors of my mother, overbearing in your rapacity,
> now let us dine and take our pleasure, and let there be no
> shouting, since it is a splendid thing to listen to a singer
> who is such a singer as this man is, with a voice such as gods have.
>   [Lattimore]

Later in the poem Odysseus himself identifies with the rhapsodist in
the several episodes in which a professional minstrel plucks the harp and
tells his tales. The bard and he eventually change places, with Odysseus
relating his own adventures. The first such episode occurs in Book 8 at the
palace of King Alcinous of the Phaecians. Nausicaa, after encountering
Odysseus on the beach, had taken him to her father's palace. In order to
entertain his guest the king says: "Call in Demodokos, our Laureate, whom
the gods have inspired with song. Let him ease our hearts singing on any
theme he wills." The minstrel sings about the legendary clash between

Odysseus and Achilles, and as he spins his tale Odysseus has to hide his face behind his mantle in order to conceal his tears.

After the story is finished there are track and field events among the seafaring Phaecians. One of these, named Seareach, taunts Odysseus about having no skill in the contests of fighting men, so the old warrior picks up a discus of stone larger than any of the others and hurls it far beyond that of his nearest competitor. Still nettled, Odysseus challenges them all in wrestling, boxing, archery, spear throwing, and distance racing, but King Alcinous demurs and calls for a return to feasting and song.

A servant runs to get the polished and clear-toned harp, and the young folks begin to dance as "Odysseus marveled at their stamping feet and the flashing ring." The minstrel then tells his story: an adulterous affair between two gods. Aphrodite was married to Hephaestus, the limping god of the forge, but she was carrying on with Ares, the god of war. Hephaestus got wind of this and made an almost invisible net of gold which he concealed over the bed, and when the two adulterers began their dalliance, it fell and trapped them "so that they were held tightly entwined and unable to separate." As a result they were caught red-handed and Ares was forced to pay a huge fine, but Apollo and Hermes made it clear that they envied him all the same. It was worth any fine, they thought, to be able to "lie beside the golden girl."

The unique characteristic of this minstrel Demodokos is that he is blind, like Homer. Perhaps he is Homer's alter ego. In any case, he occupies an important place in the palace of the king, and Odysseus is so impressed with his talent that "he sliced off for him a choice piece of his loin of pork, edged with crisp fat." As this is given to Demodokos, Odysseus proclaims his admiration for the blind bard: "Let him eat and rejoice, for out of my own sorrow I bid him hail, and I say to you that all people should honor the poets, for they are dearly loved by the Muse who gives them voice to sing the paths of life." Later, speaking to the blind minstrel, Odysseus added: "You sang so skillfully and shaped your songs with such great feeling that you must have seen those things yourself, or else you heard the tale from someone who was there. Now switch to another theme and sing of the wooden horse . . ." Again Odysseus weeps as he hears about the ruse that won the Trojan War.

After this introduction to the art of poetry Homer in Book 9 has Odysseus himself take over the minstrel's role and tell the fantastic story of his own life to the assembled Phaecians. Inspired by Demodokos, Odysseus now becomes the rhapsodist par excellence, Homer's true alter ego. He begins with a proper tribute to Demodokos:

Alcinous, great monarch, and a wonder to all men,
How moved I am to hear this harper sing;
The gods have touched him with their gift of song!
There is no happier day for any man
Than to sit in a great hall at a table
Filled with bread and meat, hearing a bard perform
As a steward passes about filling each cup with wine,
And fellowship spreads joy throughout the land.
This is the finest thing in life!

Then Odysseus launches into his own story, first giving his name and identifying Ithaca, his mountainous island home, then boasting that men far and wide respect him for his guile in peace and war, for "my name has spread beyond the sky's great rim . . ." His tale spins forth weaving, as some have said, the strange magic of the world's first novel. Episode follows episode in the fulfillment of destiny: the Lotus Eaters, the Cyclops, Polyphemus' cave, the winds sealed in a bag, Circe's island, a visit to Hades, where he speaks with the shades of the dead, Scylla and Charybdis, the Sirens, lovely Calypso, and then at last landfall on Phaecia, man's lost paradise.

In exile, nearing fifty, Odysseus recaptures the heroic past and in memory relives his lost youth. He thus comes to represent symbolically the lost youth of Everyman and certainly the lost youth of the Greeks, who in the generation of Homer were still in their time of troubles, an age of darkness out of which they were not yet quite ready to emerge into the splendid Classic period.

The last time a minstrel is mentioned in the *Odyssey* is just after Odysseus has slain the suitors. He calls for the minstrel to play a light-hearted dancing air "plucking the strings of his resounding lyre" so that any neighbor passing by will think there is a feast going on, and will not cry the deaths about the town. The minstrel was not slain with the other hangers-on, because not only was he not guilty but he represented the continuance of life, the continuance of tradition.

In addition to exalting poetry the *Odyssey* repeatedly goes into familiar detail concerning ships, shipbuilding, navigation, the maritime world, and clearly reveals that the author not only knew about these things firsthand, and undoubtedly loved them, but that in telling of the sea wanderings of Odysseus he was probably incorporating a goodly portion of his own life on the sea. This cannot of course be proved, but the maritime overtones of the *Odyssey* are so strong that the conclusion is almost inescapable. In this poem Homer thus unknowingly links the great sea power of Crete of

Minoan times with the yet to come sea power of Athens which later enables the Greeks to win their glorious victory over the Persians.

In Book 5, where Calypso helps Odysseus build a raft for his departure from her island, she offers him her best-seasoned timber and brings him a two-bladed ax with a handle of hard olive wood, a polished adze, an auger to drill his boards, stout pins to bolt them, and other necessities of the shipwright's trade. Odysseus felled twenty trees, trimmed them with the bronze ax and deftly smoothed them, cut a mast pole and a proper yard, then "bored each plank and jointed them, making them fast with wooden pins and dowels. Next he set up the deckings, fitting them to the close-set ribs, and finished them off with long gunwales, and therein he set his mast with the yard-arm fitted to it, and to his craft he fastened a rudder, and drove willow into all the seams to keep out the water, and ballasted the whole with heavy logs."*

On this craft Odysseus spent seventeen days on the open sea, driven by windy blasts through ugly waves that smote him near to death, finally to be cast up on an island beach swollen and half-drowned with sea water gushing from his nose and mouth. He staggered to a secluded spot and prepared himself a bed of leaves:

> There like a wanderer in a far country
> Who hides a glowing brand among the ashes
> To save his fire until the morning comes,
> So lay Odysseus in his bed of leaves;
> Athena came to close his eyes in dreamless sleep
> That his ordeal at last should have its end.

Among the Phaecians Odysseus finds proper sailor company, for these people are a seafaring lot, and the poet even goes to the absurd length of giving nearly all of the athletes who take part in the track and field events "seaside names." The list of these names, if merely reproduced in their original Greek form as is done in many translations, signify nothing, and appear only to be a list of proper names. But each has a specific meaning connected with the sea: Sparwood, Topmast, Tiderace, Hullman, Sternman, Beacher-man, Bluewater, Runningwake, Seabelt, Shearwater, Boardalee, Shipwrightson, and finally Seareach, the man who had insulted Odysseus and spurred him to outreach them all by throwing the discus.†

The manner in which Homer describes sailing in a ship on the "fish-cold, salt-immortal sea'.' leaves little room for doubt that the poet knew

---

* From Homer: *The Odyssey.* Adapted from Butcher and Lang.
† Robert Fitzgerald's translation of these names.

well what he was writing about. The unpredictable roaring hurricanes, the maddening calms that lasted for days on end, the violent pitching of the vessel in a heavy sea, and the great avalanches of sea water which swept the decks and on one occasion even washed Odysseus overboard—all these indicate a sailor's familiarity with the ocean. But there are also moments when the ship moves across the Mediterranean like a proud bird and Odysseus is touched by the dark miracle of life upon "the flawless brimming sea" (Fitzgerald).

In Book 5, as he takes leave of Calypso, the beautiful sea nymph provisions his ship with water, wine, boiled meats, and other foods, then

> She called for him a warm and gentle wind
> to blow off land, and as he hoisted sails
> and saw them catch the breeze, Odysseus rejoiced.
> He grasped the helm and straightway steered his craft
> unerring on its course; at night he did not sleep
> but sought the Pleiades, and bright Arcturus
> of the Great Bear, also called Big Dipper,
> a star that pivots in one place, its vigil
> fixed upon Orion, never to sink beneath the sea.
> The fair Calypso bade him keep this star
> on his left side as he traversed the deep.

In Book 9, after escaping from the one-eyed giant Polyphemus, who had devoured several members of the crew, the surviving men sleep on the shore above the rippling surf, and then:

> When Dawn lifted her fingers tinged with rose
> I woke the men and sent them to the ships;
> They first cast off the mooring cables,
> Then took their seats on benches by the oarlocks
> And every oar as one dipped in the sea.
> We flew toward the blue offing, sad in our hearts,
> Our lives secure, but gone our dear companions.

In Book 10, after surviving both storm and calm, Odysseus at last finds a sanctuary which has been compared with the protected bay of Corsica:

> Beyond the narrow passage was a bay
> Enclosed by mountains and by walls of stone
> Whose cliffs we almost touched as we sailed·by.
> My ships took shelter here, their black prows
> Moored in a long row on the still water . . .

In Book 13, as Odysseus takes leave of the Phaecians, he loads his ship with gifts and then makes ready to depart. Homer now takes over and describes the leavetaking, saying that the sailors

> Slipped the hawser through its mooring stone,
> Then bending on their oars they churned the sea.
> The vessel sheared a passage through the waves,
> And left the waters in a violet swell, while at her stern
> A white wake foamed upon the night's dark face.
> Not even the swiftest falcon kept abreast
> As they sped like an arrow through the sea.

Homer had intimate knowledge of the winds that soughed up from the northwest, of clouds that darkened foreboding a storm, of the mad help-lessness of a ship becalmed and unable to move, of all the arts of the shipwright and of the navigator, and he had both a deep love and a cautious fear of "the wine-dark sea," to use his most often repeated image. He mentions the different constellations with knowledge, and feels a sailor's joy in watching the prow of a ship as it shears through the night into the dawn. The *Odyssey* is a maritime adventure from beginning to end. In it the sea rather than the earth or living men is the real peril. Symbolically the poet attributes this to Poseidon's fury at Odysseus for having blinded his son Polyphemus. We might interpret: man angrily strikes out at natural law (or at a god), and the blow is angrily returned.

The *Odyssey,* far more than the *Iliad,* gives the real flavor of life on Greek shores in Homer's own day many hundreds of years before the time of Christ. The sea is the great highway, the great lure, the hard master, the stern judge, and the cruel tester of the mettle of men. It offers the wine-dark magic of adventure, and it offers death. Without the sea the ancient culture of Hellas could not have developed as it did. Without it that culture, once it had developed, could not have survived.

Odysseus foretells and epitomizes the period of Greek expansion, ex-ploration, and colonization which takes the Greeks into Sicily, Italy, and then into France and Spain. It is possible that this period of expansion had already begun at the time the poem was composed. In any event, the adventures of Odysseus clearly suggest this universalization of Hellenic culture. Contrariwise, these same adventures, as is the case in all great literature, offer the reader a reckless and courageous journey across the sea of life.

Before taking leave of Homer let us try to recapitulate the Homeric code. Fame, courage, excellence, manly nobility were the qualities that the

Homeric hero thought would endure after he was dead. Even the vocabulary reflected this universal search for survival in courageous action. A. W. H. Adkins, the British classicist, has pointed out that "the same word in Homer is used to mean to pray, to vow, to boast, to proclaim one's merits, to mention one's ancestry, and to utter a victory shout." Why did the Homeric hero use the same term for activities which seem to us very different? Adkins answers the question as follows:

> He was the head of a small group, for whose security and prosperity he was responsible, and whose very existence was precarious. Beyond that group was the rest of mankind, competitive, hostile, or indifferent; and then the gods, capricious, malicious, regarding ephemeral mankind as pawns in the great game of life. Neither gods nor men accorded him rights merely as a human being. Every association was of a contractual nature. He had rights only in the context of some particular relationship, some claim to consideration which he could produce.
>
> His fame, synonymous with his name, was the most lasting and satisfying possession that he could leave behind. In a society without written records, if other men overlooked him or forgot him, he vanished from memory, as if he had never been. On his tiny island, surrounded by the hostile darkness, the Homeric hero was driven psychologically into doing something which we translate sometimes as "to pray," sometimes as "to boast," sometimes as "to utter a shout of victory," without ever catching the complete meaning.*

---

* Adkins expressed these thoughts at the Classical Conference held at Oxford University in September, 1968. Reported by Philip Howard in the *Times* (London), Sept. 6, 1968.

VII

Rise of the City-State:
Chronology of Greek History

Man is by nature a political animal.

Aristotle

*A state cannot go on existing if its judgments
are made null and void by private individuals.*

Plato

Our word *chronology* is from the Greek *chronos,* meaning "time," and *logos,* meaning "knowledge and understanding." *History* also is a term derived from the Greek *historia,* which means "story learned by inquiry." We cannot escape the Greek roots of our own civilization. The chronology of Greece's own history is often summarized in the following periods, which may possibly make for an easier recall. The names of all these periods have been invented by later historians; the Greeks did not know any of them, and their value is merely suggestive.

1. *Greek Bronze Age: 3000–1100* B.C. Metalworking people enter Greece around 3000 B.C. Minoan civilization flowers in Crete (1900– 1400). Around 2000 first Greek-speaking tribes enter Greece; they bring horses. These Greeks (Homer calls them Achaeans) create the Mycenaean civilization on the Greek mainland (1700–1100). Their citadel centers at Mycenae, Argos, Tiryns, Pylos, etc., are ruled by strong kings. Their culture is deeply influenced by the Minoan. According to legend they wage war on Troy around 1250. In the century 1200–1100 new waves of Greeks, the Dorians, enter Greece and destroy the Mycenaean civilization. Large groups of Achaeans emigrate to Asia Minor.

2. Greek Dark Age: 1100–800. Mycenaean palace culture is now broken up, its strong kingdoms are fragmented, even writing is forgotten, only to reappear at the end of this period with a new alphabet. The Dark Age is a time of troubles and of wandering of peoples. There are no written records, but history is kept alive in oral poetry. By 800 B.C. the nature of the new society is clear: there is a proliferation of small city-states (the *poleis*) ruled by aristocrats. In Crete, for example, where once a single great king had ruled, there were fifty of these small city-states. In the latter part of this so-called Dark Age the Greek Renaissance begins; it is a blend of Dorian, Achaean, Cretan, and Near Eastern elements.

3. Archaic Period: 800–500. Olympic Games begin in 776. This is the starting point of the Classic Greek calendar. The Greek Renaissance continues to develop, the new Greek alphabet re-establishes the art of writing, a period of expansion commences, Greek colonies are established in Italy, Sicily, France, Spain, Asia Minor. First stone statues appear; temples of stone follow in the sixth century. Written literature flourishes at the end of this Archaic period. Greek city-states assume new political, philosophical, cultural dimensions under aristocrats, lawgivers, and "tyrants."

4. Classical Period: 500–323. This period extends from the attempted Persian conquest to the death of Alexander; it represents the high-water mark of Greek civilization. It is an age of unparalleled achievement in literature, architecture, philosophy, and the fine arts. Greek humanism lays down the basis for the further development of Western culture. Historians arbitrarily date the end of the Classical period with the death of Alexander the Great, who carried Greek culture over a great part of the then known Western world, Hellenizing Egypt, the Near East, Persia, and parts of India.

5. Hellenistic Period: 323–31. After Alexander's death his empire breaks up and his generals divide the fragments. Greek-Macedonian dynasties supported by Greek-Macedonian aristocracies control the separate regions of the Hellenistic world. During this period the Roman Conquest gets under way (in 146 Rome destroys Corinth on the Greek mainland), but it is not until Augustus Caesar defeats Anthony and Cleopatra at Actium in Greece in 31 B.C. that the domination of Rome is complete.

6. Roman Period: 31 B.C.–A.D. 330. The emperors of Rome continue great works of construction in Greek territory. Hadrian completes the immense temple of Olympian Zeus (begun in the sixth century B.C.) in Athens. Many Greco-Roman amphitheaters are constructed, often upon the foundations of Greek originals. Nero, Hadrian, and other Roman emperors take great quantities of Greek art back to Rome to decorate their temples, palaces, gardens, and public buildings. This period ends when the capital of Rome is moved to Constantinople, founded in A.D. 330 by the Emperor Constantine near ancient Greek Byzantium.

7. Byzantine Period: A.D. *330–1453.* The eastern portion of the Roman Empire, which is Greek-speaking, survives the fall of Rome itself, and Hellenic-Byzantine culture continues until Constantinople is captured by the Turks in 1453. The mainland of Greece is occupied by the Turks soon thereafter.

The English word for Greece and Greeks derives from *Graeci,* the Latin name of an insignificant tribe which had participated in founding a Greek colony at Cumae near Naples. The Romans were soon calling all Hellenes by this name, and from the Romans it came to us. It is a name the inhabitants of Greece never applied to themselves. In Homer their word for Greeks in general was Achaeans; later it became Hellenes, and the over-all term for the area occupied by Greeks was called Hellas. Both were cultural rather than political terms, and simply linked together all people who spoke Greek, regardless of country and regardless of whether they lived in the territory we know as Greece or in Asia Minor, Egypt, or Italy, in all of which places there were populous and wealthy colonies of Greeks.

Until the nineteenth century the country known as Greece did not exist, but in ancient times there were innumerable separate states whose common language was Greek. Language and a common cultural background provided the only unity that existed among a people whose sense of separatism was incontrovertible. Athens once tried without success to mold all Hellenes into an empire, and so did Sparta. Even Philip of Macedon and Alexander the Great, who conquered all the separate states of Greece (except Sparta) and strove to weld them together, were only briefly successful. The Greeks, left to their own devices and lacking the presence of a permanently all-powerful conqueror, immediately splintered politically. This was the fundamental reality of their cultural, social, and political nature.

Why was Greek political unity impossible? The Egyptians many centuries earlier had found a way to nationhood. So had the Persians. And the Greeks were in no way inferior to the Egyptians or to the Persians. They produced a cultural unity which is still the marvel of history, and yet political oneness was foreign to their nature. Many of their greatest and most characteristic figures were not from the Greek mainland. Homer, who was probably a Greek from Asia Minor, was the fountainhead of their

cultural and educational system. Their first philosophers also were from Asia Minor, as was Herodotus, the father of history. Archimedes was born and reared in Syracuse, in Sicily. Euclid, the mathematician, was from Alexandria, Egypt. But all these Greeks were firmly in the mainstream of Greek civilization.

None of them, however, indeed almost no Greek, believed in a super-state which would include all Hellenes. Plato in the *Republic* speaks of his *ideal state* as consisting of 5,040 citizens, meaning males who could vote. The total population of such a state would have been in the vicinity of 50,000. Aristotle in his *Politics* says the state ought to be small enough so that each citizen should be able to know every other citizen by sight. This only goes to prove that the Greek impulse toward political fragmentation was still strongly alive in the Classic age, after more than a thousand years of Greek history. The actual total population of the city-state of Athens at its peak around 430 B.C. was approximately 300,000 men, women, children, resident aliens, and slaves. This made it the most populous city-state in Greece. Sparta, Corinth, and Thebes were much smaller, and there were many city-states which had far less than Plato's ideal 5,040 citizens. Syracuse in Sicily was Athens' only rival in size. Plato's curious figure reflected Pythagorean number-mysticism and was the product of $1 \times 2 \times 3 \times 4 \times 5 \times 6 \times 7$.

Such a mosaic of small political fragments might conceivably have arisen for geographic and economic reasons, but Greek mountains (the Pindus range) which separated the country into a series of valleys were not all that divisive, and Greek economy was not all that regional. The principal reason for separatism was probably that the Greeks preferred to live this way. Their religion and their culture both pointed in this direction, and their feeling for "fatherland," a concept that was psychological as well as cultural and philosophical, was deeply rooted in ties of local religion and family. The Greeks loved the small circle and rejected the large.

We use the term *city-state* to define Greek political organization; the Greek word was *polis,* which had emotional correlations not suggested by either "city" or "state." The *polis* took in both the city and the country around it, with all of the population. *Polis* meant home town, country and nation, kinfolk and friends, religion, culture, and native land. Its overtones were even stronger than our present-day concept of nationalism, for the solidarity and separatism of the *polis* were basic to Greek civilization, which viewed "the whole man" and "the whole polis" as inextricably and intimately blended. Every citizen participated *directly* in the life and government of the *polis* in a manner which would have been impossible had the *polis* been larger. This fundamental concept of the collective life as a living organism in which each man played his part just as each organ and blood vessel does in the human body was one aspect of the Greeks marvelous creative power.

Religion was intrinsic to the life of Greece in all its manifestations. Death was the first mystery, and from it arose those beliefs which molded character, provided the basis for family religion, gave form to social and political organization, and were the primary impulse in literature and art. The prevailing Greek belief was that the soul and the body remained together after death. The soul continued to live after the body had died, but it was so intimately connected with the body that in order to find peace it must be properly housed in the same burial place. If a body was left unburied, the soul was forced to wander about as a grieving ghost and this could bring both evil and tragedy to those who remained alive. Greek graves were for this reason in the family field or yard, generally near the entrance of the dwelling, so that the surviving family members could see them on entering or leaving the house, and could murmur a prayer to the dead whose souls hovered just beneath or just above that tiny plot.

The Greek word *psyche,* which is now taken to mean "spirit" or "soul," originally meant "butterfly." The soul escaped from the dead body as a butterfly. During the period when the dead were burned, as Homer described, the soul escaped as a butterfly of fire. The flesh went up in flames, but the bones and ashes were buried and a mound raised over them. There are many mentions of these mounds or barrows in the *Iliad.* So essential was it to bury the remains that a group of Athenian admirals were hauled into court for not burying the bodies of sailors who had lost their lives in a naval battle. The officers, being enlightened men, took little stock in the creed which demanded burial in the earth in order to give peace to the soul. They thought that dissolution of the bodies in sea water was equally acceptable, but the current of popular belief was so strong that these men who were the saviors of Athens were condemned to death by the courts.

According to Greek belief, when the body was buried the soul became a god which dwelled under the earth in the same place. Burial, therefore, meant union with the gods or, as the phrase went, "marriage with the gods." In the drama of Aeschylus, Antigone's tomb is referred to as a "bridal chamber" where she had gone to meet "her bridegroom, death." Electra prays at the tomb of her father, Agamemnon, who has become a god, beseeching his help, and the entire play of *Oedipus at Colonus* revolves around whether Thebes or Athens will get the body of Oedipus when he dies and becomes a god, for they believe that as a god he can protect their cities. So strong was this belief of burial enabling the soul of the deceased to become a god that one of the worst of all curses in Classic Greek drama was, "May the earth not receive your flesh!" The rapid decomposition of the body was hoped for in order that the soul might become a free divine spirit. This belief prevails in Christian Greece today.

The dead member of a family was not just another god; he was a very private divinity shared by no other family. Greek religion, therefore, was a kind of ancestor worship. The Greeks did not conceive of a unique creative principle in the universe which was the source of all life. Instead, they worshiped the creative principle embodied in their ancestors, who had given birth to them as individuals and to whom now, as gods, they could address prayers, give thanks, lament failure, or come beseeching succor. As a consequence, family property, which enclosed the burial plot or the tombs, was itself sacred. Religion and not economics gave private property its significance in ancient Greece.

Private properties were carefully fenced and their boundaries marked with stones which also represented gods, and thus the divine nature of ownership. Any stranger who dared to encroach on the property of another was open to divine retribution. Also, since the gods created by the dead interred on each property demanded a carefully bounded plot which was their very own, two properties must never share a fence in common, or the gods would be uncertain of their abode. The concept that "good fences make good neighbors" would never have had any support in Greece. Plato sagely wrote: "Our first law must be this: let no one touch the boundary which separates his field from that of his neighbor. Let no man disturb the small stones which separate friendship from enmity."

The hearth with its ever-burning fire, which was the private altar of every Greek family, was surrounded by a wall so that it might not be visible to strangers. It was inside the house and occupied always the same place, for on this altar lived the god who would protect all the generations who were to succeed each other in this house. The hearth must always bear its live embers, and no filth could ever be tossed into it. Only certain kinds of wood could be burned upon it. The hearth was the place where the god of radiance resided, the god who symbolized and linked the generations of the family. People worshiped the hearth fire and made offerings that would be agreeable to a god: flowers, fruits, incense, flammable wine, and sacrificial animal victims. When Agamemnon returned from Troy his first religious act was to give thanks at the altar fire in his palace.

As long as a member of the family lived he must keep alive this private sacred fire. If it was allowed to become extinguished, a god ceased to exist. The hearth fire was the symbol of family kinship and of continuity. Such fires, never accessible to strangers, were the oversouls of each individual family unit in ancient Greece. Just as each family had its sacred hearth and fire, so did each city or *polis.* The family circle was expanded and repeated in the *polis,* which thus became a very personal and a very sacred, as well as a political, entity.

The ancient Greeks lived in a closely structured universe. Every person, every institution, every created thing had its place, and it was respect for this order of things that gave order to the culture itself. The *polis,* the independent Greek city-state, embodied this orderly view of life completely, and the *polis* was at the heart of Hellenic civilization. Athens led the procession, but Sparta, Thebes, Miletus, Rhodes, Syracuse, Corinth, and many other city-states made worthy contributions to Greek culture. The Greek word *polis* is the root of several English words: *politics* and all of its derivatives; also, *metropolis, acropolis,* etc. We apply the latter term almost exclusively to the Athenian Acropolis, but in ancient Greece there was an acropolis on practically every other hill. The term means simply *high city* or *heights of the city.* The English word *acrophobia,* fear of high places, indicates its meaning well.

The cities of ancient Greece never rose by degrees with a gradual accumulation of dwellings, thus growing to town or village size if enough families moved in. When the early tribes of Greeks reached the country they simply selected a spot, generally on a hill, for this made defense easier, and there at once in a single day they established their *polis,* or city. Founding a city was always a religious act. There were pious chants, sacrifices, and prayers to the gods to "live with us in our city."

As the town expanded, dwellings and market places arose on the fields below the original citadel, which always remained the official city center. For on the acropolis were the temples to the gods, the altar with its sacred fire, and the place where the assembly met to discuss the affairs of government. This spot was sacred. The gods of the city lived here, so the city could not conceivably move to another location. There might be another *polis* only a mile or so away, but its patron gods were different, and it represented a completely separate society.* A profound gulf lay between

* Sometimes these patron or city deities had the same name in different cities, but they were not the same gods. The Athena of Athens was quite different from the Athena of Corinth, for example. Many gods were of course universally accepted, but these were not patron deities: Zeus, Apollo, and most of the Olympians.

them. So closely intertwined were gods and *polis* that when one city was conquered by another there often followed the complete destruction of the conquered city and the enslavement of its inhabitants. But these inhabitants could not be made citizens of the conquering city in the early centuries.

Before the Hellenistic period the Greeks never united two cities in a single state, mingling the populations and associating them under the same government. Nor was there any possibility of sending in an outside group to govern the conquered city, for those who ruled any *polis* must worship the gods of that place, as they were not only political rulers but also officiants of the native cult. The only exception was when the conquerors took over the vanquished city lock, stock, and barrel, expelled the inhabitants, moved in and actually "refounded" the place, as the Ionians did in Miletus in Asia Minor and as the Athenians did at Aegina, Melos, and Salamis.

It was quite all right for the citizens of one city to detest and even to ridicule the gods of a neighboring city, but the gods of their own *polis* must always be treated with respect. There was no dogma, but neither was there "freedom of religion," for everyone who was born into or who on rare occasions might be allowed to become a citizen of a given city was obligated to accept the tutelary gods along with his right of residence. Anyone who did not do so was an enemy or a traitor, and even Socrates himself, the wise and good philosopher, was to suffer death because he had disregarded or regarded improperly this ancient law.

The history of a city started on the day of its foundation. All that had taken place before this was quickly forgotten, so almost nothing is known about the Greek-speaking tribes before they settled in Greece. Every city worshiped its founder as one of its very special gods, and when Pausanias traveled throughout Greece in the second century of the Christian era every city could still tell him the name of its founder, with all the legendary details of his life. These details were recalled every year in the sacred ceremonies, so could not pass into oblivion. Whether they were historically true or not is another matter; what is important is that they were believed and guided the thoughts of the people.

The laws of the city were originally religious laws and were believed to have come straight from the gods; these gods, of course, despite their power and glory, were but the beliefs of men. The annals of the city were carefully kept by the priests, and they became the bible of the inhabitants. Everywhere the living were ruled by the dead. Custom was the pact between gods and men. Religion and love of the *polis* were one; the piety of the ancient Greek was his love of his *polis*. "It is our *polis* that preserves us," wrote Sophocles, and Plato said, "Our *polis* begets us, nourishes us, educates us."

When the Dorians came into Greece between 1200–1100 B.C., bringing weapons of iron and thus starting the Iron Age, there occurred a crucial change in the Greek way of life, customs, religion, and government. As this was also the beginning of the Greek Dark Age, which lasted three or four centuries, the importance of this change was not at once noticeable. But in the end the old primitive religion based on the Earth Mother, the python snake goddess of fertility, was replaced by a set of new gods, the Olympians, who dwelt on Mount Olympus and represented both the dynamic, driving sky energy and the basic human emotions derived from that energy.

These primary life forces were deified in the forms of the twelve Olympian gods. We say, "God is love," and the Greeks said, "Love is a god." That is the difference. These new gods left the hearth and were worshiped in the first temples, which were of wood. The king lost his supreme power as high priest, and his place on the Acropolis was taken by the aristocrats, who increased the beauty of the temples thereon. The city moved down from the heights and extended itself below. The government also descended outside the ancient citadel.

The administrative buildings of the government and the main market place of the city were now gathered around a great square below the old heights, which was known as the *agora*. This word derives from the verb *ageiro,* which means "I gather." In the old days speakers got up to address the crowd and people gathered around him to listen. He was soon replaced by a second orator, and he by a third, and so on, as succeeding clusters of people assembled to hear what they had to say. Farmers and peddlers brought in their goods, and before long shops rose around the open square. A permanent orator's stand was built, and the *agora* was born.

The *agora* was the commercial and political center of the city. The courts of justice were there, the mint, some temples and shrines, porticoes for shops, for bargaining, for debates in the shade, the state dining hall, and fountains for drinking water. The *agora* was clearly marked by its boundary stones, as were all other properties, and in Athens today one such stone still remains carrying this inscription: "I am the boundary of the agora."

One of the main temples on the *agora* of Athens was the Hephaesteum, or Theseum, which still stands and is the most perfectly preserved Greek temple in the world. Hephaestus (Vulcan) was the smith of the gods, and the blacksmiths of Athens built their shops around his temple. They are still there. In a place of honor on the *agora* was the great altar to Zeus, and there was also a sanctuary for all twelve Olympian gods. The various walks were decorated with statues, and during the daylight hours they teemed with activity. The Greeks delighted in life in the open air. Sky, sun, wind, religion, and art were inseparable from the routine of their daily lives.

What was life like when Greek culture began to emerge from centuries of oral tradition into the clearer light where written records made history possible? As the Dark Age comes to an end and the Archaic period begins (800–700) we have the conflicting reports of Homer and of Hesiod.

Homer presents an idealized picture of Achaean society in his stirring epics. Hesiod, a Boeotian poet who followed him, balances the ledger with a very down-to-earth survey of the vices of the ruling caste and the humdrum daily activities of the dirt farmer of the eighth century. Homer's heroes are displayed for the admiration and reverence of all Hellenes; he makes short shrift of the ordinary man and even of the Assembly, which was supposed to be the place where ordinary men could be heard.

Hesiod's point of view in the *Works and Days* is the exact opposite. He himself had been a victim of the Boeotian aristocrats, his brother had cheated him out of his inheritance by paying off the important authorities, and Hesiod lashes out at the "bribe-guzzling judges and princes who do not know what justice is." In Hesiod the corruption of the aristocratic governing class clearly indicates that all is not well in the Greek way of life. Pressures are building up in the multitude which before very long are bound to explode.

Hesiod highlights many other unpleasant aspects of Greek life in Boeotia in his day. He complains of the sweltering summer heat and he detests the cold blasts of winter which "make the earth and woods bellow aloud." Great oaks and pines are brought low by winter's gales, "the unnumbered trees of the forest cry out, and the wild beasts shiver and set their tails between their legs, even those whose hides are covered with hair."*

Hesiod was a small farmer whose father had come from Asia Minor, so undoubtedly he had heard many times how much better things were in the old home country. But Hesiod knew his own Boeotia well. He saw its wealth in land, in oak trees filled with acorns, in flocks and hives of bees and barns of golden wheat. The accumulation of gold or silver was not

* Translated by A. W. Mair in *The Greeks* by H. D. F. Kitto.

known to his epoch. Homer's "golden Mycenae" and "luxurious Corinth" and frequent mention of articles in these precious metals are to Hesiod relics of a forgotten day.

Hesiod loved the earth, which brought forth its fruits for the treasure of mankind. In his suggestions for the good farmer he wrote that "the cry of the crane signals the time for winter plowing, and when the constellation of Orion is visible the grains of wheat must be winnowed from the chaff." Hesiod provides a Greek *Poor Richard's Almanack* filled with popular maxims, a calendar of the best times to do and not to do things, and a considerable amount of fatherly advice, such as "always marry a girl of your own neighborhood, a girl young enough to be trained in habits of thrift, one who will be willing to do hard work without complaint. She will make a man a good wife."

Hesiod also wrote of the five ages of man, of the creation, and of the gods. He begs the Muses to give him inspiration:

> They plucked a branch of laurel for my head,
> And breathed their gift of music into me.
> "Sing of the race of gods and men," they said,
> "And of things past, and of what is to be."

In his *Theogony,* properly inspired, he describes the creation in these words: "In the beginning was chaos, then came the wide-bosomed Earth, the firmament of all the deathless gods who dwell amidst the snowy peaks of Mount Olympus." The five ages of man are described in *Works and Days.* The first age was a veritable Eden inhabited by "a golden race of mortal men . . . who lived like gods without knowing sorrow, free from all toil and hurt. Wretched age did not rest upon them, but with bodies never failing they made merry and feasted beyond the reach of evil. They lived in peace on their lands with all good things, rich in flocks and loved by the blessed gods."

All this, of course, was before the fall of man, and before Pandora had let the evils escape from her legendary box. But in Hesiod's story man falls only to rise again. In the fourth age Zeus created another race of men, "a nobler and more righteous breed, a godlike race of heroes who are called demigods, the race before our own . . . Some of these went in ships over the great sea gulf to Troy for Helen's sake, she of the shining hair."

The fifth age of man, in Hesiod's own time, was an ugly age of iron, and Hesiod writes that he wishes he had not been born in it. In this age "men never rest from labor and sorrow by day, and from perishing by night, and the gods shall lay sore trouble upon them." This race will be destroyed "when children turn against their fathers, when brother turns against brother, guest against host, friend against friend." Hatred, conflict, and dishonor will bring about the destruction of the fifth race of men.

Hesiod gives his stories about the gods a moral tone which was not evident in Homer. For example, the tale about Prometheus and Pandora parallels the biblical story of Adam and Eve in the Garden of Eden. After Prometheus has stolen the sacred fire from heaven in order to help mankind cloud-gathering Zeus cunningly devises a bane to counterbalance Prometheus' gift to man. Zeus commands his Olympian artificer, Hephaestus, to create a beautiful woman for this purpose. Hephaestus mixes earth and water, shapes it to resemble a goddess, endows the form with speech and life. Athena teaches this beautiful woman, who is Pandora, the art of skillful weaving and Aphrodite gives her beauty and "eager desire and passion that wasteth the bodies of mortals." Lastly, Pandora is endowed with "a shameless mind and a treacherous nature." Then, as we all know, this lighthearted girl released misery into the world; as in Genesis, curiosity brings about the fall of man. After this man must live by the sweat of his brow because he has fallen from what might be called a state of innocence, a state of grace. Hesiod does not use the latter words, but they are implicit in the way he tells his myth.

Hesiod also points out that rapine is natural for animals, but should not be for man. One of his stories is about a hawk and a nightingale which the hawk held in its claws and was about to destroy. Trembling, the sweet-singing bird cried out and begged for mercy. The hawk screamed back: "Why cry, my friend? I'll eat you if I will, despite your song. He is a fool who rails against his fate, for he still loses and only calls down shame to share his tears."

But in a sequel to this Aesopian-like fable Justice reports to Zeus about the actions of men, and after weighing their deeds Zeus rewards the good and punishes the bad. Hesiod points out that when a single man commits an act of evil the whole state suffers and must atone his wrong.

> But they who never from the good have strayed,
> Who both the citizen and stranger aid,
> They and their cities flourish; genial Peace
> Dwells in their borders, and their youth increase.*

Their lives are sweet and sure. The oak is on their hills, the topmost tree bears the rich acorn, and the trunk the bee. Burdened with fleece their flocks roam in the fields, and they prosper mightily. Hesiod clearly upholds the

* Translated by C. A. Elton in *The Greek Poets,* by Moses Hadas.

right action, he denounces evil and sinfulness, and in his works a system of ethics begins to emerge. Hesiod is for the good man and the simple country life; even in his mythical stories there is no praise for the rapacious aristocrats who rule in the cities.

By 750 Hellas had not only emerged from the Dark Age, but her culture and her population were both expanding in a new burst of energy. Sailors and traders fanned out all over the Mediterranean. The thin soil of the mainland would not support a large population with the primitive methods of agriculture then at hand, so when these travelers returned with tales of abundant fertile lands and protected harbors in other parts of the world, the second period of Greek emigration and colonization began. The first had been that wave of Greeks who fled to Asia Minor around 1100 in order to escape the Dorians. This second exodus was longer lasting and extended much farther. It consisted of two waves, one moving east and one west. Colonies were planted along the shores of Italy, Sicily, the Black Sea, and eventually even in France and Spain.

The Euboeans founded Neapolis (new city), today's Naples, and from their settlement the Romans first began to learn from the Greeks. The Roman name for this town was Cumae. The Achaeans from middle Greece founded several colonies along the arch of the Italian boot. An Ionian colony was established halfway along that same arch in their midst. The Spartans planted a colony at Taranto; a group of Messenians escaping from Spartan despotism colonized Messina.

Corinth sent colonizers to Syracuse in Sicily, which became the most populous and wealthiest of all the Greek cities in the West. Plato visited the court of Dionysius at Syracuse in order to instruct the aristocrats. Gela, also in Sicily, was colonized by men from Crete and the island of Rhodes. The great Aeschylus came to Gela, where he died and is buried. Later, this colony pushed farther west and founded a colony of its own at Acragas (Agrigento) in western Sicily. The colonists of Sybaris, in the middle of the arch of the boot, sent colonists along the western coast of Italy and founded a settlement at Poseidonia (Paestum), south of Naples. Three lovely Doric temples still stand above the uninhabited swamp in the midst of wild roses. The inhabitants of Sybaris were so pleasure-loving that they added a new word to the language, *sybarite*.

The Greek colonists were mostly men who took up with the women of the land and produced hybrid families in their new homes overseas. The stronger influence of the father kept their language and culture Greek and a continual trade with Greece maintained a close contact with the homeland. These new cities were all colonies in the original sense of the word, that is, settlements away from home.

*Temple at Segesta, Sicily, not far from Palermo. Built by the Hellenized natives
(barbarians) of the land, but never completed. Late fifth century B.C. Goethe
lavished great praise on this temple in his record of his trip through Italy.*

All the important colonies constructed beautiful temples and theaters.
The Doric temples at Paestum are noteworthy even today; so is the lovely
unfinished temple at Segesta, not far from Palermo, lovely and majestic
on its abandoned hill. This is the most spectacular Greek temple in Italy.
Like most of the other Greek temples in the West, it is not made of marble
but of ocher-colored sandstone. Agrigento also boasts several temples, one
of which is the best-preserved outside of Greece. Selinunte has the remains
of half a dozen temples, all violently toppled by an earthquake but still
impressive for their size and splendor. Today's Syracuse boasts of its
magnificent Greek amphitheater carved out of solid rock, and the museum
at Gela contains many beautiful objects of the same ancient days.

The Greek colonies in Italy were so plentiful and so successful that the
whole area was called Greater Greece, *Magna Graecia* by the Romans,
Megale Hellas by the Greeks. The Romans acquired their Greek culture
from these colonies rather than from the Hellenic mainland, and they even
took over the entire pantheon of Greek gods as well. The twelve Olympian
gods with their Greek and their Roman names were:

GREEK NAME		ROMAN NAME
Zeus	*King of the gods*	Jupiter
Hera	*Wife of Zeus,*	Juno
	goddess of marriage	
Apollo	*God of light, truth, music*	Apollo
Athena	*Goddess of wisdom, justice*	Minerva
Poseidon	*God of the sea*	Neptune
Aphrodite	*Goddess of love, beauty*	Venus
Artemis	*Goddess of the hunt, youth*	Diana
Ares	*God of war*	Mars
Hephaestus	*The gods' smith*	Vulcan
Hermes	*The divine messenger*	Mercury
Hestia	*Goddess of the hearth*	Vesta
Hades	*God of the Underworld*	Pluto

Dionysus, Demeter, Persephone, and Orpheus, who were not among the twelve Olympians, symbolized the strong undercurrent of mystery which took root in Greece at an early epoch and held its position against all comers until the arrival of Christianity finally absorbed it.

All the Greek cities in Italy and other regions far from the Greek mainland were independent communities. They were not colonies like certain African, South American, or Asiatic lands which later belonged to and were exploited by European nations. Each Greek city abroad was a transplanted bit of Greece, and some of them surpassed their original *polis*. The strong point of them all was invariably culture, not conquest. They did not extend themselves over great areas or govern large native populations; they concentrated on keeping their culture alive, not on extending their sway. They universalized the Greek ideal. Their alphabet was first taken over by the Etruscans and then by the Romans. They gave their culture, their art, and their religion to Rome. From these small seeds came the impetus which started the forward march of Western civilization, a march which has not been arrested even today.

The Greek emphasis on physical culture is well known and was one of the things to which the *polis* gave very special attention. The Hellenic ideal was "a sound mind in a sound body," and the two were regarded as inseparable. The civic authorities of each town established and ran a gymnasium to which the young men came in the afternoons, took off their clothes, oiled their bodies, powdered themselves with a coat of dust or fine sand, and then commenced their exercises, which consisted of calisthenics, wrestling, boxing, jumping, running, or throwing the javelin.

It was to be expected that a people to whom the body was so important should also come together publicly for athletic games and competitions. In such a manner arose the Olympian Games, which probably developed out of the local athletic competitions held in Olympia. The date given for the First Olympiad is 776 B.C., but this is only a guess, based on Hippias and Pausanias. Plutarch in his "Life of Numa" refers to the list of the various Olympian Games and champions that go back to 776, as being purely conjectural. In Book 23 of the *Iliad,* which may be a later addition to this work, there is a long description of a series of funeral athletic competitions, and these correspond fairly well with the events at the Olympian Games. In any case, by the 600's the competition at Olympia was widely recognized, and Solon at the beginning of the next century is reported to have awarded a prize of 500 drachmas to the winners from Athens.

The original event was the sprint of one *stade* (one *length* of the track), which was about 207 yards long. The length of this race gives rise to the word *stadium.* At first this 207-yard sprint was the *only* event, and later it always began the games. With the passing of time other events were added: longer races, wrestling, races in armor, chariot races, boxing, the broad jump, throwing the discus, and hurling the javelin or spear. Throwing the discus was for length, but the spear or javelin was hurled at a target, and tested accuracy. The standard competition at the Olympian Games, however, was narrowed down to five events, which were called the *pentathlon:* 207-yard dash, broad jump, spear throw, discus throw, wrestling.

The sprint was at first run on soft sand, for early vases picture runners with hands outspread eagle fashion and feet scattering the sand behind. Later, tamped earth was used on the track, and speed picked up accordingly. The time for these sprints could not have been anything phenomenal, for the techniques of the race were not well developed. Concerning the broad jump, tradition reports that one contestant leaped 49 feet, almost double the present world record. There is no reason to believe the report.

In the seventh century, when the tyrants took over control of the cities and made a great thing of order and progress, the Olympian Games became fantastically popular, and Olympic champions were honored like victorious generals, statues were put up to them at Olympia, and in their own towns they were great heroes. Pausanias mentions 200 statues at Olympia, representing only a selection of the total. These statues glorified the male body and were an important step in the development of Greek sculpture. Not one of them has survived.

The diet of the athletes consisted mainly of cheese from wicker baskets, and occasional servings of fish, fruit, and vegetables. There was almost no meat in the fare until a certain Dromeus adopted a regime based primarily on the eating of large quantities of meat, and his successes were so striking that other athletes followed his lead. In fact, after Dromeus had won ten victories in long-distance races at various Greek games including those at Olympia (around 485 B.C.), it became a set training rule to stuff the athletes with so much meat that they became sluggish in their ordinary daily activities. The Greeks obviously thought that the more meat a man consumed the more strength he would have, and thus missed the real secret of proper athletic training.

In the beginning there were only two judges, but the number was gradually increased until it became fixed at ten. The position was regarded as one of great honor, and the men chosen were called "judges of the Hellenes." They lived in a special public building, were given very strict training in their work, and when the games began they put on their purple robes and sat at the semicircular end of the race track. When the contests took place the crowd shouted and cheered just as it does today. There was little sportsmanship on the part of either the public or the winners, for the losers became the butt of gibe and ridicule, and often tried to sneak home without being seen.

As the intellectual and artistic life of Greece developed, interest in athletic competition decreased. Going to the drama and hearing the recitation of the ancient Homeric poems took the place of going to the games. Euripides looked down on the games, so did Xenophon, and the historians took little note of them. Intellectual gymnastics replaced physical competition as the supreme goal, yet the games did not die, people still attended in large numbers, and the contests at Olympia were not finally abolished until nearly 1,200 years after their inception.

One of the most important aspects of the Olympian Games was their national character. Greeks from all the city-states competed, and during the time the games lasted a sacred truce was proclaimed throughout the territory where the Greek language was spoken. The competition took place every four years, as it does today, and often proved of inestimable benefit if the date fell in the middle of a long and bitter war.

Garlanded heralds went forth from Olympia to all the cities of Hellas to announce the opening date. Friends and enemies then met in an atmosphere of peace, and worshiped at common shrines. There was a chance for rethinking; there was a chance to negotiate an end of hostilities. Greek culture and Greek athletics drew all Hellenes together, made them feel as one, while Greek politics tended always toward separatism and fragmentation. War was a constant of Greek political life, but it was not, of course, to be equated with genocide or annihilation. The games, coming at regular intervals, were another constant. They renewed the unique pride of all Greeks, inspired them to sharpen and further develop their points of difference from other peoples, gave them a feeling of achievement and of identity as the leaders of their world. *Polis,* courage in war, athletic competition, culture = Hellas—this was the noble equation.

VIII

The Burgeoning Vine:
Athens and Sparta

Democracy is a charming form of government, full of variety and disorder, dispensing a sort of equality to equals and unequals alike.

Plato

In the early days of Greek history Athens was an unimportant village. A settlement did exist on the Acropolis in the Mycenaean period, but Homer put it in a category far below Mycenae, Sparta, and Pylos. During the Dorian invasion, really a mass infiltration which extended over a century (1200–1100), this citadel was never occupied by the invaders. Thucydides said because it was not worth taking. In any case, refugees from the Dorians poured in from the surrounding country, and without forgetting its Mycenaean roots Athens grew. The light that burned on the Acropolis was never extinguished. Indeed, on the Greek mainland Athens was the only unbroken link between the old civilization and the new.

Her growth was not phenomenal, but by 900 the small *polis* and its inhabitants had acquired a measured importance. Revealing the flexibility which later enabled them to become the school of Hellas, the Athenians held on to what they knew, learned from the refugees they had received, and absorbed from the Dorians who encircled them.

After the Dark Age it was in Athens that the revival took deepest root and spread out its widest branch. Slowly but surely this Attic melting pot became a blend of Ionic grace and Doric strength, producing the proud, creative spirit which made possible the glorious fifth century. The dynasty of Athenian kings was replaced by aristocratic rule and a new epoch began. Yet between 900 and 600, while Sparta and Corinth asserted their primacy, Athens was only a second- or a third-class power. Cultural maturity seldom comes as readily as statehood; the processes of mind and heart are intangibles that are not responsive to the best-laid laws of gods or men. The inquiring mind will blossom under all conditions and adversities except total repression, but freedom nurtures it best, and freedom is a culture's last flower.

Athens began to resemble the Athens that history has made famous toward the end of the Archaic period, around 600 B.C. Very much like Britain, she found a way to "muddle through" all difficulties. The general picture of her inhabitants at this time was not a very happy one, and recalls Hesiod's rugged pages on Boeotia. The poor were getting poorer, the rich richer, and the aristocrats who ruled were getting more greedy and more arbitrary. The thin crust of soil in Attica made the production of wheat increasingly difficult.

Then came a year or two of bad weather and most of the farmers were destitute. Among the masses debts became so burdensome that many lost their lands, others were sold into slavery (some in foreign lands), because they could not meet their mortgages. Nearly all of the lower classes owed far more than they could possibly hope to repay. Seeing those who did not meet their obligations lose both lands and freedom filled them with frustration and hatred.

The rapacious aristocrats, for their part, were sitting on the lid, unwilling to yield an inch. They had recourse to the old laws in order to protect their vested interests if those laws sufficed; if they did not, they arbitrarily invoked new laws of their own making. Slave labor, the dearest of all labor in the end, performed nearly all of the necessary work in Attica, and there was no honor or dignity in anyone who used his hands. The exploited majority was seething with anger. There was neither law nor justice, and Attica was on the verge of a social upheaval.

One of the miracles of Greek history is that at this point in time there appeared the great lawgiver of Hellas, Solon, who later was reputed by all as one of the seven wise men of Greece. He was also the first in the long and glorious list of Athenian writers. Solon himself was an aristocrat; he was also an honest, a just, and a widely educated man. He was not aligned on either side, and he believed that greed and injustice were the source of all misery. He had already distinguished himself as a poet and as a man of tolerance and ideals. Fortunately, before the volcano exploded both sides agreed to his appointment as chief archon of Athens, with dictatorial powers to lay down laws, to arbitrate, and to govern as he saw fit (594). Solon used his powers sparingly, and was so successful in walking the tightrope between the two extremes that five hundred years later Cicero was able to write that Athens was still governed by Solon's code.

The first thing Solon did was to repeal all the excessive punishments of

Draco's laws. He then canceled all debts, returned to their former owners lands confiscated for debts, restored to freedom those who had been disfranchised or enslaved for not paying their debts, put a limit on the size of landed estates, encouraged an awesome respect for the *spirit of law,* and did all he could to give the people a wide knowledge of the various statutes.

The Athenians conceived of two main aspects of the law: first, the fundamental ethical principle involved; second, the detailed statutes which applied in the various cases. The first aspect was the more important of the two, because it defined and revealed the heart of the law. All succeeding statutes were calculated simply to make these fundamental ethical principles more effective in action. After inspiring his people with the concept of ethics, Solon exposed them widely to the most important statutes by having these printed on wooden tablets or rollers, which could be turned around and were easily accessible in the courts. He also made the lowest class of citizens eligible for the jury and so equalized men before the law.

Solon instituted the right of appeal, established the validity of wills, placed special emphasis on the dignity of agriculture and the crafts, compelled the idle to work, and passed many statutes limiting the degree of luxury and behavior. He decreed that each father must teach his son a trade, encouraged foreign craftsmen to come to Athens with the promise of citizenship, used the influence of the government to increase specialization, industry, the development of ceramics, the production and exportation of olive oil, but not of other fruits of the land.

Persons who might have produced and sold surpluses of these other products he thus pushed toward industry and the crafts. Athens soon had a monopoly of the export of ceramics throughout the Mediterranean area. Her production of grapes, wine, and olives also took a great leap forward. Another of Solon's extremely important decrees was that the sons of men killed in war must be educated at state expense. This gave a great boost to the morale of the Athenian soldier.

In his regulations concerning luxury and behavior Solon put a check on the dowry of brides, he curbed by law extravagant lamentations or tearing of the hair at funerals by professional mourners, he decreed that an adulterer caught in the act could be killed, he cut down on sacrifices of animals, and decreed that only three articles of clothing might be buried with the deceased. He also legalized prostitution and provided state-regulated brothels for the relief of the young men of Athens. One of his most important laws was that in time of extreme unrest or rebellion—the Greek word is *stasis*—it was a crime for any citizen to remain neutral, for indifference might result in a take-over by a militant minority.

Solon also opened the Assembly to all citizens, removed the qualification of birth formerly required for membership in the inner council, invigorated the courts, and, once he had restored properties confiscated on account of debts, made property rights inviolable. He further decreed that no man could mortgage his body, thus exposing himself to slavery, for any debt or encumbrance whatsoever. In general the constitution that Solon gave to Athens was an enlightened one, but when asked if he had laid down the *best* laws, his reply was "I gave my city the best laws possible." With him the age of custom, verbal tradition, the will of aristocrats and kings made way for written law as the bedrock of the state. Incidentally, in honor of this great Greek lawgiver, we call our own senators "solons."

After Solon had invoked these laws and got them to operating smoothly he appeared before the Athenians and persuaded them to take a solemn oath that for ten years they would religiously follow his code. If they failed to do so, the most horrible curse would fall upon them. Content with this vow, Solon then left the country and traveled widely and long in Egypt and Ionia. Herodotus tells a fascinating story about his being entertained at the palace of King Croesus of Lydia, and although the chronology may be wrong, the story was as widely accepted and as fundamentally Greek as the story of George Washington and the cherry tree is American.

Croesus showed Solon all his treasures, which were among the richest of antiquity, and then said to the Athenian lawgiver, "Solon, I have heard of your great wisdom, and I would like you to tell me who is the happiest man in the world?" Solon gave him the name of an unimportant Athenian who had reared a contented family and then had died in battle at the peak of his life, receiving a state funeral on the same spot. Croesus was taken aback, for he had expected to hear his own name. Solon expatiated: "Count no man happy until his last day has passed. Until then all that a man may know is good fortune, not happiness."

Years went by and Croesus laid plans to wage war on the mighty Persian Empire of Cyrus the Great. He had great faith in the oracle at Delphi, so after making lavish gifts of gold and silver he asked the oracle what the result would be if he crossed the river Halys, which was the boundary between the two countries. The oracle answered in that double-talking manner which was customary with all the great oracles: "A great empire will fall." Taking this as a favorable response, Croesus attacked Persia and was disastrously defeated and taken prisoner. It was his own empire that had fallen.

Cyrus ordered that he be executed by being placed on a pyre and burned to death. As the flames began to rise Croesus recalled Solon's words, and three times cried out his name: "Solon! Solon! Solon!" Intrigued that a man at the point of death should make such a cry, Cyrus asked Croesus who Solon was. An explanation was quickly given and Cyrus then tried to extinguish the blaze, but could not do so. Croesus prayed to Apollo to quench the flames if he had found the offerings formerly made to him acceptable. Although the day was clear, the god suddenly produced storm clouds and a heavy rain which drowned out the fire. Cyrus untied the captive king and they became good friends; Croesus gave the Persian monarch much sage advice as to how to rule the new territories that he had won.

The legacy that Solon left to Athens was a new concept of government and social organization. He broadened the political base and thus initiated the move toward Athenian democracy, which came a little less than a century later. Although in succeeding centuries there were many "tyrants" in Athens, many oligarchic coups, many periods of relative chaos when it appeared that everything would go down the drain, and finally the conquest of all Greece by Macedonia and then by Rome, Solon's code survived every vicissitude and endured in its main principles until the Roman conquest.

The political organization that Solon instituted was this: The aristocratic *Areopagus,* or Senate, which was the highest power, was made less exclusive and shorn of its birth qualifications, but property qualifications were continued.

The *Boule,* an elective executive council of 400, came next in order of importance. Each of the four Athenian "tribes" elected 100 members to this council, which submitted bills and business to the general Assembly.

The *Assembly,* the old *Ecclesia* of the Homeric poems, was revitalized and broadened to include all citizens, who were invited to join directly in its deliberations.

In earlier times this Assembly had been much more perfunctory in its operation. We will recall what happened when a commoner rose to challenge Agamemnon and was brutally attacked by Odysseus. Actually, the old Assembly was "more akin to a rally of aroused tribesmen than to a meeting of informed citizens prepared to vote," as Finley Hooper, a sensitive American specialist in Greek history, has stated. Kings called the people together in times of danger merely to get their vocal support; such a gathering of the crowd at a moment of crisis was often a persuasion to near-unanimity. Later, when the aristocracy replaced the monarchy (by 800 this was in effect all over Greece), the Assembly began to have a limited voice in the government but its membership was open only to citizens of property. When Solon made all citizens members of the Assembly he greatly broadened participation in the government.

The last branch of government was the Heliaea, a body of 6,000 citizens chosen by lot to be the veniremen, or jurors, for the various courts. Solon made all citizens eligible for membership. Perhaps eligibility for this body even more than membership in the Assembly, which obviously everyone could not and did not attend, gave citizens of the lower and middle classes a sense of political importance.

The total effect of the system was still oligarchic rule, but oligarchic rule in motion toward democracy. When democracy came to Athens it meant, of course, *direct* participation in the government, not representative participation. In the United States today we have not a democracy but a republic. Our government is run by representatives; we do not control it directly as did the Athenians, but elect others who do so for us. We have gained in efficiency but have lost in responsiveness and in responsibility.

As Greek history proceeds we will notice that the word *king* appears with great frequency. In Greek the word is usually *basileus,* the term used in Homer, but as the centuries passed *basileus* came to have quite a different meaning, and eventually we find it applied even to those chief magistrates, or archons, whose term of office was but a single year. On the other hand, the word *tyrant,* or *tyrannos,* which is not a Greek word at all but a term borrowed from the Lydian, was applied to any man who illegally seized control of the government. He did not have the constitutional authority of a king. However, the word did not originally have the unsavory connotations attached to it today.

In general, the Greek tyrants were civilized and politically well-trained aristocrats; even the worst of them were not anti-intellectual vulgarians of the Hitler type. But in the later centuries many were military dictators who became tyrannical in the present sense of the word. Sparta was the only *polis* of Greece that never had a tyrant as ruler, but in Sparta the whole governmental setup was so strictly regimented that this signified not freedom but merely a totalitarian concept of government sanctioned and operated by the citizenry as a whole.

Solon was one of the great lawgivers of antiquity, but he wielded no magic wand. He successfully canalized the ethical and legal basis of the Athenian state, but he was unable to provide it with a fixed *form* of government. However, for almost forty years things went well in Athens, despite the dissatisfaction of the two extremes, one wishing to retrench its lost power and the other eager for a broader revolution and more drastic reforms.

Toward the mid-century, circa 562, another aristocrat, Peisistratus, a man of considerable charisma, came to the fore as spokesman for the small farmers and the city laborers who still felt deprived by the oligarchic system. Solon, uneasy at the growing disorder, warned his countrymen of a possible coup, but his words went unheeded. Finally, in despair, he called the Athenians "a bunch of geese," placed his arms and shield outside his door to signify that he had left politics for good, and devoted his final years to writing. Peisistratus twice seized control of the government and was twice overthrown before he finally established himself firmly in power. His dictatorship lasted for the last nineteen years of his life, 546–527, and after this he was succeeded by his sons, who ruled for another seventeen years. The "tyranny" finally ended in 510, and three years later, under Cleisthenes, a third aristocrat, Athens became a democracy.

Peisistratus was typical of the better-grade Greek tyrants. He was a great builder and promoter. Indeed, who among the dictators of history was not? Order and progress are the cure-all of every dictatorship from Peisistratus to Porfirio Díaz, Stalin, Mussolini, Francisco Franco, and the military junta that is ruling Greece today. Peisistratus, at least, comes at the top of the above series of six, both in what he accomplished in material well-being and in his application of the law. He followed the code of Solon almost without change excepting only the way he seized power and doled out to supporters and friends some of the choice plums of office. Aristotle called his rule "temperate, more like that of a statesman than of a tyrant."

He constructed a long aqueduct and gave Athens a good water supply. He gave seed corn to the poor, expanded trade, planted colonies at the strategic Dardanelles, built up the navy, and opened the wheat basket of southern Russia to importation. He initiated a public works building program to take care of the unemployed and began construction of the great temple to Olympian Zeus, which was not finished until the Roman Emperor Hadrian came to power six centuries later. A few of its soaring Corinthian columns (the original columns were Doric) still brighten the heart of Athens today. Paraphrasing the words of Augustus, we might almost say that Peisistratus found Athens a city of wood and brick and left her a city of marble. Peisistratus also sent judges traveling through the countryside in order to bring justice to the rural folk and, no doubt, to keep the rural element from coming to the city, where they might cause trouble.

The most remarkable innovations of Peisistratus, however, were in the sphere of organized state festivals. He reorganized the festival of Dionysus and gave it strong state support. A large stone outdoor theater was constructed on the south side of the Acropolis for this specific purpose. This "theater of Dionysus," as later remodeled, is still one of the landmarks of Athens. Out of the festival of Dionysus the tragic drama of Greece was born.

Peisistratus also reorganized the Panathenaeic Festival, the festival of all Athenians, which took place in August and was marked by a great procession up to the Acropolis and by the recitation of the Homeric poems by professional bards. There is acceptable evidence that as tyrant of Athens he was responsible for the restoration and editing of the Homeric poems, particularly the *Iliad* and the *Odyssey,* giving them the form in which they have survived.

After the death of Peisistratus in 527 control of the government passed into the hands of his sons, and for a time it appeared that a new dynasty might emerge. These two sons continued the works of their father, proceeded with his building program, and invited to Athens the two famous Ionian poets Simonides and Anacreon, who found the Attic intellectual environment to their liking. But the masses grew more and more disaffected and so did the aristocrats, who disliked the vested family interest which Peisistratus had established. The dictatorship became more oppressive as opposition mounted. There was a period of unrest and violence, followed by a tug of war, until Cleisthenes "took the people into partnership," as Herodotus says, and gave Athens a democratic government in 507.

Cleisthenes also instituted the custom of legal ostracism of a political leader who was considered to be a menace to the state. The members of the Assembly wrote their votes on fragments of pottery (*ostracons*) and it took a minimum of 6,000 votes to ostracize a man. The period of ostracism was ten years; it was not considered a disgrace. The man's property was not confiscated, and exiles often returned to become great leaders. Aristotle called it democracy's way of protecting itself by lopping off "the tallest ears of corn."

It might be said that in sixth-century Athens Solon represented thesis, Peisistratus antithesis, and Cleisthenes synthesis. The Athenian democracy born under Cleisthenes endured for almost two centuries. The Roman Republic was fashioned in imitation of it, and so in greater or less degree were all democratic or republican forms of government of a later date. The founders of our Republic were particularly inspired by it, especially the trio of distinguished writers, Hamilton, Madison and Jay, whose clarion call to union in the classic papers of *The Federalist* clearly reveals that they had imbibed at the Attic spring.

The course of democracy in Athens was not always smooth. Indeed, as the distinguished historian M. I. Finley points out, one can easily compile "a catalogue of cases of repression, sycophancy, irrational behavior and outright brutality in the nearly two centuries that Athens was governed as a democracy. Yet they remain no more than so many single incidents in this long stretch of time when Athens was remarkably free from the universal Greek malady of sedition and civil war." There were two brief oligarchic coups, a generation of demagogues, and the execution of Socrates as a menace to the state. But in the United States in our less than two centuries of independence we have had a bloody civil war, the assassination of four Presidents, several hundred lynchings, organized crime with which our government seems unable to cope, and widespread violence in our cities today. Athens fared well by comparison. Her period of democracy did not end until the Macedonians conquered most of Greece and closed this chapter finally in 338.

SPARTA

After Athens, Sparta is the best known city of Greece. Homer described her as rich and powerful, a fit home for the gold-studded palace of battle-roaring Menelaus and Helen of Troy. Telemachus paid a long visit to this palace in the *Odyssey* when he was searching for his father. Homer also wrote of the goddess Athena's flight "into this land where greens are wide for dancing." The city's situation was attractive; it lay in a fertile area in one of the southernmost valleys of the Peloponnesus. A ring of high mountains provided an excellent national defense. When the Dorians arrived they destroyed the Mycenaean city completely, and on its ruins established their own. From this time on Sparta was dominated by Dorian ideals. She was a military state and represented the closed society par excellence. Flexible, democratic, artistic Athens stood at the opposite pole.

The story of Sparta is largely traditional. The city had no historians to record the deeds of her people or to sing their praise. Therefore, Spartan history, much like that of Carthage, survives mainly in the chronicles of her enemies. This implies a quality of exaggeration which enemies are prone to exploit for their own purposes. The Sparta that was known throughout Hellas was a stern, uncompromising, courageous, self-disciplined, single-minded, self-sacrificing *polis*. Among the other Hellenes there were some who admired her but none who loved her. The following chronicle, re-

Relief on base from Mantinea: Apollo pitting his lyre against the flutes of Marsyas, a priest of Cybele. Apollo won the contest by adding his voice to the music of the lyre.

corded by these other Hellenes, but with a Spartan kernel as its base, must be regarded as legend rather than history. But myth and legend, despite the distortions of history, reveal the dark river of the unconscious and are the soul of a people told in symbolic terms. The story of Sparta fits within this fragile frame.

In her formative years (1000–600) Sparta showed a lively interest in the arts. The Spartans, like all Greeks, expressed themselves bounteously in poetry and in song. The "Doric mode" was born and plaintive music filled the air. But in the seventh century, exactly why we do not know, the spring went dry. From this time on, unlike Athens, Sparta did not create, she imported talent. Terpander, the musician who added a string (or was it two or three strings?) to the lyre, came from Lesbos to live in Sparta. His choral lyrics once quieted a mob and prevented a riot, but his meddling with the lyre was not liked and he was exiled. Two other famous immigrant artists were Alcman, the poet of love, and Tyrtaeus, whose martial rhythms stirred Spartan youths like a military band. Lycurgus, who gave Sparta her traditional code of laws which Plato so admired, was her one true son.

Lycurgus is said to have lived in the ninth century, but if he never lived at all the Spartans would have had to invent him in order to give the sanctity of tradition to their onerous constitution. Perhaps he only codified laws and customs that already existed, but was credited with their authorship as the Jews credited Moses with the Ten Commandments, Genesis, and Deuteronomy. Perhaps he was just a myth and existed only in the minds of the Spartans. In any case he was the legendary embodiment of the Spartan spirit.

Both Herodotus and Plutarch say that Lycurgus was responsible for most of the regimentation of Spartan life. After extensive visits to Crete and Egypt he brought back to Sparta many new ideas about law and social organization. He was particularly impressed by the Egyptian practice of separating the soldiery from the rest of the population. He insisted on a more equitable distribution of the land, which had been concentrated in a few large estates, and then "he declared an outlawry of all needless and superfluous arts," particularly those which involved the use of gold or silver.

Sparta had great iron deposits, but was lacking in silver, which was plentiful in Attica. Lycurgus, therefore, established an ideal of austerity: let the spirit of iron rule our city. Silver and gold, he was persuaded, soften a race and make it useless. The Spartans even used an unwieldy iron currency, while the easily handled silver currency of Athens became the monetary standard throughout the Mediterranean world, even in faraway Gaul.

Lycurgus went a little too far with his next provision, which Plutarch calls the "most masterly stroke of this great lawgiver." In his effort to combat luxury and the desire for riches he decreed that all citizens should eat in common, of the same bread and the same meat, and of the kinds that were specified. The rich thus being obliged to share a common mess with the poor would lose their vanity and the poor would lose their hostility and feel that they truly belonged to the commonwealth. This ordinance did not go down well with some of the aristocrats, and a group of them chased Lycurgus out of the marketplace. He outran them all except for one young man named Alcander who caught up with him and as Lycurgus turned this young man gave him a mighty blow in the face with his stick. The blow struck out the lawgiver's eye and left his cheek a bloody mass. Plutarch describes what then took place:

Lycurgus, so far from being daunted and discouraged by this accident, stopped short and showed his disfigured face and eye beat out to his countrymen; they, dismayed and ashamed at the sight, delivered Alcander into his hands to be punished. . . . Lycurgus, having thanked them for the care of his person, dismissed them all, excepting only Alcander; and, taking him with him into his house, neither did nor said anything severely to him, but, dismissing those whose place it was, bade Alcander to wait upon him at table. The young man, who was of an ingenuous temper, without murmuring did as he was commanded; and being thus admitted to live with Lycurgus, he had an opportunity to observe in him, besides his gentleness and calmness of temper, an extraordinary sobriety and an indefatigable industry, and so, from an enemy, became one of his most zealous admirers, and told his friends that Lycurgus was not that morose and ill-natured man they had formerly taken him for, but the one mild and gentle character of the world.

Thus, the giver of stern laws became a national hero.

Every material thing in Sparta was marked by its simplicity. Houses were poorly finished with their timbered ceilings and walls neither evened nor paneled; the temples were similarly poor in their construction. Furniture and domestic utensils were strongly made and possessed the beauty of strength and form while lacking that of embellishment or precious value. Clothes also were poor and rough. For these reasons all that the archaeologist can find today where proud Sparta once stood are a few scattered stones and a mass of rubble. Thucydides, the Athenian, in his history of the Peloponnesian War, points out the great lack of temples and public buildings in Sparta and states that the *polis* is "composed of villages after the old fashion of Hellas. And I suppose if Sparta became desolate," he continues, "and only her ruins remained, posterity would be strongly inclined to question her power, and yet she rules the whole Peloponnesus."

In the political and social spheres everything in Sparta pointed toward the production of topflight professional soldiers. All citizens, both male and female, were given a rigorous physical training from infancy. Newly born babies were bathed in wine instead of water, as in the other Greek states. Then each baby was examined by a council of elders and those found defective were thrown off a cliff to die on the rocks below. This, at least, was the tradition in the early centuries. Those who survived were exposed to the elements and either became inured or died.

At an early age (Plutarch says at seven) all boys were taken from their parents and sent to live in a barracks. There was only one career for them: that of the soldier. They lived in these military dormitories even after they were married, and invariably shared a common mess. A visitor from another Greek city, Sybaris, after dining among these young men, is reported to have remarked that now he understood why it was that the Spartan soldier was not afraid to die. Having to eat such food was almost as bad as death.

Spartan children were taught absolute obedience, and Spartan nurses were much sought after in the other Greek states, particularly in Athens. Children were also taught not to flinch under punishment, and cases were known of their dying under the whip rather than letting out a cry of pain. The story of the boy who stole a fox and hid it under his tunic and then, with an expressionless face, allowed the fox to devour his entrails rather than admit that he had taken it may not be true but it is typical.

The Spartan attitude toward marriage and sexual relations was quite different from the norms prevailing in the rest of Greece. In many of the public processions both the men *and the women* went naked. Plutarch writes: "These public processions of the maidens, and their appearing naked in their exercises and dancings, were incitements to marriage, operating on the young with the rigor and certainty, as Plato says, of love, if not of mathematics." Besides, if a young Spartan male was not married by age thirty he was disfranchised by law, a punishment none were willing to endure.

The groom, after choosing his bride, carried her off by a sort of force, and this, perhaps, gave rise to the tale of Helen being carried off by Paris. An older woman then came to cut the bride's hair and to dress her in man's clothes and leave her lying upon a mattress in the dark. "Afterwards comes the bridegroom, in his everyday clothes, sober and composed as having supped at the common table, and, entering privately into the room where the bride lies, unties her virgin zone and takes her to himself; and, after staying some time together, he returns composedly to his own apartment to sleep as usual with the other young men." This separation of wife and husband was supposed to increase and to lengthen their mutual affection and their mutual delight.

However, Plutarch reports, when a man grew old or was ill it was expected that he would lend his wife to a younger man in order to have her produce strong children. Lycurgus was of the opinion that children were not so much the property of their parents as of the state, and therefore the Spartan mother should be carefully bred. The laws of other nations in this regard seemed absurd and inconsistent to him. It was indeed strange that "people would be so solicitous for their dogs and horses as to exert interest and to pay money to procure fine breeding, and yet kept their wives shut up to be made mothers only by themselves, who might be foolish, infirm, or diseased." The story of Helen and the Trojan War warns us to take these statements about sexual freedom with a grain of salt.

The Spartan citizen was noted for his lack of eloquence and was characterized by his monosyllabic, or "laconic," language. In the Assembly speeches were not at all like the persuasive oratory of Athens, and in order to be heard a man had to outshout the others; voting also was judged by the loudness of the shouts. Spartan soldiers used short swords as well as short words, and when a visiting Athenian laughed at them saying a juggler could easily swallow them, the king answered sententiously: "They are long enough to reach our enemies."

Spartans were the only Greek soldiers to whom war was a relief. Their appearance and behavior in battle often frightened their enemies into flight before the fighting was joined. They placed garlands upon their heads, the pipers played a religious hymn and the king himself began the paean of attack. "It was at once a magnificent and a terrible sight to see them march on to the tune of their flutes, without any disorder in their ranks, any discomposure in their minds, or change in their countenances, calmly and cheerfully moving with the music to the deadly fight."

When the enemy was met they fought with a deliberate skill and assurance, never overtaken by either fear or fury. Once they had the enemy on the run they pursued him only far enough to ensure victory, but unlike many other Greeks they did not cut to pieces those who had abandoned all resistance, considering such a base act unworthy of a Greek people. This custom, wrote Plutarch, saved Athens from complete destruction after her defeat by Sparta in the Peloponnesian War. Thucydides (of course, he was an Athenian) was not so complimentary; he describes the Spartan massacre of the major portion of the captives at Plataea in 431 and the ruthless destruction of the city.

Sparta could not possibly have been the successful military state that she was had it not been for the Spartan slaves. All of Greek civilization was based on a slave society, but in Sparta the slaves were a special breed, called helots. They were very much like serfs tied to the soil, but they were slaves of the state, not of any individual. Occasionally one obtained his freedom, but this was rare, and more than occasionally these helots, fed up with their lot in life, rose in rebellion only to be put down in the bloodiest possible manner. The Spartan ruling caste forced the helots into a slave psychology. Potential leaders among them were regularly picked off in a very deliberate fashion.

Thucydides tells of one occasion after a battle in which the helots had acquitted themselves well as auxiliaries. Those who had performed most bravely were singled out so that they might be rewarded. They were invited to a special celebration in their honor, were given their freedom and their heads were garlanded, but shortly thereafter all disappeared and not one of them was heard of again. In such a way was potential leadership among the helots destroyed before it had time to express itself in overt action.

As a result of such practices, the helots became almost a subhuman class whose sole purpose in life was to work and to produce so that the citizens of Sparta might enjoy that leisure which would permit them to become superior soldiers. No Spartan citizen was supposed to engage in agriculture or any menial trade. Between the helots and the citizens was a class of free farmers and craftsmen who lived in the surrounding villages. These villages, under strict Spartan domination, labored at many necessary tasks and also tilled the fields but had no share in the government. On the basis of these two classes the very rigid Spartan economy was raised and the exemplary Spartan aristocracy thrived.

Sparta was never a very populous city-state. The total number of Spartan citizens *with their wives and children* probably never exceeded 30,000. There were probably four or five times that number of helots, and perhaps half as many free villagers. This small group of citizens man for man, throughout Greek history, made the best soldiers of Greece. Sparta lost only two battles in five hundred years. Once in 425 the Athenians forced a contingent of Spartans to surrender, and once again their army was defeated near Leuctra by Thebes in 371, long after Sparta had passed her peak. Greece shuddered to her foundation after Leuctra, and Sparta never recovered from this blow.

The largest number of Spartan soldiers ever to take part in a battle were the 5,000 who fought at Plataea in 479. The smaller contingent of 300 or so who held the pass at Thermopylae in 480 and died almost to a man along with their king is even more gloriously remembered. At Leuctra a century later the city was barely able to muster a thousand men.

When news of the disastrous defeat at Leuctra reached Sparta, the people were compelled to appear in public with happy expressions, even those who had lost sons, brothers, or a father in the battle, while those who heard that a family member had been spared appeared afflicted and wept. The Spartan mother's farewell to her son as he left for war tells the whole sad story: "Come back with your shield, or lying on it." They were not empty words. Die for Sparta, but *never* turn and flee.

Yet in such destructive heroism did Sparta gut herself of all future life. She turned her back on culture in order to preserve the state. She cut her own veins and let the lifeblood flow away. She left no literature to posterity, no great art, no philosophy except a totalitarian concept of the law. But Spartan law embodied the Spartan ideal: individual sacrifice for community welfare. Spartans did create and follow a system of ethics and of behavior which was the envy of their neighbors. Many Athenians profoundly admired Sparta's rigorous constitution, and Plato was persuaded that its basic tenets should be embodied in the legal code of his ideal commonwealth. But if in fact Plato had lived in Sparta instead of Athens he would have been gagged before his prime. The miracle of the free mind was an Athenian, not a Spartan, concept.

Today when we think of the heritage of Greece we think of Athens, and it is fitting that we should. But unfortunately the romance of history deludes the general observer into lumping all ancient Greek cities together, as if Athens were multiplied a dozenfold in Hellas, and this was never so. Even in Greece there was only one Athens. Her leadership in the wars with Persia and her subsequent rivalry with Sparta helped to create the dynamic tension out of which her great culture emerged, but the Attic seed was unique in history. Other Greek cities had their great achievements, their noted figures, their glorious temples, their moment in the sun, yet none repeated Athens. Sparta, perhaps the most frequently remembered of them all, had her incomparable disciplined society and her soldiery, but in today's world there are few who would ennoble the ideal of the soldier the power of whose weapon has far outstripped the wisdom of its handler.

IX

The Persian and Peloponnesian Wars:
Herodotus and Thucydides

*Fix your eyes on the greatness of Athens, until you become filled
with the love of her. . . . Future ages will wonder at us, as the
present age does now.*

Pericles, Funeral Oration

If all the world were just, there would be no need for valor.

Plutarch

The fifth century begins with the wars between the Greeks and the Persians, and in these wars "Greece suffered more sorrows than in twenty previous generations," wrote Herodotus. We might also add "and won more glory." First, Darius the Great, and then Xerxes, invaded Greece with large armies whose sheer weight of numbers appeared to give them all the advantage. These were troops which had already won a series of notable victories in Asia and Africa, and they had the support of a vast empire behind them. The very name "Persians" inspired fear all over the Mediterranean world. They were not carefully trained and highly disciplined soldiers like the Greeks, nor were they a homogeneous and close-knit army. They were, indeed, a heterogeneous multitude assembled from various subkingdoms with the Persian soldiers as their elite. These were bound to their king with ties of strong personal loyalty, and their archers were the world's finest. At this point the apparent advantage ends.*

Herodotus, who admired the Persians, points out the different philosophies behind the armies: once in a great storm a group of Persian soldiers

---

* The Persians under Darius I had conquered Afghanistan, northern India, Turkestan, Mesopotamia, northern Arabia, Egypt, Syria, Thrace, and Macedonia.

had thrown themselves overboard in order to lighten the ship and thus secure the safety of their king. The Greeks, when they heard of this episode, were confounded. They were willing to die for their *polis* or because a man could achieve a glorious memory by dying nobly, but to commit suicide for a king was unthinkable. The Greeks considered this a mark of Oriental slavishness, in the same category as the ritual of bowing and scraping before the monarch, whereas it was really a different concept of nobility and honor.

The discipline of the Athenians was nurtured by a free society and arose from love of country and from open discussion and decisions democratically arrived at. Sparta was not a democratic society, but she was small, homogeneous, highly disciplined, and proud. In facing the Persians the Greeks knew what the risks were and felt that the odds were against them, but their whole way of life led every man among them to rise to the occasion regardless of the consequences. This war would be the test of their individual worth and public value; it was the moment of truth, man's final measurement.

The Greeks looked down on the Persians and considered them barbarians like other primitive peoples who talked with a "ba-ba-ba . . ." sound to their language. The Greeks also looked down on the Persian Empire, which was so huge that it sprawled across half of known Asia like some great unwieldy monster. How could any country that large have worth? The Greek states were small and intimate and every citizen contributed his small part to make them great.

The chronology of events was as follows: In 499 the Greek cities of Ionia which had fallen under Persian rule rebelled. Athens sent help, but to no avail, for the revolt was mercilessly suppressed. Darius, the Persian king, dispatched emissaries to Greece demanding earth and water as tokens of submission. His emissaries were thrown into a well and the Greeks shouted to them: "Help yourselves. There's plenty of both down there."

Darius decided to invade Greece proper in order to teach these upstarts a lesson (490 B.C.). He had with him the son of Peisistratus, who was to be installed as puppet tyrant. The army of Medes and Persians landed at the bay of Marathon only 26 miles northeast of Athens. The Athenians mustered their entire citizenry, even enlisting their slaves, and with the aid of 1,000 men from Plataea they faced the enemy. Athens had sent an urgent note to Sparta asking for reinforcements and beseeching her not to allow the barbarians to overwhelm one of the oldest and most noble cities of Hellas. But "it was the ninth day of the first decade, and the full moon was not yet out, and the Spartans could not break their tradition and send an army until that day had come." So writes Herodotus, explaining the Spartan absence on the field that day.

The plain of Marathon is a crescent-shaped strip of land along the bay, backed by an amphitheater of hills. The plain measures about 6 miles by 2, and a large mound 35 feet high still marks the place where the Athenians buried their dead. Centuries later Lord Byron reported that he might have purchased the entire plain for 900 pounds sterling. The Persians had landed at the northern end of the plain, probably because the water offshore was deeper there, so they had their backs to the sea. The Athenians and Plataeans occupied the southern end of the plain. Some Ionians had brought news to the Greek command that the Persian cavalry had temporarily left camp, probably in order to water the horses, and the Athenian general knew this was the chance he had been waiting for.

He mustered his 10,000 men, who were outnumbered about two to one, in a line which was just as wide as that of the enemy. In order to achieve this distribution he made the center of his line very thin, whereas the two flanks were several soldiers deep in men. He decided to attack on the run, the first time in history, says Herodotus, that this had been done. This was in order to throw the Persian bowmen off their mark. The Athenians certainly did not run the entire mile that separated the two armies under the burden of their heavy shields and armor, but they undoubtedly did charge the final few yards. The Persians must have thought them out of their minds.

In any case, the more numerous army of Darius hit the center of their ranks, rammed clean through, and began to pursue the Greeks they had scattered. The Athenians wheeled their heavier flanks and closed the pincers on the disorganized Persians with their full force. The invaders began to turn and run with the Athenians hotly behind. Herodotus says that the Persians lost 6,400 dead that day, to 192 for the Athenians. We can take his larger number as an almost certain exaggeration, but the figure of 192 Athenians killed in action was probably accurate.

The story goes that one of the Athenian soldiers ran the 26 miles back to Athens to announce the victory, and then fell dead. However, Herodotus, who knew all the details of the engagement and wrote only forty years afterwards, does not mention this episode which gave rise to the Marathon race in present-day Olympian Games. In fact, the story does not appear in Greek literature at all until six centuries after the battle, and so is no doubt one of those legends invented by a later generation in order to glorify a long-past event.

Herodotus does state that the Athenians were the first Greeks who had dared to look the Persians in the face and that they fought that day at Marathon "in a manner worthy of being recorded." However, the importance of the battle of Marathon was in reality more symbolic than real. The engagements at Salamis and Plataea a decade later were both more hotly contested and of greater importance. Marathon was only the initial skirmish in a long-range war, but it quickly became the literary property of the Athenians, who made the most of it.

The dramatist Aeschylus took part in the battle and survived, but his brother was slain. Themistocles, a later hero of Athens, also was on the field that day. After the battle was over hundreds of Athenians went to the battlefield to look upon the bodies of the dead Medes and Persians, whose strange appearance and dress seemed to them to belong to another planet.

The victory at Marathon gave the Greeks a respite of ten years, and they made good use of that decade. A rich vein of silver was discovered near Sunium, south of Athens, and the city became very wealthy. At first it was proposed to divide the proceeds from the mine among the citizens, but Themistocles persuaded the Athenians to build a fleet instead. This fleet later saved Greece and made Western civilization possible.

Darius of Persia died in 486 and his place was taken by his son Xerxes, who was determined to avenge his father's defeat. Amassing a much greater army—Herodotus says it consisted of an incredible 2.5 million fighting men—he crossed the Hellespont and entered northern Greece. The figure is pure fantasy, but reports do indicate that Xerxes' army was among the largest ever assembled in ancient times. (J. B. Bury reduces it to about 300,000, but even this total is beyond my own belief.) In any case, confronted by this horde, many northern Greek cities gave up without a fight, while the Persian army, like a swarm of locusts, moved toward the south. This time the Athenians did not face it alone; Sparta and other city-states joined hands with the victors of Marathon and, united as never before, the Greeks readied themselves for the inevitable blow.

The first encounter was in 480 at the Pass of Thermopylae, held by King Leonidas of Sparta with 300 Spartans and about a thousand allied soldiers. The result is well known. The Spartans died there almost to a man, along with their king. Over the mound of earth which marks their mass grave stands a simple stone monument with this inscription of Simonides:

> Go tell the Spartans, stranger passing by,
> That here obedient to their will we lie.

The Persians poured through the pass and onto the plains that led to Athens. The inhabitants of the city were instructed to save themselves in any way they saw fit; Athens was not to be defended. The united Greek army and fleet retired to Salamis, and there awaited the Persians. The oracle at Delphi had been consulted and had responded that "Athens would be saved by her wooden walls." Themistocles, their commander, had persuaded the Athenians that this meant their wooden ships. The city was easily taken, but when the Persians arrived they found an almost completely abandoned town, for most of the population had fled to Salamis and other nearby islands. The invaders burned Athens to the ground and left the Acropolis in rubble.

At this point the greatness of the Athenians reveals itself for the second time. Two of the strongest allies, Corinth and Sparta, were unwilling to risk everything in a battle with the superior Persian fleet, but the Athenian general Themistocles prevented their flight. To the Corinthian commander he said bluntly, "The Athenian fleet is big enough to take Corinth if you desert us now," and to the Spartan general he said, "If you withdraw we will leave you alone and put all of our citizens on these ships and sail for Italy where we will re-establish our *polis.*" Then to make certain that the allied fleets would not slip off by night he sent a trusted slave to Xerxes telling him that he really wanted Xerxes to win but that the Greeks were planning to escape in the night unless the Persians bottled them up in the harbor. All these bluffs paid off, and the following day the battle was joined in the narrower waters which Themistocles considered more favorable to his heavier ships (September 23, 480 B.C.). The result was a smashing victory for the Greeks.

It was Themistocles who had wisely determined to make Athens into the greatest sea power of Hellas, and although he had only a short time to achieve his purpose he was eminently successful. Greek ships had improved greatly since Homeric times when the mainstay of all fleets was the vessel of twenty oars. However, in the *Odyssey* the fifty-oared ships of the Phaecians are mentioned as the new racers of the seas; these were called the "penteconters."

By the end of the eighth century the Phoenicians, the master shipbuilders and navigators of the Mediterranean, had produced a revolutionary type of ship no longer than the old penteconter but with twice as many oarsmen, the extra manpower being made possible by placing a second tier of rowers above the first. This vessel, called the "bireme," had a much greater speed than the older penteconter. Before the bireme had been adopted by the Greeks, however, the Phoenicians had made even further improvements and introduced the "trireme," a vessel with three tiers of oarsmen, one above the other. The trireme carried a complement of 170 rowers and became the standard Greek warship. These vessels had a heavy bronze ramming piece over their prows, and were thus able to shear a lighter ship in two. The combined Greek fleet which was to meet the Persians at Salamis was composed of 300 triremes and less than a dozen penteconters. The Persians had twice this number of lighter vessels.

Themistocles lured the Persian fleet into the narrow straits of Salamis, which were only about one mile wide, where there would be very little room for maneuvering and the lighter enemy vessels could not gain any advantage from their superior numbers or mobility. He then attacked the Persians from the side and crushed many of their ships. Xerxes himself sat on his throne on the slope of Mount Aegaleo opposite the straits watching the engagement. He saw Persians falling into the sea by the hundreds and drowning, for none of them knew how to swim. The Greeks who fell or were thrown overboard quickly swam to shore.

One Persian ship was captained by the Carian Queen Artemisia, and when this lady saw that her vessel was bottled up she rammed one of the Persian ships in order to make the Greeks think she was on their side. Xerxes saw the ramming and believed that a Greek vessel had been sunk. Herodotus says that he exclaimed, "My men are fighting like women, and my women are fighting like men!" It was the cry of a defeated king, for by nightfall the greater part of the Persian fleet had been destroyed, and Xerxes gathered his army and retreated as fast as he could.

A few months later, after the Persians had regrouped, they were ready for the final land engagement of the war. This was fought at Plataea in Boeotia, where approximately 100,000 Greeks from practically every city-state of Hellas (except Thebes) met the vastly more numerous Persian army (479). Again, as at Marathon, their superior hoplite forces out-maneuvered and then routed the enemy. The Spartans distinguished themselves in this engagement. The second naval battle of the war took place at about the same time along the coast of Ionia, and this also resulted in a great victory for the Greeks. The power of Persia was repulsed and Greece was left free to work out her destiny alone.

It had been a fight between a Greek David and a Persian Goliath, and as in the Biblical tale David had won. He had the superior intelligence, the superior weapon, the superior society, and he was fighting for his homeland. Clearly the better man had won. The Mediterranean was kept free for the expansion of trade and for the exchange of ideas. But it might so easily have gone the other way, and had this been the case Europe would not be what it is today. Oriental ideas and peoples would have merged with those of the Continent to form a new civilization, with what results no one can tell. In any event, the battles of Marathon, Thermopylae, Salamis, and Plataea made possible the Europe that our history knows. They canalized an energy which almost immediately resulted in the flowering of fifth-century Athens, the bedrock of our culture. That handful of Greeks who defeated the Persians secured the foundation upon which has rested ever since the tenuous structure of our lives.

It is unpalatable for one who believes that a good seed in man strives always for his improvement to recognize that so much of this improvement has come about as a result of the application of force. In the process of history power, pride, and hatred have often been more important elements than goodness of heart or social ideals. A quick look at the Greek soldier during the key periods of Hellenic history will clarify the point.

In the Homeric battles the common soldier had very slight importance. The conflict was between individual nobles and kings; mass encounters counted for nothing. The king ruled the battlefield as he ruled the state. By 800 B.C. things had begun to change and by the middle of the following century the Greek population and economy had grown so much that a period of exploration and colonization began. Colonies were established all over the Mediterranean and produced a flourishing commerce. With this growing trade came increased wealth and increased commitments. More soldiers were needed to protect these growing interests. Fortunately, at this stage in Greek history more citizens were able to equip themselves with good armor, and a new warrior class emerged: the Greek hoplites. Economically and politically they represented the new middle class, not the aristocrats, who still formed an elite cavalry.

The hoplites were so heavily armed that they could fight effectively only in close formation. This presupposed a careful period of military training. The hoplite carried his heavy shield firmly fixed on his left forearm in order to protect his own left side and his neighbor's right. In battle the hoplites formed an unbroken phalanx, often several soldiers deep, and slugged it out with the adversary. Sometimes sheer weight and power could crack the enemy line. Fighting was unglamorous and the best-trained contingent usually won. By training and fighting together the hoplite class acquired a feeling of solidarity and of importance. The influence of the aristocrats was weakened. Dominant on the field of battle, the hoplites soon demanded more participation in the government. The move toward Greek democracy, therefore, was initiated and made possible by a new concept in military tactics.

Much later still, after 400 B.C., the Athenians made another fundamental change in their army. They hired numerous mercenaries, removed the heavy hoplite armor and gave these soldiers only a very light shield for protection. Mobility on the battlefield was the new goal. These more lightly equipped troops could dart around the heavier hoplites and pick them to pieces. Spartan soldiers trained in the older tradition found it difficult to cope with the more mobile Athenians, and so despite the defeat of Athens by Sparta in the Peloponnesian War, the vanquished city soon rose again and demanded anew her place in the sun.

It would be a pity in a book of this kind, based as it is on the oldest chronicles as well as the newest, not to give some very special credit to Herodotus, the "father of history," who wrote about the wars between the Greeks and the Persians in a style so zestful that even today it is a pleasure to read him. Herodotus (484–430 B.C.) was born in Halicarnassus in Asia Minor, a Persian subject, for these Greek provinces were then under the Persian yoke. King Xerxes was assassinated by his powerful grand vizier when Herodotus was in his early twenties, just starting on the extensive travels which were to become the basis for his famous history. Before he began to write, therefore, Herodotus had a great amount of firsthand knowledge and had pondered much upon the lands and peoples that were to be his subjects. The writing itself was done with a facile hand, and the father of history never passed up a good story.

When Herodotus returned to Halicarnassus and began to read his history to the people there, they paid him little heed. Nettled by this cool reception, in 447 he emigrated to Athens, the center of Greek intellectual life. The Athenians received his work much more favorably, and hearing Herodotus read aloud from his work became an enjoyable pastime among them. The city awarded him a prize of 10 talents for his work, approximately $10,000. This makes it easy to understand why Herodotus could so readily refer to the Athenians as the saviors of Greece. On the other hand, he knew the Persians well, and also did them justice. It is clear that he admired them, their loyalty to their king, their absolute truthfulness, and their primitive chivalry. He made them the tragic heroes of the struggle, and in the story that Herodotus tells they do not suffer by comparison with the Greeks except that they are the vanquished and not the victors.

Herodotus intersperses all kinds of fascinating information and anecdotes in his history. He describes almost clinically the art of embalming in ancient Egypt. He goes into detail about many of the mythical and religious ceremonies of both Egypt and Greece. He gives a vivid account of the love affairs of the Persian kings, their lengthy discussions with their counselors, and he inserts many timely bits of philosophy, both private and political, in the midst of his dramatic narrative.

Herodotus begins his history with these words:

> *These are the researches of Herodotus of Halicarnassus, which he pub-lishes in the hope of thereby preserving from decay the remembrance of what men have done, and preventing the great and wonderful actions of the Greeks and the Barbarians from losing their due meed of glory; and withal to put on record what were their grounds of conflict.*

Then he goes on to state that the Greeks many centuries previously had gone to Asia and absconded with two kings' daughters before Paris of Troy decided to come to Sparta and carry off a princess of his own.

> *Now as for the carrying off of women, it is the deed, they say, of a rogue; but to make a great stir about such as are taken, argues a man a fool. Men of sense care nothing for such women, since it is plain that without their own consent they could never be forced away. The Asiatics, when the Greeks ran off with their women, never troubled themselves about the matter; but the Greeks, for the sake of a single Spartan girl, collected a vast armament, invaded Asia, and destroyed the kingdom of Priam.*

And this, wrote Herodotus in his rather naïve way, was what lay at the back of the enmity which the Persians felt toward the Greeks.

In Book 7 of his history Herodotus describes Xerxes observing his hosts which were spread out over the whole Hellespont just prior to their entry into Greece. The king congratulated himself on his good fortune to be the commander of such a vast army, then suddenly he began to weep. The king's uncle saw that he was in tears and asked the reason. Xerxes replied:

> There came upon me a sudden pity, when I thought of the shortness of man's life, and considered that of all this host, numerous as it is, not one man will be alive when a hundred years have passed.

In Book 6 one of the king's generals is bolstering up the courage and confidence of Xerxes by telling him how powerful he is, how great his kingdom and conquests, and how divided the Greeks are. The statement was quite factual and revealed the essential character of the Greeks and their concept of political life. The Persian general said:

> I am told that these very Greeks are wont to wage wars against one an-other in the most foolish way, through sheer perversity and doltishness. For no sooner is war proclaimed than they search out the smoothest and fairest plain that is to be found in all the land, and there they assemble and fight; whence it comes to pass that even the conquerors depart with

great loss: I say nothing of the conquered, for they are destroyed altogether. Now surely, as they are all of one language, they ought to interchange heralds and messengers, and make up their differences by any means rather than battle.

As we well know, the Greeks achieved such a mutual understanding and unity only once in history: when they came together in order to defend themselves against the Persians.

In Book 8, when Herodotus is describing the speed and efficiency of the Persian military couriers, he writes that the best possible horses and horsemen are stationed at regular intervals along the route to be traveled so that the news can be relayed from one to the next without the loss of a second. Then he adds: "These men will not be delayed from covering at their greatest speed the distance they must travel, either by snow, or rain, or heat, or by the darkness of night." This passage with only a slight change of wording is inscribed on the Central Post Office in New York City and has become famous throughout the world. The inscription reads: "Neither snow, nor rain, nor heat, nor gloom of night stays these couriers from the swift completion of their appointed rounds."

At the end of Book 9 Herodotus recalls the occasion when the courtiers of Cyrus came to the king to plead that they be led into a fairer kingdom than their own where they might enjoy an easier and more tranquil life. "Let us quit this land of ours," they said, "for it is a scant and rugged land, and let us choose for ourselves some better country. Many such lie around us." But Cyrus answered his courtiers, saying: "Go if you like, but do not in that case expect to continue as rulers, but rather prepare for being ruled by others. Soft countries give birth to soft men. There is no region which produces very delightful fruits, and at the same time men of a warlike spirit." And Herodotus adds: "So the Persians departed with altered minds, confessing that Cyrus was wiser than they; and chose rather to dwell in a churlish land, and exercise lordship, than to cultivate plains, and be the slaves of others."

A brief paragraph from Book 7 so completely embodies the Greek idea of *hybris,* or excessive pride, that one might almost think the words were written by one of the tragic dramatists. The old uncle of Xerxes is advising the king to think twice before he decides to invade Greece, which is inhabited by "a people distinguished above all others both by land and by sea." The uncle continues:

Do you not see how God with his lightning smites always the biggest animals, and will not suffer them to become insolent, while those of a lesser bulk chafe Him not? How likewise His bolts fall always on the highest houses and on the tallest trees? So plainly does He love to bring down everything that exalts itself. Thus oftentimes a mighty host is discomfited by a few men, when God in His jealousy sends fear or storm from heaven, and they perish in a way unworthy of them. For God allows no one to have high thoughts but Himself. Again, hurry always brings about disaster, from which huge sufferings are wont to arise; but in delay lie many advantages, not apparent, it may be, at first sight, but such as in course of time are seen by all. Such then is my counsel to you, O king!

As we have already seen, King Xerxes did not pay any attention to this advice, and as a result the great Persian Empire, which then occupied an area larger than that of Rome at her peak, suffered its first crucial defeat in the annals of history. A century and a half later Alexander delivered the *coup de grâce.*

After the defeat of the Persians the Greek spirit rose to new heights. The Athenians returned to their *polis* with their families and possessions and with renewed zeal began to rebuild their city. The Acropolis was a shambles, so Themistocles ordered that the broken statues be buried in deep trenches before new temples were erected. Sparta, Corinth, and Thebes recovered even more quickly from the wars than Athens. The Greek cities in Sicily flourished. A dynamic spirit flooded all Hellas. There was nothing that the Hellenes could not accomplish if they set their minds to it.

Their enthusiasm recalls the zeal of Spain in 1492, that miraculous year in which the Moors were conquered after eight centuries, a Spanish pope was elected, the first Castilian grammar appeared, and America was discovered. There was one critical exception: Spain was united, while Greece was not. What, then, would the Greeks do next? They had boundless energy and the field was open before them. The answer, oversimplified no doubt, is that they created the world's greatest civilization.

They did not unite into one or two strong nations. They did not live together in peace. They did not re-create themselves in a vast colonial empire overseas but had as many colonies as there were Greek states. They did attempt to maintain a "balance of power," that perennial excuse for man's belligerent instincts. They did achieve fifty years of relative peace and stability. They did accomplish miracles of creation during those glorious fifty years. How often in modern times has a similar half century been the boon of man? It seems beyond his nature to create a peaceful society that will endure.

Athens had led the fight against Persia, so after the wars she took it upon herself (or found it thrust upon her) to prevent a recurrence of the Persian threat. Her fleet was the most powerful in Greece; her statesmen, writers, and philosophers were the leaders of Greek thought. She organized what was known as the Delian League, composed of several Greek city-states, with its headquarters on the sacred island of Delos. The members of the league contributed ships, arms, or funds to the central agency for their mutual protection. Athens persuaded, cajoled, coerced vacillating states to join. Why should they reap the benefits of protection without helping to defray its costs? Sparta, primarily a land power, was not interested, and tightened up her own Peloponnesian League which had been formed in the late sixth century. Each of the two great cities was infected with the age-old sin of pride. The Greeks were squaring off and choosing sides.

The headquarters and treasury of the Delian League were transferred to Athens in 454, and the group of allied city-states began to resemble an empire. However, it was an empire on shifting sands. Were the Athenians stupid, shortsighted, rank amateurs in political organization? If the Romans could mold an empire, why not the Athenians? The answers are philosophical, not political, and rest on the completely different system of values in each case. Athens never even considered the possibility of offering a member *polis* citizenship, and had the offer been made it certainly would not have been accepted. The *polis* was the great strength and also the great weakness of Greek political life. It was a kind of superfamily which one could never abandon. It distinguished the Greek from the barbarian, with his great empire. The *polis* embraced the heart and soul of every Greek. The naked isolation of an individual in today's world was unknown to him. He was involved, he knew that he belonged, he felt no separation. Alienation to the Greek was an incomprehensible term, but to give up the *polis* was to give up life. Athens' attempt at dominion, therefore, met increasing resistance.

In spite of this, at first the Delian League flourished. Commerce expanded, Athenian ships crisscrossed the seas, many products and great riches accumulated on the wharves of Athens. Her fleet protected this trade with vigor and with vigilance. With the excess funds that accrued from the contributions of the league's members, plus a sizable lump of her own funds, imperial Athens embarked on a program of fortification and public construction which made her the most beautiful city in the world, and one of the strongest. The Acropolis sprouted temples and statues, the Parthenon was built, the marketplace below was embellished, Phidias chiseled his incomparable friezes and statues, Greek drama and Greek art enjoyed their Golden Age.

Sparta watched all this with fear and envy. When walls went up around

Athens, and other walls linked the city safely to her port, Sparta sent emissaries who proposed the destruction of all walls in Greece. Athens refused, and slapped an embargo on one of Sparta's allied cities. The members of the Delian League became restive, and many of them looked toward Sparta in the hope that she might head a crusade for their "freedom."

Athens, for her part, began to reveal that even she was not beyond the fatal arrogance of power. Under the redoubtable Pericles, who for over thirty years (461 to 429) was by far the most influential orator in the Assembly, the city grew richer and more powerful every day. Pericles would brook no concessions. "Give the Spartans an inch and they will take a mile," he said. "Make one concession, they will interpret it as timidity and their demands will become overwhelming. Let us stand firm before the Spartans; we have our walls and fleet." So Athens stood firm and war became inevitable. In 431 Spartan troops invaded the farms of Attica, and for twenty-seven years thereafter the terrible conflict continued.

We have a history of this Peloponnesian War written by one of the Athenian generals who fought in it, Thucydides. It is one of the great histories of ancient or modern times. Thucydides characterized his history in these words:

> The lack of the fabulous may make my work dull. But I shall be satisfied if it be thought useful by those who wish to know the exact character of events now past which, human nature being what it is, will recur in similar or analogous forms. My work has not been composed to court temporary applause but as a lasting possession.*

Thucydides made every effort to be objective and accurate in what he wrote. He did improve on Herodotus in these regards, but he lacks some of the anecdotal flavor of the father of history. None the less, his proud sad pages have made of this war between Athens and Sparta one of the great wars of history, which in fact it was not. Athens was certainly humiliated by her defeat, but she was not destroyed. Her culture was yet to Hellenize half the known ancient world.

Among the most famous passages in the history of Thucydides is his report of the Funeral Oration of Pericles. A few months after the war had begun the Athenians gave a funeral at public cost for those who had fallen. The bones of the dead were laid out in a tent raised for the purpose; then in the funeral procession they were borne in cypress coffins mounted on

---

* From *The Complete Writings of Thucydides*. This quotation is translated by John H. Finley, Jr., in his introduction.

carriages, one for each tribe. One empty bier was decorated and carried for those whose bodies had not been recovered. It was the custom that a man chosen by the state should pronounce a panegyric over those fallen in battle, and Pericles was the orator selected. Among his remarks that day were the following often quoted words:

> I would have you day by day fix your eyes upon the greatness of Athens, until you become filled with the love of her; and when you are impressed by the spectacle of her glory, reflect that this empire has been acquired by men who knew their duty and had the courage to face it.
>
> We are called a democracy, for the administration is in the hands of the many and not of the few. But while our laws secure equal justice to all alike in private disputes, the claim of excellence is also recognized; and when a citizen is in any way distinguished, he is preferred in the public service, not as a matter of privilege, but as the reward of merit. . . . There is no exclusiveness in our public life, and in our private intercourse we are not suspicious of one another. We cultivate the mind. We are lovers of the beautiful, yet simple in our tastes, without loss of manliness. In short, I say that as a city we are the school of Hellas.
>
> The sacrifice which these dead have made is now being repaid to them, for they have received the noblest of sepulchers. I speak not of that in which their poor remains are laid, but of that in which their glory survives. For the whole earth is the sepulcher of famous men; not only are they commemorated by columns and inscriptions in their own country, but in foreign lands there dwells also an unwritten memorial of them, graven not on stone but in the hearts of men.*

The people of Athens received these words with pride and satisfaction, but a sadder day was soon to come to them. When the war began the countryfolk of Attica reluctantly had taken refuge in Athens behind her towering walls, as had been planned. They hated to abandon their farms and villages which had so laboriously been restored after the Persian Wars. They crowded into the city without proper shelter or furniture, sleeping in sheds or in the semiprotected nooks and angles of the streets. They lacked all sanitary facilities, found it hard to keep clean, and suffered from exposure and mutual contagion. Outside the walls they saw their homes and farmlands go up in flames. What generations of hard labor had accomplished was destroyed in a few horrible days. Before many months had gone by a devastating plague hit Athens and hundreds of people died.

Pericles addressed the Athenians in a lofty and dignified tone, trying to give them courage. "You have a great *polis* and a great reputation," he

* From *Thucydides.* Translated by Benjamin Jowett.

said. "You must be worthy of them. Half the world is still yours—the sea. You must think of our Attica as only a small garden, surrounding a mansion. If you shrink from the responsibility of sovereignty, do not claim its honors. The blows of the enemy we must bear with courage; those of the gods, with resignation. You must not blame me for misfortunes which are beyond calculation, unless you are willing to credit me with successes which were uncalculated."*

The reception of this speech by a desperate people was not very favorable. Pericles was fined for his errors. "But not long afterwards," adds Thucydides, "for such is the way a crowd behaves, they elected him general again, and committed everything to him." (Kitto.) The conflict continued unabated, and Pericles, after losing two sons and a sister to the plague, himself came down with the sickness. At first he seemed to be recovering, but then succumbed. And only two years of the war had passed. Almost all of the states of Greece were by now fighting on one side or the other, as democratic Athens and regimented Sparta went at each other tooth and claw.

There is no point in dwelling on the details of the various battles and leaders. For several years the Peloponnesian War was a stalemate, then the Athenian Assembly decided to send a fleet to Sicily in order to overcome Syracuse. It was an attempt to extend the "empire" and acquire new resources with new dominion. The Assembly was acting on something of which it was almost ignorant, and the decision was calamitous. A great armada set out but, undermanned and undersupplied, the attacking Athenians were soon put on the defensive. Instead of returning loaded with supplies and new wealth, the entire fleet was destroyed when Nicias, who was in command, failed to save his ships because the moon was in eclipse and religion demanded that there be a waiting period of twenty-seven days. In 405, the Spartans caught a second Athenian fleet in the Dardanelles, and it too was destroyed. A single ship returned with the sad news, and no one slept in Athens that night. With imports cut off the city was soon starved into submission. Sparta demanded the destruction of the great walls and they were demolished.

Sparta's allies, Thebes and Corinth, wanted to destroy Athens completely, kill her men, and sell her women and children into slavery. Sparta would not consent to this, and her mercy made possible the resurrection of Athens. With Sparta now commanding Greece, the old status continued, with only a change of masters. And when finally Sparta herself was

* From *The Greeks*. Translated by H. D. F. Kitto.

humbled by Thebes in 371, there was no dominant power left in Hellas. This might have been but did not turn out to be a blessing, for wars between the smaller states multiplied senselessly and the whole land was stained with the blood of victims and of soldiers. Greece was an easy prey for Philip and Alexander of Macedon. The only state that profited from the Peloponnesian War was Persia, who got back her Ionian colonies.

X

The Resurrected Gods:
Religion and Literature

Only the gods never grow old or die.
Everything else melts away
In the hands of all-powerful time.

Sophocles

Overreaching glory is a ruin,
The flashing glance of Zeus consumes the proud! *

Aeschylus

The Greek victory over the Persians made possible the Classic period, the marvelous fifth century B.C., one of the high-water marks, perhaps the highest, in the history of mankind. There was a great flowering of Greek literature, architecture, and art, all deeply rooted in the ancient myths. Among these myths certainly the most enduring was that of the resurrected gods. Orpheus, Demeter, and Dionysus all represent the cycle of death followed by a resurrection. Not only that, but in the cases of two of them, Orpheus and Dionysus, the god is killed, his body is torn into pieces, is buried, and comes back to life again. Oftentimes this second appearance is in the symbolic form of an animal. The god's worshipers sacrifice that animal and eat its raw flesh. This transfers a portion of his divine strength to those who have partaken of the sacrifice.

According to Greek legend, Orpheus was a pre-Homeric poet of Thrace who was the son of Apollo and Calliope. The music of his divine lyre could even move inanimate objects such as the rocks, the rivers, and the trees. When his wife Eurydice died he followed her to Hades and so

* From Aeschylus: *The Orestes Plays of Aeschylus.* Translated by Paul Roche.

charmed Pluto with his music that she was freed and allowed to return to the world above on condition that Orpheus would not look back until they were both again on earth.

At the moment of setting his foot on earth Orpheus turned around and Eurydice vanished forever from his sight. He heard her whisper a single word, "Farewell." The inconsolable grief of the god at this final loss of his wife so enraged the women of Thrace that in one of their orgies they tore him to pieces. The Muses gathered the fragments of his body together and buried them at the foot of Mount Olympus. He came back from the dead to assure his worshipers of an immortal life.

Orpheus, thus, was one of the first gods to suffer a violent death followed by a resurrection. Belief in him became the pervading faith of a mystic form of worship which extended over all of Hellas and even into southern Italy. Philosophy is the heir of myth, and later the Orphic belief in immortality inspired both Pythagoras and Plato, who expressed it in more "scientific" terminology. Orphism even held the doctrine of original sin. The soul was enclosed in the body as in a tomb or prison, to punish a very early crime committed by the Titans who had killed Dionysus.

Orpheus was "the founder of those mysteries which ensured the salvation of mankind." He revealed to the ancient Greeks the knowledge of the divine world. The picture of Orpheus charming the beasts with his lyre is the one mythological motive which is reproduced again and again in the Christian paintings of the catacombs. The Church Fathers considered Orpheus the disciple of Moses and regarded him as the teacher of mankind. Whether or not he ever existed is beside the point. Orphism existed and it revitalized the religious history of Greece. It not only permeated the literature, philosophy, and art of the ancient world; it outlived them and reaffirmed itself in Christianity.

The Orphic cult in Greek religion and the Demeter rituals at the Eleusinian Mysteries, which perpetuated this belief, were the most powerful religious undercurrent in the Greek countryside. In the Eleusinian Mysteries Zeus, the sky force, was joined in symbolic union with Demeter, the Corn Mother or earth force. A priest representing Zeus simulated the sex act with a priestess of Demeter. The union was only symbolic because the priest took a small dose of hemlock in order to deprive himself temporarily of his virility. The act took place in the semidark and after it the priest suddenly appeared in a blaze of light holding up an ear of corn, which the union had brought forth. This all went back to the cycle of vegetation and growing. A seed buried in the earth in order to emerge in another form of life was seen as a parallel with human destiny. The awed worshipers felt themselves saved; after death their own spirits would spring up again in a bright hereafter.*

Demeter's daughter Persephone embodied the very principle of resurrection. She was snatched away from her mother in the fresh bloom of youth and carried down to dark Hades. There she ate the forbidden pomegranate seeds and for this was forced forever afterward to spend six months out of every year in Hades, going above ground for the remaining six. It is easy to see in this myth a symbolization of the earth's seasons, the cycle of life and death, of things that grow and die as spring and winter alternate in their eternal sequence. Primitive life "at the height of its vitality has always spoken this language." The spirits of the dead were always present at the awakening of nature.

Dionysus is the resurrected god whose influence was so strongly felt in Greece that every year in early spring they held a splendid festival in his honor. Out of these festivals Greek tragedy, one of the great forms of world literature, was born. Dionysus, like Orpheus, was killed and resurrected; there were several places in ancient Greece where people would show his grave. But in the spring he always came back again, as the frenzied joy of his festival announced. Dionysus himself was both the symbol of fertility and the violent destroyer. He was the god of many forms; he could take the form of a bull, a goat, an ass, a snake, all strong male sexual symbols, and he could also take the form of a lion, a panther, a lynx, all destroyers.†

Sometimes Dionysus even became a tree, fire, or water, the water which is the source and nutriment of all life. He represented both the moment of birth and the moment of death, those two sacred experiences when the death and life principles of the universe are merged in a dark embrace.

Dionysus was the son of Zeus and of a mortal woman, so he was half human and half divine. The "official" wife of Zeus was Hera, but the father of gods was invariably in love with another woman, frequently a mortal. Once he fell in love with Semele, a beautiful princess of Thebes, and with her conceived a child. Hera, in a rage at what had happened but unable to harm Zeus directly, told Semele that she had fallen in love with a horrible monster in disguise.

---

* From *The Golden Bough,* by Sir James Frazer.

† All the animals associated with the Greek gods were at an earlier totemic stage of Hellenic religion regarded as the gods themselves. Thus we have the eagle of Zeus, the owl of Athena, the deer of Artemis, the dolphin of Poseidon, the dove of Aphrodite. Later the sacred animal became the companion of the god, but sometimes it also figured as his enemy or his victim, and often it took on a magic dimension when it became the sacrificial beast.

The seed of doubt causes Semele to deny her charms to Zeus until he can prove who he is. The god reluctantly appears to her in all his majesty, wielding his thunder and lightning. Poor Semele has her curiosity satisfied but she is consumed by the bolts of lightning. Zeus snatches the unborn child from her burning body and hides it in his thigh. Three months later Dionysus is born. It might be said that he emerged directly out of the "divine fire." Hermes is called to take him to Mount Helicon where he is placed in the care of the Nymphs. The famous statue of Praxiteles, dated circa 340 B.C., and now at the Olympia Museum, is called "Hermes with the Infant Dionysus." It is the only surviving piece of Greek sculpture which may with certainty be called a work of one of the great Classic sculptors.

The legend of Dionysus goes on to tell us that over the baby's cradle grew a new vine; Dionysus pressed its fruit to his lips and the Nymphs did the same until they all were in a state of happy intoxication, dancing and singing merrily. Hera, still unforgiving, drove Dionysus mad, and he roamed over the known world spreading the culture of "the vine." Eventually he was cured of his madness and became the God of Fertility.

The cult of Dionysus was officially adopted by Athens in the sixth century B.C., and four yearly festivals were held in his honor. The first of the two main ones was held in February and the second, called the Great Dionysia, in April. The February festival was to celebrate the drinking of the new wines and the April festival was a celebration of the rites of spring, the fertility of the earth. At this festival processions were held, a goat was sacrificed to the god, baskets of flowers and fruit were placed on the altar of Dionysus. The people drank and made merry and rejoiced in the consecration of life.

Dionysus as the intoxicated god, the mad god, epitomized the divine madness which was necessary for any great creative art. This was the divine madness of inspiration, the frenzy of creation. When the ancient Greeks sacrificed an animal and poured a libation of wine to him, they were offering a sacrifice to the magic and mystery of life which manifests itself in opposites. Dionysus epitomized and incarnated the ambivalence and wild spirit of human emotions: love and hate, life and death, creation and destruction, tragedy and comedy. He balanced these antitheses, these positives and negatives, these elements of yin and yang, in his own life, death, and resurrection.

His great festival, which corresponds closely with the Christian Easter and the spring equinox, initiated the spring season when the earth was becoming green again and new flowers were emerging from the dark moist ground. The power to create and the power to destroy, this is the manifestation of the undying life force. At this point we should draw attention to the fact that the Greek word *theos,* which is always translated into English as "god," often means "force." This makes the gods inseparable from the reality of the Greek universe.

Dionysus was mad even in his mother's body; he had danced in her womb. He was torn from her body in flames, and the dance was his especial delight when he grew older. Often the young god had horns which recalled his "bull" spirit. When he went from Thebes to Pieria, "the Muses received him decked with ivy, with festive songs." He threw caution to the winds and exulted in the intoxication of life. He was the blind and reckless drive that creates all life, the primitive will and impulse to perpetuate itself that defies the canons of restraint and civilization. Life that is self-generating is touched by madness. Dionysus was also the moment of insanity necessary for genius, the spark of madness necessary to keep aglow the divine fire, a gift of the gods to man. To this day he is widely but unknowingly respected in Greece, where insane persons are shown a respect and awe which are in striking contrast to the manner in which they are treated in most other countries.

The festival of the Great Dionysia was very much like our present-day Mardi Gras, but even more licentious. Its main elements were a phallic procession, the singing of dithyrambs to Dionysus, the killed and resurrected god, followed by great revelry. Those participating in the procession were not only dressed in goat costumes with a long tail, but the most distinctive feature of their costume was a large artificial phallus usually made of hard red leather. The revelry terminated with a symbolic marriage, which was believed to stimulate the soil and make things grow.

The principle of fertility was linked with the rite of sacrifice to form the heart of these early phallic festivals. The sacred phallus was part of the clown's costume until the fifth century A.D. in Western Europe, and was retained for many centuries longer in the Byzantine Empire. It was still used in the rural areas of Thrace in this century. The Dionysian revels gave rise to the "satyr plays" of a later date which continued to be an integral part of the Dionysian Greek drama until the time of Euripides, last of the great tragic dramatists.

Both tragedy and comedy had their origin in these Dionysian revels. During the festival a group called the *komos* entertained the crowd with ribald horseplay and humorous dialogues. Their revelry was known as *komodia,* and out of this comedy arose. The other side of the picture was represented by the men dressed in goatskins who danced and sang around the altar of Dionysus, performing scenes from his life. This enactment was called *tragodia,* or goat-song, which linked the life of man with that of the gods, and from it arose Greek tragedy.

Under the tyrant Peisistratus the Greater Dionysia festival became a well-organized competitive event for those who aspired to write. The actor Thespis was the first to stand apart from the chorus with which he then carried on a dialogue. He was the first "thespian" in history. This was the first stage in changing pure ritual into drama. Thespis won the contest at the Dionysian festival of 534 for having presented the best dramatic piece for that particular year. A generation later (499) Aeschylus made his first appearance on the Athenian stage and the Golden Age of Greek drama was at hand. Aeschylus added a second actor to his plays, and thus made possible the refinement of the element of conflict.

On the second day of the Greater Dionysia festival at Athens five comedies were put on, and after this came the competition in tragedy. The preliminary competitors had by then been narrowed down to three finalists, each of whom was allowed a full day for his performances, which consisted of three tragedies and a single satyr play. The audience arrived at dawn, and the performance lasted all day.

The original seed theme of these tragedies was the suffering, death, and resurrection of Dionysus, which later was transformed into the tragic life and death of a Greek hero. This kept classic drama on a lofty plane, linked it with religion and history, made it the enlargement of the epic and heroic struggle of man. Aeschylus himself stated that his dramas were "slices from the banquet of Homer." He meant that the Homeric poems in their entirety had given him the bases of his plays, not strictly the *Iliad* and *Odyssey.*

The famous theater in which these performances took place in Athens, the theater of Dionysus, was excavated by the Germans in the last century. It is the oldest theater in Greece, and was originally constructed in 490 B.C. Despite massive rebuilding and remodeling it is still a worthy monument, especially the carved stone seats for the priests and high officials. An even more ancient structure of wooden stands had collapsed in the year 500 killing several spectators, and it was decided to rebuild the theater in stone. The oldest part of the theater that we see today dates from about 340 B.C. when the last major remodeling was done before Roman times.

Before the plays began a statue of the god (Dionysus) was brought in and placed in the center of the circular area (*orchestra*) to be used by the chorus. From this point of vantage the god might witness the spectacle. An animal was sacrificed and with proper invocations the performance then began with the entrance of the chorus marching to music. The theater was hallowed ground and any sacrilegious behavior on the part of the audience received harsh punishment. Myth had been transformed into fertility ritual and fertility ritual into literature. Symbolic marriage, as in modern literature, was the original conclusion; then came suffering and tragedy to take its place. Such is the hard course of all the dreams of man.

Greek literature must be judged by what has survived, and fortunately the few works which have survived are among the best. Perhaps they are the best, for the hands of history, left to their own devices, are a fine sifter. Nevertheless, the lost literature of the Greeks, much of it known by title only or by a few lines quoted in some other work, has for centuries fascinated the scholars.

There were almost four thousand plays produced at Athens during the two centuries of Greek drama's Golden Age. Fewer than fifty of these have come down to us intact. Aeschylus wrote about ninety plays; we have the titles of eighty and fragments of seventy, but the complete texts of only seven. Only a single one of his trilogies has survived, the *Oresteia,* and it is perhaps the greatest series of plays in Greek drama, possibly in world literature. Sophocles wrote 123 plays, and only seven of these have survived intact. Of the ninety dramas of Euripides we have the texts of nineteen. Nothing has been preserved of these men's younger years; the only plays of Aeschylus that we have were written after he was fifty; all extant plays of Sophocles and Euripides were written after the writers were over forty. There were more than 150 other writers of tragedy whose names have been preserved of whom not one play has survived.

Aeschylus won the dramatic prize at the Greater Dionysia thirteen times, Sophocles won it twenty-four times, Euripides four times. By this standard alone Sophocles was the most successful of the Greek tragic dramatists, having won more times than Aeschylus and Euripides combined. But there are many who consider Aeschylus, despite the limitations of his time, as the greater writer. In the field of comedy we have the works of only one man, Aristophanes, who wrote forty comedies, of which eleven have survived. He won first prize in comedy only four times. The work of all the other writers of comedy, except for one complete play and portions of three others by Menander, have perished.

Literature in the other genres also has disappeared in great quantity. There were about fifty historians writing during the two great centuries, but we have the works of only three. Of lyric poetry, which spans an even longer period, we have much less, sometimes only a few verses on which we must judge a prolific and gifted poet. Every one of Aristotle's 27 dialogues is lost, and over 350 of his 400 monographs have suffered a similar fate. During the last days of the Roman Empire and the Dark Ages that followed, thousands of Greek manuscripts were lost or burned or rotted away. Only in the dry climate of Egypt did some of them withstand the ravage of centuries.

When the Arabs destroyed what remained of the library at Alexandria in A.D. 640 a great and precious heritage came to an inglorious end. Fortunately, very soon after this, in Greek-speaking Byzantium of the ninth century, there was a reawakened interest in Greek antiquity, and the Byzantine scholars became a bridge between the ancient Greeks and the European Renaissance, which shared this enthusiasm. Sadly we may bemoan the lost literature of Greece, but happily we may also rejoice that almost everything which has survived is first-rate. The classical age we know is not cluttered with inferior rubbish, of which there must have been a great deal.

Greek classical drama cannot properly be compared with that of the modern period. Modern dramatists depict the lives of average men and women. The Greek writer would never do this. His characters had to be heroic. As Moses Hadas, the well-known classical scholar, has pointed out, the sad fate of Willy Loman in Arthur Miller's *Death of a Salesman,* would not be acceptable as tragedy either to a Greek writer or to a Greek audience. Miller's use of a very Greek-like flute melody to give Willy a tender quality adds an interesting dimension to his character but does not render his fate truly tragic. For tragedy to be great to the Greeks the person suffering it had to be a person of heroic proportions. His capacity to suffer and his actual suffering on the stage must be exceptional and must involve the audience to an exceptional degree. Willy Loman too often flitted over the surface of life like the average American father playing with his sons; his suicide was pathetic, not tragic.

The modern dramatist is preoccupied with contemporary problems, while Greek drama was focused mainly on universal problems, independent of the flux of time. The modern dramatist makes up his own plots, creates suspense in order to hold interest, bases his drama on the observation of contemporary life. The Greek dramatist used as his source material stories which were already thoroughly familiar: well-known myths, stories of the Homeric heroes, traditions and, history. There was nothing new in the plot, and the element of suspense was lacking, at least in so far as the events themselves were concerned. Everyone knew in advance what the outcome would be. There *was* suspense in regard to *how* the writer would delineate his story, *how* forcefully poetic his language would be, *how* impressively acted the story would be, *how* effective the total theatrical production.

The Greek dramatist viewed life from quite a different angle than his contemporary counterpart. He saw and he presented a "life by values," whereas the modern writer sees and presents "life in a time frame." The modern writer is caught in the historic particular; the classic dramatist saw things in a timeless or universal dimension. Time is the crucial dimension of today's fictional universe; it meant nothing to the Greek.

Greek drama was not written or presented in order to entertain or in order to improve social conditions. It was primarily a ritualistic experience, a catharsis, a working off of tensions while the drama was enacted. The Greeks knew that human passion was the one subject of permanent interest to all mankind. To examine and exalt passion was to reveal the secret of life.

Each carved stone seat of the front row at the theater of Dionysus in Athens has the name of a priest inscribed on it. Drama to the Greeks was very much like a high religious service: the prebendaries occupied a place of honor, the tragic dramatist was the teacher of morality, the stage took the place of our church pulpit, and the play took the place of the service and of the sermon. Greek drama did not lose its ritualistic tone until after the Golden Age had passed. It had a kind of solemnity to it, a kind of sublimity which is missing in modern drama. It was a combination of religion-ritual-pageant-music-drama. So that the accumulation of emotional tension would not be destroyed the play was presented unbroken by any intervals, like a religious ceremony.

There are two art forms today which in very limited degree suggest the emotive quality of Greek drama: grand opera at its best and the Spanish bullfight. In both of these art forms the spectator already knows what the outcome will be, but the beauty of the ritualistic presentation is what holds him. In Greek drama the chorus begins the play and remains as a background accompaniment to the action throughout, much as the orchestra in an operatic performance first plays the overture, then provides a continuous accompaniment to the singers. The bullfight, of course, revolves around the repeated cycle of suffering and death.

Greek drama was always presented out of doors, and the productions lasted from dawn till dusk. Nearly all of the action on the stage also took place out of doors, at the portals of a palace, outside a temple or a tomb. The seats were hard, at first of wood, later fashioned in stone. Many in the audience brought pillows or mats to sit on. They also brought food and wine, because they would be in the theater all day, and they ate during the intervals between plays. Occasionally, if the play was very bad, they ate during the performance itself, as Aristotle points out, and were even known to have hissed and booed bad works off the stage. Once they attacked Aeschylus bodily because in his play he had said a few lines about the goddess Demeter which they took to be a blasphemous revelation of the secret mysteries of Eleusis. Aeschylus was tried and acquitted of the "crime."

The largest theaters held around fifteen to seventeen thousand spectators, but the acoustics were so excellent that a normal voice on the stage could be heard quite clearly in the back row. The theater at Epidaurus, which is the most perfectly preserved of all the ancient Greek theaters, shows what these theaters looked like originally before the Romans came and cut in half the circular choral ring, called the orchestra.

The form of the orchestra was derived from the circular threshing floor which first became the community dancing area and finally the choral ring. The altar to Dionysus always stood in its very center, indicating clearly the religious origins of Greek drama. Back of the circular orchestra (which was never occupied by spectators) there was originally a tent or closed-off space among the trees where the actors dressed. This was the original "green room." Later a rectangular structure back of the orchestra replaced this early green room among the trees. The stage on which the drama itself took place was the narrow area which lay between this structure and the orchestra. In the early days it was level with the orchestra, but after the classical period it became a raised platform.

The structure behind the stage (called the *skene*) was at first made of wood, then of both wood and stone. It became larger and higher with time, and it was painted to represent fixed scenes. Occasionally there was a second story where flying figures and gods might appear. There was generally a machine (a crane) which could lower the figure of a god (*deus ex machina*) to suddenly unravel the plot.

This entire structure, of course, formed a kind of sounding board behind the actors and helped to throw the voices forward. Sometimes at each side of the acting area stood a large wooden prism of triangular shape which could be revolved in order to represent three different scenes. The background scenery was painted on wood or canvas, much as ours is today, and in the early days this must have been very crude, because a certain Agatharchus became famous by using the art of perspective to give the quality of distance.

The performances were always held in the open but as their literature indicates the Greeks seldom romanticized landscape and doubtless took little note of the sky or surrounding earth forms. Indeed, the high back-drop often shut out all prospect, even if at Epidaurus the surrounding hills were an ever-present setting. In any event, Greek drama did not poeticize nature as such. "In the second place, the Greeks came to the theater to enjoy poetry, and the poetry of character, of passion, of the relation of man and his destiny to the course of Divine Providence and Divine justice . . . in short, to assume a frame of mind perfectly inconsistent with the distractions of landscape." (Mahaffy, *Rambles and Studies in Greece*.)

The acoustic qualities of the Greek theaters are marvelous. In the theater at Epidaurus one can hear a whisper or a match being lighted from the back row. However, the actors in Classic drama wanted not only to be heard and understood, they wanted to be emotionally impressive. The most careful training was given to their voices so that these would acquire a resonant and noble quality which would *appear to be* completely natural, but which in reality was not natural at all, because men do not talk like that.

Today's presentations of Greek drama are generally very poor, because there is a tendency to overdo everything, to shout, to be overly sonorous, to use a pompous or oratorical tone, to gesticulate stiffly, all of which produce an element of falseness. Again, by way of comparison, grand opera comes to mind; fine singing and acting in opera appear to be natural, but are not so at all. They need an orchestral accompaniment in order to be most effective, as Greek actors needed their chorus. Both forms of art represent an interplay of the one with the many, symbolically of individual man and all mankind. Here, however, the comparison ends, because the subject matter is entirely different. True, there are gods in Wagner, but they are not our gods.

The scope of action in Greek drama expanded slowly. Thespis detached himself from the chorus and became the first individual actor, Aeschylus added a second actor, and Sophocles a third. The original actor was called *hypocrites*, which meant simply "answerer," that is, he answered the chorus, often intoning its theme. The word later came to mean *hypocrite*, because the actor *impersonated* someone else. The actors were always men, and when a woman was called for, her role was invariably acted by a man in a woman's costume. In addition to the three principals there were supernumeraries, retinues, pages, etc.

Although the rising tiers of seats provided unobstructed visibility, it was not easy to observe facial expressions from the back rows, so the actors wore masks. Each role displayed only a single primary emotion, and these larger-than-life masks caught and magnified that attitude. The masks were

Theater at Epidaurus, called by Pausanias the most beautiful theater of ancient Greece. Built in fourth century B.C. *(circa 350) by Polycleitus the Younger. The theater seats 14,000 and is almost perfectly preserved.*

Orchestra and stage of theater at Epidaurus during one of the recent presentations of ancient Greek drama.

also amplifiers which helped to project the voices, perhaps giving them a strangely unhuman tone. Often an actor would play more than one role and would change his mask. During the fifth century high-soled shoes were not used to add height to the actors, but later they were adopted in order to give a greater-than-life-size dimension to the actor. A high headpiece was also added, but these are not properties of the Golden Age classic theater.

The chorus played an extremely important role in Greek drama. Originally it consisted of fifty persons, but Aeschylus reduced it to twelve, and Sophocles later added three, making it fifteen. In Euripides the chorus becomes less important, but it cannot be omitted from the play. The chorus did not ever *speak* in unison, but it did *chant* in unison when the verses of the dramatist's odes were performed. When the chorus *spoke* this was either managed by the leader of the chorus talking alone, or by individual members of the chorus speaking in turn. The movements of the chorus were also closely synthesized so as to give the impression of a single massman.

With Aeschylus the chorus entered the dramatic action. It involved the audience, which identified with the chorus and felt itself speaking or chanting the choral words. The chorus, therefore, was a link between writer, actors, and spectators. It represented the populace. Sometimes it summarized events, meditated upon them, clarified moral implications, commented on the characters, poeticized the theme. The chorus might occasionally set forth the dramatist's own feelings. The Greek audience was not like the modern theater audience, drawn mainly from the middle and upper classes; it included Everyman. Greeks from all stations came to see their heroes and their gods enact the drama of man's life before their eyes.

There was always music: the chorus marched in to the sound of a flute, and there were frequently also drums, trumpets, and occasionally a lyre. We do not know what this music sounded like. Present-day Greek music, even in the most remote back country, has absorbed so many other influences that it could not be very close to that of ancient Greece. There was also choral dancing, if by dancing is meant rhythmic movement in unison.

The choral dancing was mimetic and epitomized through group gesture the prevailing emotional quality of the drama. The chorus would cower in fear, lift arms in triumph, writhe or swirl in agitation or excitement. There was very little moving about the orchestra, no great leaping or rapid pirouettes. The trunk of the body was generally at rest; its extremities bore the burden of the body's emotion, as the branches express through their motions the moving symmetry of a tree.

Actors, chorus, music, costumes, poetry, myth—all these combined to produce the classic drama of the fifth century. In it man's incoherent impulses were given a form.

There were many themes, but perhaps the most important of all was the theme of presumption against the gods, *hybris,* which the ancient Greeks considered to be the greatest sin. The heroes or royal houses that carried pride too far suffered an evil fate. The tragic hero was always confronted with a choice, and if he made the wrong choice it was because of what Aristotle called his *hamartia,* or fatal flaw. His punishment, then, was inevitable. "Wrong" choice did not mean sinful choice or cowardly choice; it meant simply that man could not be a god.

The defeat of the tragic hero did not mean the defeat of man. The audience which saw the hero defeated or slain felt purified by that sacrifice. A burden was lifted from its head. Man was always the measure. His dignity survived every disaster. His own godlike quality endured if the poetry was great enough. There was a transcendent importance to the word itself, which must be just right and must be spoken or intoned just right. Poetry and emotion were the goals, not clarity. Indeed, clarity might easily destroy the fragile world of imagery which the poet had devised.

Let us take an example from our own heritage: *I will lift up mine eyes unto the hills.* These words are from the King James version of the Bible, and our example could be multiplied by the hundreds. Now let us suppose the translator had written down instead of the above poetic phrase the clearer and more ordinary: *I'll keep my chin up,* or *I won't lose hope,* or *God will help me.* The clarity is there, no doubt, but all poetry is gone from the words. Clarity without poetry was not drama to the Greeks. Poetry without clarity, on the other hand, could often be, for emotion transcended the precise meaning of the phrase, and emotion was what was important; it was, indeed, the unique quality of man.

In a way, then, Greek drama was dramatic poetic declamation. It carried forward the tradition of the earlier poetry declaimed or intoned by the professional bards. This is in the Mediterranean tradition, where poetry for its own sake is not only a written but also an oral art form. Hence in Greek drama the speeches are often directed toward the audience rather than toward the rest of the dramatis personae. This is true sometimes even when two characters are talking to each other. Much of what they say is for the public and not for the other person on the stage.

This often gives a sluggish and heavy quality to much of the dialogue if we compare it to the dialogue of present-day theater, which epitomizes the rapid conversational tone. The longer speeches in Greek drama are not soliloquies in a Shakespearean sense, that is, dialogues of a man with his inner thoughts, but are recollections, announcements, explanations, or poetizations needed to reinforce or to sustain the author's viewpoint or to clarify the action. In one such passage in *Oedipus at Colonus* of Sophocles a messenger talks for three unbroken pages.

Greek tragedy, unlike modern drama, was all of one substance. Fate was hostile to man's desires but not to his glory. The gods denied to man omniscience, perfection, and immortality but not the longing and striving for omniscience, perfection, and immortality. The defeated tragic hero was greatest at the moment of his defeat, which gave his life meaning. A reasonable course of action led to a fated tragic conclusion, but the hero's integrity provided victory over his tragic fate.

Romantic love did not exist in the Greek classic drama, nor did sentimentality as we know it. There were evidences of both in Greek lyric poetry which reached back into the Archaic age, but this was never transferred to the stage. What the Greek theater did was to view life itself as a tragic drama. It always revolved around the duality of reason versus feeling, with the latter being nobler, higher.

Apollo was the god who represented reason, restraint, and form, Dionysus was the god of instinct, intuition, the force of life, the blind and reckless will that seeks to perpetuate itself. Greek drama and Greek art struck a perfect balance between these two extremes. Its harmony has never been surpassed by any other art or any other age or any other people.

Aristotle in his famous analysis of tragedy in his *Poetics* gives the following definition:

> Tragedy, then, is a representation of an action that is worth serious attention, complete in itself, and of some magnitude; in language enriched by a variety of artistic devices appropriate to the several parts of the play; presented in the form of action, not narration; by means of pity and fear bringing about the purgation (catharsis) of such emotions. By language that is enriched I refer to language possessing rhythm, and music or song; and by artistic devices appropriate to the several parts I mean that some are produced by the medium of verse alone, and others again with the help of song. . . . Fear and pity may be excited by means of spectacle; but they can also take their rise from the very structure of the action, which is the preferable method and the mark of a better dramatic poet.*

Aristotle goes on to say that it is the poetry which brings about the involvement of the audience, causes it to identify with the actors on the

* From *Aristotle, Horace and Longinus, Classical Literary Criticism.* Translated by T. S. Dorsch.

stage, while the dramatic process itself brings about a catharsis of the emotions.

The tragic concept permeated Greek life. As the distinguished American classical scholar Moses Hadas points out, not only was the history of the individual conceived as tragic but so was history itself. "The historians, Herodotus and Thucydides alike, gave the events they recorded tragic meaning and even tragic form." Athens was started on its rise to greatness by the defeat of the Persians between 490–479 B.C. Aeschylus presented his drama on this struggle, *The Persians,* barely seven years after the events. Herodotus wrote at length of this same encounter only a generation later. Both authors tell the story from the Persian point of view. "It could not be otherwise," says Moses Hadas, "if history is tragic, because though the audience is Athenian the tragic actors and sufferers were the Persians." Aeschylus makes the Persian realm, not King Xerxes, the tragic hero of his drama. The Persian enterprise to invade and take over Greece was too grandiose; it was *hybris* on a national scale and must suffer a terrible national fate. The Greek victory "was a divine instrument for subduing overweening pride." The theme of *koros-hybris-ate* (too much prosperity-presumption-doom) is the eternal cycle of Greek tragedy and of Greek life.

There is not space in a book of this kind to go into the various forms of Greek literature; a few examples will clarify the differences that lie between the Hellenic approach and our own. The best Greek plays are the *Oresteia* (also called the *House of Atreus*) trilogy by Aeschylus, which won the prize in Athens in the year 458, two years before the death of the dramatist; and the *Oedipus* trilogy of Sophocles, which strangely failed to win first place in 429.

The plays of Euripides do not reveal the heroic defiance or resignation of his two predecessors, but he is the most modern of the three, and his *Medea* is one of the most powerful Greek plays. The characters of Euripides are more ordinary and find the cause of tragedy within themselves; his gods are less godly. Athens was not quite ready for this, so Euripides never won great acclaim in Attica. After his death in voluntary exile in Macedonia, where he had gone because of the indifferent response to his dramas in Athens, Euripides' reputation began to grow and in the following generations surpassed that of either Aeschylus or Sophocles. When the Athenian fleet was defeated in Sicily in 413 the natives of Syracuse allowed all Athenian soldiers or sailors to go free if they could quote a reasonable number of lines from Euripides, who was their own great favorite.

In the realm of comedy *The Birds* by Aristophanes is probably that writer's masterpiece. It placed second in the comedy competition of the year 414. This play was written to ridicule the disastrous Athenian expedition to Sicily, but it is also a marvelous commentary on the weaknesses of man and of social institutions generally.

The *Oresteia* of Aeschylus, produced at the height of the Golden Age of Classic Greek drama, typifies the best qualities of that drama. The first play of the trilogy, the *Agamemnon,* is the most powerful play of the three, and stands with Sophocles' *Oedipus Tyrannus* at the pinnacle of the Greek classic theater. The *Oresteia* trilogy deals with the cult of violence, the curse of blood, the pedigree of sin. Violence begets more violence, murder multiplies itself in generation after generation. The hot-blooded temperament of man increases the unbalance of universal justice.

King Atreus was Agamemnon's father. Many years preceding the opening of the play Atreus had killed the young children of King Thyestes and served them to him in a banquet of reconciliation. Aegisthus, son of King Thyestes, swore to get revenge. The course of events leading up to the play is then as follows:

(a)   Helen deserts King Menelaus of Sparta and elopes with Paris, Prince of Troy.

(b)   Agamemnon, King of Mycenae, joins forces with his brother, Menelaus, and their combined fleet sails for Troy.

(c)   The fleet is becalmed at Aulis, and a seer tells Agamemnon that he must sacrifice his daughter, Iphigenia, to the goddess Artemis, if he wishes to get favorable winds. He makes the sacrifice.

(d)   Clytemnestra hears of the sacrifice of her daughter, and she, too, vows to take revenge. Aegisthus comes to her court at Mycenae and becomes her lover; together they plot to kill Agamemnon when he returns from Troy.

At this point the play itself begins, but the above points must be borne in mind if we are to understand the emotions involved. Many of these points are clarified in the play in flashbacks, not flashbacks of stage action but of choral explanation. As the drama begins, the watchman on the walls of Mycenae sees the beacon fires leaping from peak to peak which signal that the siege of Troy has ended.

Clytemnestra orders that the fires at all the palace altars be rekindled. Intently, then, she recalls the past. She listens in silence as the chorus gives a graphic account of the death of her daughter "lifted like a goat above the altar, her mouth gagged to stop her cries" (Roche). Iphigenia's saffron dress is slipped to the ground, she glances with piteous eyes at each bloody officiant, her own body "caught as in a painting, her lips about to speak: she who had so many times shed luster on them at her father's feasts" (Roche).

The news of the fall of Troy is made known to all in the palace at Mycenae and is received with exultation, but when Clytemnestra speaks it is to express her suffering for the Trojans. They are the tragic heroes of the war. In her mind she hears "their wails from lips no longer free" and thinks of all the corpses of the defeated Trojans: husbands, brothers, children, as the undisciplined hordes of Greeks pour into their conquered city to loot and slay. Clytemnestra's lines are a strong indictment of the war, waged for a woman. After Clytemnestra the chorus takes up the lament and sings of the cruelty of war, the sin of pride:

> *Overreaching glory is a ruin.*
> *The flashing glance of Zeus consumes the proud.*
> [Roche]

Not long afterward Agamemnon's herald arrives to say that the king is not far away. The herald greets the soil of his fathers with joy; his safe return is "the one bright truth of ten years' hopes in shreds! Oh blessed earth!" (Roche). He says that the remnant of the army which has been spared is nearing home. The herald then recalls the horrors of the war: the constant drizzle, the damp and rotting uniforms, the tangling of lice in the soldiers' hair on the hated fields of Troy:

> The winters there—you can't imagine them—
> The cold left birds dead in the snow,
> And mountain blasts chilled soldiers to the bone.
> Then summer came with burning sun and sea,
> No wave, no ripple, not one breath
> Moved on its blazing deep.
> But why complain? It's over now,
> The dead are in the earth,
> They'll never rise to breathe again,
> So what's the use of calling out their names?
> And what's the use of grieving over fate
> Or life's misfortunes?

Clytemnestra asks the herald to tell her husband to hurry home, for he will find her as faithful as he had left her. She has been his "own sweet palace watchdog," fierce toward his enemies and utterly loyal to the marriage bond. Of course, the audience knows this is a lie. Finally, Agamemnon enters with Cassandra, daughter of the king of Troy, beside him in his chariot. She was one of the spoils of war. Clytemnestra recalls the ten desolate years that her husband had been away. She had suffered from countless rumors of his being wounded or dead. If he had as many wounds as these rumors reported he would look like a net, she said.

Clytemnestra then insists on spreading crimson carpets on the ground before Agamemnon alights. He objects saying such a reception would be for a god, but she persists and accuses him of fear. Agamemnon gives in, a slave takes off his boots, he gets down and enters the palace to thank the gods for his safe return. Clytemnestra remains outside and confronts Cassandra, her husband's new mistress, with hatred.

Cassandra gives the impression of a wild and primitive thing who does not wish to be where she is. She is possessed by the gift of prophecy, and finally cries out that great tragedy will soon befall this house. She writhes in fear and winces at her coming fate. Reluctantly she follows Clytemnestra into the palace.

Behind its closed doors the double murder then takes place. Agamemnon cries out that he is mortally hit. The chorus recoils outside. Three times the sword in Clytemnestra's hand strikes home. She slays Cassandra too and then reappears on the stage with the bloody sword still in her hand. She feels no guilt, indeed she says that when the spurts of blood gushed from her husband's body "it freshened me like drops from heaven when the earth is bright and sprung with budding" (Roche).

Aegisthus now arrives and states that the scales at last are balanced, the crime against his house has been wiped out in blood, and he will take over the throne of Mycenae. As the play comes to an end, the chorus intones a threat that Orestes, Agamemnon's son, is yet to be reckoned with.

The killings do not take place on the stage. It was against the tradition of Greek drama for any violence or high passion to be enacted before the eyes of the audience. But the certainty of doom hangs over King Agamemnon from the very first line. Clytemnestra emerges as the epitome of affronted womanhood. She had more than enough reasons to hate her husband, and many might even agree that she had enough justification for killing him. But for a Greek wife to slay her husband was an unforgivable crime, because the man was the source of the family, the center of its power and its succession. Besides, Agamemnon was a powerful king, and in killing him Clytemnestra had struck a blow at the authority of the state which he embodied. She committed not only an individual crime but an offense against social and religious institutions. And so the human passions are weighed against those of tradition and of the gods. Thus after Agamemnon has been slain Clytemnestra's expression of her relief is that she feels that the whole earth is again in bloom, which suggests that what she had done was in a symbolic sense to offer her husband up as a sacrifice to her own unbearable inner tensions. With his death she felt momentarily freed, and she could again flower as a woman.

Clytemnestra is womb unforgiving, the vengeful mother, the affronted and murderous wife. Deep womb, dark flower. It was not just a wanton or witless murder that she had committed. Agamemnon had insulted (blasphemed against) her motherhood by sacrificing their daughter, Iphigenia. Then he had affronted her wifehood by being absent for ten long years at the siege of Troy. Since Agamemnon had denied both her motherhood and her wifehood, she as a woman no longer felt respect for him as a man, so she deliberately took Aegisthus as her lover and together they plotted the murder.

Clytemnestra is perhaps the most powerful woman character in Greek drama. She is, in her lifetime, woman triumphant. She embodies the life force, and in pursuing her ends nothing can deter her; she never falters. She is the blind and reckless will to life, the spark of being which seeks completion whatever the obstacle, whatever the odds. Agamemnon, despite his victorious return from Troy, seems pallid beside her. He is stereotyped majesty; she is flesh and blood. He is not the great king of kings that he is historically purported to be. He is accompanied by his own doom: Cassandra.

We remember his fears before Troy, his desire to sail away, his senseless arguments with Achilles. The Trojan War itself was called senseless, even in Homer. When Agamemnon kills his daughter we sympathize with her. The Athenians, too, considered this a hideous crime. Clytemnestra, on the other hand, is a stronger woman than legend or history has made her because in the mind of Aeschylus she was the creative force of the universe, which is also the destroyer.

The drama blends the dark river of Greek prehistory, when human sacrifices were offered to the gods, with Mycenaean times, when the king was a godlike hero, the source of family authority, and the symbol of statehood. Aeschylus has tapped the mythological unconscious of the Athenians, who belonged to neither of these two periods but whose culture was the hybrid flower on their grafted and united stems.

In the second play of Aeschylus' trilogy, *The Libation Bearers,* Orestes and his sister Electra slay Clytemnestra and Aegisthus, and in the last play, *The Eumenides,* Orestes is pursued by the Furies who want to damn him eternally because he has killed his mother, a person of his own flesh and blood. Orestes resists them and denies his guilt, pointing to his mother's crime. But the Furies are relentless and pursue Orestes all over Greece. Finally he calls on Athena for help; she, unwilling to decide a matter of hot blood, arranges a trial for him before twelve jurymen at a special court (the Areopagus) on the Acropolis.

She and Apollo both appear at this trial as defenders of Orestes, while the vengeful Furies are his prosecutors. During the trial Apollo points out that the mother is not the real parent of her child, but merely the person who nurses the seed that is placed in her. The father is the only true parent. Therefore, Clytemnestra's crime in killing her husband, the king, was far worse than that of Orestes.

Athena agrees, for she had no mother at all but had sprung full grown from the mind of her father, Zeus. Thenceforth she always favored the male. She favored the Greeks at Troy, she was the guardian angel of Odysseus, the patron goddess of Athens, and now the defender of Orestes. After both the defense and the prosecution have finished presenting their cases Athena readies the jurors for a vote. She states that they are judges in "this first of murder trials," and then goes on to say that this court will be perpetually set up for the people. She expresses the hope that the people will make good laws and that the juries will render just decisions. The vote of the jury is tallied and comes out six to six; Athena's vote breaks the tie and Orestes is acquitted and dismissed.

In this trilogy of Aeschylus' private vengeance has given way to legal justice and the dramatist is showing the birth of a new day. Both Sophocles and Euripides later retell the story of Agamemnon, Clytemnestra, Orestes, and Electra in dramas of their own but without the strong ethical and religious implications inherent in Aeschylus. Sophocles does not go into the trial itself or into the search for a system of justice. His Electra is filled with hate and memories. She floods the entire play with her dark passion.

Euripides insinuates a more than sisterly love for Orestes on the part of Electra and shows a vengeful Electra almost bullying her brother into killing their mother. Euripides' Electra hates her mother because through Clytemnestra's adultery and vengeance she, Electra, has lost her position and glory as a princess. It is this that she longs to regain. The murder itself is a vicious crime; no gods push Orestes to avenge the death of his father.

Greek Classic drama has thus run the gamut of emotions and history. It has moved from the noblest moral and religious considerations down to the narrower psychology of the individual participant. It has moved from the arena of the universal down to the particular, from the godlike hero-kings to the king as but another man, from a strong belief in the gods to a not so strong belief in man as the maker of his own destiny.

This was undoubtedly one reason for the failure of Euripides in Athens. He took some of the glamour away from the gods. He did not disavow them completely, but he did call them into question. He disclosed their weaknesses and their evils. He also turned away from the older concept of the heroes and made them into ordinary human beings. He sympathized with the kinds of people who were not particularly sympathetic to the Athenians, and he ruthlessly probed into the foibles of the Athenians themselves.

Aeschylus died in 456, Sophocles in 405, Euripides in 406, and Aristophanes in 385. With them the great Classic drama came to an end. For centuries nothing in a similar vein was written; then came Shakespeare and finally Racine, but the perspective of these dramatists was, of course, quite different. Man was living in a different age; the old gods had passed away.

The magnificent intensity of Aeschylus often suggests the Old Testament, Sophocles reminds us of Job, while the attitude of Euripides is much like that of Ecclesiastes. In all of them man is reconciled to the human condition through suffering, for suffering is what gives man dignity, purges him of guilt, makes his humanity possible in a hostile universe.

XI

The Idealized Image:
The Visual Arts

The beauty of an object depends on the harmonious relationship of all its parts.

Polycleitus, classical sculptor

Art has a double function: it must both imitate and transcend nature.

Aristotle

The Greek Bronze Age (Before-Iron Age) came to an end around 1100 B.C., and was followed by three centuries of darkness during which even the art of writing was forgotten. After this began the artistic revival which led to the greatest centuries of Greek creativity. Historians have more or less arbitrarily divided the high-flowering centuries into three successive periods: Archaic, Classic, and Hellenistic. While these divisions may be helpful, they are by no means absolute. They do characterize a recognizable ascent followed by a decline. The Archaic period begins with relatively crude forms in the visual arts, but ends on the high Classic plateau. The Hellenistic period begins on this plateau, then slowly makes its descent. The lines of demarcation are never clearly drawn.

The river of history flows continuously, sometimes with a fuller body of water, sometimes at a faster or a slower pace, but it is never dry. The procession does not end. There is a mingling of influences, races, cultures, ideas. Humanity reaches always for a star; the human mind and heart are an ever-blooming spring. The earth burgeons along history's river and man never ceases to look beyond himself with the divine frenzy of poem or picture. There may appear to be sudden ends when one civilization is vanquished by another, as was the Mycenaean by the Dorians, or Carthage by Rome, or Rome by the barbarians, but even in these cases much of the defeated culture survives in the new—a dark current that seeks again to find its outlets into the sun.

The Archaic period (800–500 B.C.) begins with the poems of Homer and a flourishing of beautiful urns and vases. Toward its middle point sculpture and temple building in stone commence. Stiffness in handling the material characterizes these early efforts to create a new art form in stone.

During the Classic period (500–323 B.C.) Greek sculpture and Greek literature reach their zenith. In sculpture this is the age of idealized beauty reflected in the statues of Phidias, Praxiteles, and countless other sculptors of genius. The Parthenon and its companion temples are constructed on the Acropolis. Several large classic statues in bronze and a few broken ones in marble have survived in Greece, but not one classic marble statue is intact.

The Hellenistic period (323 B.C.–A.D. 31) is so called because after Alexander's conquests Greek culture spread to vast new areas whose population was not Greek in blood. Many Greek artists left their old city-states to set up shop in centers far from their original homes. Sculpture became more individualized and more realistic. Architecture became more ornate. Colossal bronzes were cast, all of which have perished. The marble "Laocoön," the "Venus de Milo" and the "Winged Victory of Samothrace" are examples of the Hellenistic stonecutter's art. The end of the Hellenistic period is marked by a hurried carelessness in execution.

Today we must examine the art of Greece in museums or in ruined monuments which have become points of touristic delight. During the Golden Age of Greece art was inseparable from daily life. It embodied the harmony and order of that daily life. Great imagination and a strong sense of beauty are required to reconstruct from museum pieces and fragments a body that is no longer alive.

The traveler who enters a Greek museum with a high heart too often comes out feeling rather dizzy about it all, and especially plagued that he has wheeled by so many pots—big pots, little pots, middle-sized pots, tall pots, fat pots, slender pots, black pots, red pots, and multicolored pots. Certainly of all the Greek visual arts pottery is the one which has had the best survival rate. This is due both to the number and the material of the pieces of pottery.

In the first place, there must have been millions of pots of all sizes, shapes, and embellishments made during the days of ancient Greece. And these were scattered over the entire Hellenic world, from the Black Sea to Italy. Second, a piece of clay which has been properly prepared and is then fired is a good risk against the perils of both climate and the years. It can be broken, to be sure, but once buried under debris or under the earth it has a good chance of survival; unless every single fragment is smashed something will endure.

This is why the Greek museums, and all museums, are so full of pots. What these museums should do, of course, is to take away about 90 percent of their collection and exhibit only a very few of their finest and most representative pieces. Perhaps in that manner something might be appreciated in this most typical and most prolific of the visual arts.

But pottery is not only typical and prolific, it is also of key importance in filling in our knowledge of Greek life. For example, no Greek garments or draperies have survived, but the pictures on Greek pottery exhibit an abundance of every conceivable kind of dress and drapery from lowest to highest degree. Pottery also illustrates the various Greek tools and farm implements, the different kinds of armor and weapons, the many kinds of ships and furniture, examples of what Greek mural painting looked like, illustrations from scenes of daily life, rituals and religious scenes, games, processions, battles, musicians playing the ancient instruments, dances, sacrifices, scenes of dining, hunting, of lovemaking and of revelry. In a word, pottery is what has given us almost all of the visual details of ancient Greek life.

Pottery was the first art to flower after the Dark Age. As early as the year 1000 Greek potters were busy molding the first of their post-Dorian forms, forms which ultimately would lead us step by step to the glorious art of the fifth century. The earliest pottery made after the Dark Age imitated Mycenaean designs with only small groups of black semicircles as the main motif. This style slowly developed into the use of geometric designs, the principal feature of which was the Greek key, or meander, which is still in widespread use today, particularly in chinaware.

By the ninth century the new style was firmly established. Then these geometric designs gradually made way for the introduction of stylized animals, which at first were only geometric representations of animals. After animals came the addition of human figures, and by the seventh century both human beings and animals were quite accurately represented.

At first the figures were black against the orange color of the clay, but later, around 530, the background is black with the figures outlined in the glazed orange of the clay. There are also beautiful vases and urns in polychrome shades. Of course, the older designs continue to survive and "geometric" vases are still produced in the later centuries, with their shapes, designs, and glazing all considerably more refined.

Even a cursory examination of Greek pottery quickly reveals something of profound importance about the race: the Greeks could not conceive of use without beauty. They fused the two concepts before they ever laid a hand to the material. A kitchen cup, a plate, a chair, a piece of ivory, a mirror of bronze, a simple coin, and every urn and vase of whatever size or description must always be beautiful. How often do we in our day make use so important that beauty is forgotten completely? Our steel furniture, file cases, business machines, kitchen pots and pans, and any number of other items in daily use have a utilitarian value but are, in fact, extremely ugly. This ugliness is bound to enter our lives. There is no escape.

But let us not expect too much from the ruins of ancient Greece. Go into the small museum at the site of ancient Corinth (and Corinth was a place that manufactured lovely pottery) and all we see is a collection of inferior brown and black jugs, many of them broken. The experience repeats itself in most other Greek museums. The priceless items have been taken away to Athens, London, Paris, New York, Berlin, Vienna. The best pieces, indeed, are no longer in Greece, for most of the archaeologists have been foreigners, and they always found a way to sneak the real treasures home.

A hundred and fifty years ago, long before the period of the great excavations, John Keats viewed one such treasure in London and wrote his "Ode on a Grecian Urn." He recapitulates in stirring images the sylvan scene fixed there imperishably. The purpose of all art is to capture the perishable moment imperishably, and Keats has made this the main theme of his poem. He sees on the urn "a flowery tale" more sweetly told than in his own lines: a lover reaching for a kiss, songs being played by rustic musicians, a tree which will never shed its leaves, a spring which will never become summer, a "heifer lowing at the skies and all her silken flanks with garlands dressed" as she is led to the green altar of sacrifice.

> What mad pursuit? What struggle to escape?
> What pipes and timbrels? What wild ecstasy? . . .
> O Attic shape! fair attitude! with breed
> Of marble men and maidens overwrought . . .

Outside of Keats on other Grecian urns we see in miniature the whole pageant of beauty which is this Attic attitude. The story of the *Iliad* is told in pictures on the ancient pottery, scenes from the *Odyssey* are even more popular sources of inspiration. All the gods appear in their various rituals and festivals, and the form of naked Aphrodite, "the golden girl," adorns many a vase with fixed but exciting beauty that awakens the fancy of all who see her; on other vases massed hoplite warriors ready their shields for the attack, Achilles and Ajax take time off from Troy to play a game; Jason

Red-figured crater, circa fifth century B.C.
Athens, National Museum.

searches for the Golden Fleece, musicians play the lyre, Theseus slays the Minotaur, Sappho and her poet friend Alcaeus are pictured in flowing robes, a rhapsodist recites Homer, an Attic actor holds his mask, a Greek ship sails upon the sea. Greek vases capture all these scenes and more; in faded glory they epitomize the whole great circle of Greek life.

PAINTING

Painting was a highly developed art among the Greeks in the fifth and fourth centuries and was considered on a parity with sculpture. Most pieces of sculpture were painted, and the best sculptors sought out the best painters to give life and color to their works. Only the dimmed traces of color remain on a few minor pieces of classic marble, and these give no idea at all of what the originals must have looked like in their brilliant hues.

But painters did not depend on statues or on pottery to express themselves; there were great murals in the public buildings of Athens and Delphi painted by the finest artists, and if we are to believe the reports on them they were of exceptional beauty. Originally, a four-color technique was used—black, white, red, and brown, and there was great variation in pose and gesture. Later other colors were added and facial and body expressions became very realistic. The Greeks admired these murals profoundly. Not one of them remains; indeed, not even a fragment of one remains.

Nevertheless, we are not completely in the dark in regard to Greek painting for several reasons. First, the finest vases show many of the more famous painted scenes in miniature. Then, the Romans made copies of the best known Greek paintings and some of these have survived in Herculaneum and Pompeii. Third, many centuries before Pompeii the Etruscans hired Greek painters to decorate their tombs and to teach their own artists, and at several Etruscan sites, but especially at Tarquinia, north of Rome, we may see several of these gay but faded frescoes. Last of all, some of the Roman mosaics reproduce Greek paintings and Greek mosaics, which often pictured the same subjects. The most lovely by far is the "Alexander" mosaic found in a rich man's home in Pompeii and now in the museum in Naples. It is the copy of a Greek painting of around 300 B.C. This mosaic shows Alexander fighting the Persians under Darius, and is a beautifully executed work of art.

However, everything that we know about Greek painting is learned from copies, and these at best are a far cry from the originals. One who has viewed copies of the best Greek sculptures and is able to compare them with the originals will immediately recognize and *feel* the difference. And so it must be with painting, except that in this case the comparison cannot be made, for no Greek original has survived.

By the middle of the fifth century the best Classic painters knew how to use perspective and chiaroscuro as well as a palette of many colors. Two of the most famous artists of the latter part of this century were great rivals, and it was decided that a contest between them would determine which was the master. Zeuxis painted a vine with grapes on it in such a realistic manner that some birds swooped down and tried to eat the grapes. Certain that he had won the victory Zeuxis then asked his rival Parrhasius of Ephesus to draw aside the curtain and reveal his picture, but Parrhasius indicated that the curtain *was* his painting, so Zeuxis gracefully had to accept defeat.

In the fourth century the most famous artist was Apelles of Cos, the court painter of Alexander. He painted many portraits of the young king and his horse, and was also especially fond of reproducing the voluptuous figure of Aphrodite. Fabulous sums were paid for the works of Apelles and of other popular artists, and they were given great commissions by their cities and by the local tyrants. The Greeks did not paint in oils, but used a mixture of egg white and color (*tempera*) to paint on wet cloth or wooden panels or employed the encaustic process of mixing melted wax with colors. They also developed to a high degree fresco painting on wet plaster, a technique which was lost after the fall of Rome and was not revived until the Renaissance.

Fresco painting, of course, was not a creation of the post-Dorian Greeks of the Classic age, for the Cretans had painted exquisite murals on their palace walls as far back as 1500 B.C. The art was temporarily lost during the Greek Dark Age, to be revived at the end of the Archaic period, that is, around 600 B.C.

SCULPTURE

The Cretans also were the first inhabitants of Greece to perfect the casting of art objects in bronze, an art which later was developed to a high degree by the Greeks of the Classic and Hellenistic periods who were able to produce colossal statues of 60 to 100 feet in height. The Colossus of Rhodes, which towered over or beside the entrance to the harbor on the island of Rhodes, was an immense bronze statue of Apollo about a hundred and five feet high. But these colossal statues come at the end of many centuries of casting.

Bronze workers entered Crete and Greece around 3000 B.C. from Asia Minor. Between 2000 and 1500 the casting of bronze had reached such a stage that beautiful (but small) art objects could be made of this material. Tiny statuettes of persons and of gods in various poses were produced in quantity, and hundreds of them can be seen today in the museum at Heracleum. Only a few have strayed to museums in other parts of the world.

Bronze, of course, is an alloy which is not found in nature. It is composed of a large percentage of copper, 85 to 95 percent, the remaining percentage being tin. A rather soft and malleable bronze requires only 5 percent tin content, but a hard bronze will need 15 percent. There was plenty of copper in Crete and Greece but there was very little tin. After the known local deposits had been exhausted there was a period when the making of bronze almost disappeared. But new mines were discovered, and also, by a kind of chain process of exchanges, small supplies of tin found their way to Hellas all the way from Spain and Germany. It is quite possible that the discovery of a local tin mine was the main reason for Mycenae's sudden rise to wealth and power around 1700.

Bronze art objects had a hardness and a color (besides the greenish patina added by age) which made them very desirable to the ancient Cretans and Greeks. Perhaps, too, the difficulties of casting the alloy made it a challenge to Bronze Age artists. In any case, very lovely miniature figures were cast in Crete around 1700, and their positions or poses were much more varied and expressive than the first large statues in stone which were not carved until the seventh century, a thousand years later.

There were several ways to cast bronze. Solid figures and objects were probably cast first, and obviously these could not be of very large size because of the weight involved. *Solid casting* was done in this manner: (1) A model was made in clay, stone or wood. (2) Over this hard model was placed a layer of clay. (3) While still in place this relatively thin layer of clay was then cut into segments, which when completely dry could be removed from the inner model piece by piece. (4) These pieces were then carefully reassembled and glued together. (5) Into the resulting hollow was poured molten bronze, and when this hardened the outer vessel of clay was removed leaving the solid bronze core inside.

Hollow casting. The two processes for hollow casting in the ancient world were as follows:

(A) The above rules for solid casting were first followed up through the producing of the outer clay segments. These segments were then reassembled around an inner solid core small enough to fit loosely inside while still leaving some empty space around it. This inner core did not have to be carefully wrought; it simply occupied most of the hollow in order to keep out the bronze. So that the outer clay shell would be equidistant from this core at all surrounding points the core bristled out here and there. The molten bronze was poured in around these bristles and filled all the empty space. When the thin bronze figure had hardened, the outer clay shell was removed and the inner core was gouged out from the bottom. The few marks left by the bristles could then be filled in, but these were usually located in such spots that they were not easily detectable.

(B) The lost-wax (*cire perdue*) process: The inner mold was very carefully wrought with its bristles protruding and over this was placed a thin coating of wax. The wax was covered with a coating of clay. When the outer clay had hardened the entire mass was heated and the wax was allowed to melt and flow out at the bottom. Into the resultant hollow molten bronze was then poured. When this was hard the outer clay shell was removed and the inner mold was gouged out leaving the thin bronze figure. The lost-wax process was more precise than that explained in paragraph A above, and figures of enormous size and relatively slight weight could be produced in this manner. It was not necessary that these figures be cast in a single piece. The famous "Charioteer of Delphi," the oldest life-size bronze statue that has survived, was cast in seven separate pieces which were later carefully joined together.

Hollow casting was brought from Egypt or Assyria into Greece around 530; prior to that time only small objects could be cast in bronze. Of course, sheets of bronze were often beaten into various shapes, and sometimes these were embellished with inlays of silver or gold as in the case of the marvelous shield of Achilles, described in the *Iliad*. Designs were also cut into the bronze itself, some of them surprisingly lovely. Many bronze mirrors had beautiful designs and figures on the back.

Statues in bronze were just as carefully made as sculptures in marble, and all the colossal figures of the gods were either of bronze or of gold and ivory carefully wrought over the surface of an inner core of wood. The famous statues of Phidias, most celebrated of classical Greek sculptors, were of both types. His huge statue of Zeus at Olympia (60 feet high), and his Athena Parthenos (40 feet high) in the Parthenon itself, were rough cores surfaced with highly embellished gold and ivory. Phidias wrought in bronze another statue of Athena Promachos as the warrior defender of her city which was placed in the open on the Acropolis between the entrance gate and the Erechtheum.

This statue has been variously estimated as being from 30 to 70 feet in height; a good guess is that it was about 50 feet high, and it is known for a fact that it was easily visible to mariners approaching the coast near Athens and so served as a beacon much as does our own Statue of Liberty.*

There was also a third bronze Athena slightly more than life size, and so carefully wrought in its details that most viewers considered it Phidias' masterpiece. This statue was also on the Acropolis and was known as the

---

* This statue shone in the sun during the day and in the fourth century A.D. when Alaric and his Goths laid siege to the Acropolis they thought they saw it step off its pedestal at night and walk around the walls. This so frightened them that they lifted the siege. Justinian took the statue to Constantinople, where it occupied a spot of honor for nine centuries.

Lemnian Athena because the Athenian settlers of Lemnos had paid for its construction. The Zeus at Olympia was a seated figure of the god in a golden robe and wearing a crown of gold in the form of olive branches; it was tremendously impressive according to the reports of both Greeks and Romans who saw it.

This figure would parallel the statue of Abraham Lincoln in the Lincoln Memorial in Washington. Indeed, this beautiful American building, which carefully reproduces the classic Greek style and presents Lincoln as a living spirit, is perhaps the only structure in the world which gives a true idea of what a Greek temple looked like, and what feelings it evoked among those who entered.

The Colossus of Rhodes was a much larger statue than any of those mentioned above, and stood approximately 105 feet in height. It was placed in the harbor of this thriving emporium in the year 280 and was destroyed by an earthquake which devastated the city of Rhodes in 224. Its fragments lay in the water for centuries, until at last, one thousand years later, the scrap metal was fished up and a train of several hundred camels carted it away. The Colossus of Rhodes and the statue of Zeus at Olympia were among the Seven Wonders of the Ancient World. The other five were: the Temple of Artemis (Diana) at Ephesus in Asia Minor, the tomb of King Mausolus at Halicarnassus (also in Asia Minor), the Lighthouse at Alexandria, the Pyramids, and the Hanging Gardens of Babylon. Five of these seven wonders were constructed by Greek artists.

Of the colossal statues of the gods not one fragment remains. The Roman copies that exist are stiff and poorly made and give no idea of the originals on which so much of the fame of the great Phidias rested. Nearly all of the Greek bronze pieces were later melted down to be used for other purposes and so were irreparably lost.

The great number of bronze figures actually cast by the Greeks astonished the Romans, who gazed on them in admiration. Nero plundered the Delphi sanctuary and took back to Rome with him over three hundred bronze statues. A few classical and several bronze pieces of the later Hellenistic and Roman periods have survived; one of the latter is a marvelous boxer of the second century B.C. whose cut and bruised face is convincingly realistic. This statue is in the Museo delle Terme in Rome.

Greek sculpture reveals a very clear progression from the stiff Archaic down through the much more realistic Hellenistic and Roman periods, and the pieces in stone mark this progression more clearly than do those in bronze. The first stone statues of life size were produced in Greece around 650 B.C., toward the middle of the Archaic period. The Greeks had carved wooden statues before this, but none of these have survived. The earliest stone statues were not of marble but were in softer limestone, and they were very crude.

We generally think of the Greeks as originators, but in all the arts they were at first imitators and learners before they became creators in their own right. The Greeks were one of the most absorbent and resilient peoples on earth; they possessed an uncanny talent for appropriating the discoveries and ideas of others as the starting point for their own creativity. The early Archaic Greek statues in stone clearly indicate their Egyptian and Near Eastern background, but they differed in two important ways: (1) they were always finished all the way around, not only in front, and (2) they displayed the naked male body. The first Greek figures in stone, therefore, were studies in human anatomy, which provided the proper basis for further development of the art.

The early Archaic figures invariably take the same foursquare frontal pose, body standing stiff, legs together or left leg slightly forward, but never in any other position, arms at the side, not hanging freely but affixed to the torso just above the wrist with a jut of stone, the cubic head erect and always facing frontward. These early statues were still imprisoned in their rectangular blocks of stone. They were essentially "architectural" rather than human figures. They were made to be viewed only from the front.

The faces were impersonal and expressionless until about 575 B.C. when there began to appear the vague suggestion of what is known as "the Archaic smile." The eyes reflected always a cold, abstract, stony stare. Even the details of the anatomy were geometric patterns rather than attempts at realistic or idealistic reproduction. The ears, for example, were circled scrolls, the hair was of geometric ovals, the eyes the same, the ribs were half a dozen parallel indentations on the stomach, the knees were small wedges.

Torsos, arms, hands, legs, and feet appeared to carry out stiff mathematical measurements. The necks of these Archaic statues were very thick and the additional strength added by the long stone slab of hair behind the neck so strongly attached head to body that few Archaic statues are headless today, whereas many of the later and finer pieces have their heads missing.

As the Archaic period moves forward (sixth century), marble replaces limestone as the sculpturing material, the geometric stiffness begins to disappear, and the figures embody more and more of the grace and mobility of the freedom-loving Greeks. The vase painter had displayed such realism much earlier, but the Greek artist was not then accustomed to working in stone and picked his way with care.

The first evidences of a more flexible handling of the human body came

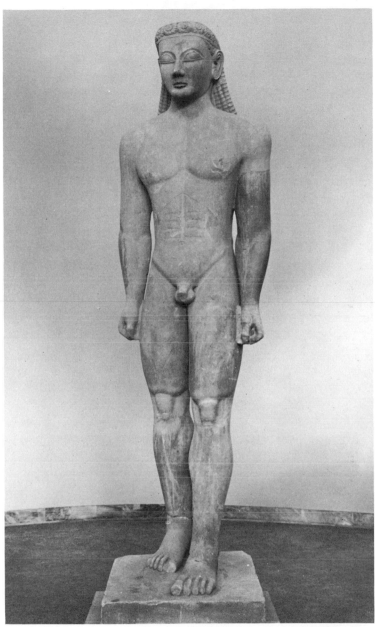

Kouros from Sounion, early Archaic period, circa 615–590 B.C. *Note the block-like character of the figure which has not yet emerged from the imprisoning stone.*

in the stone reliefs carved only halfway around, then about 500 B.C. the statues themselves begin to emerge from their Archaic stiffness. Legs and hands assume a more mobile position, and the body is more naturally proportioned. The Archaic smile appears more relaxed, and the figure as a whole comes out of its block-like character. Sometimes the face takes on an almost sulking aspect. There is growing confidence in the carving of marble as chisels replace the earlier punches and abrasives which the first Greek stonecutters had used. All early Archaic statues are colored in bright red, green, blue, but as the period ends some artists prefer to let the color of the stone suggest the human skin.

The earliest life-size statues in stone of the Archaic period were of young men and were probably used as tombstones. The archaeologists who dug them up originally called them "Apollos," because they were idealized figures, but it is dubious if any of them represented a god. More recent art specialists call such an Archaic figure a *kouros,* which means simply "young man." Some of the statues were probably of athletes. These young men were always carved naked, for the Greeks participated naked in the Olympian and other athletic contests, and it was natural for the sculptor to reproduce that nudity.

The female figure, however, known as a *kore* (young woman), was always draped in the early Archaic statues. By the fifth century the drapery began to fall away; the first step was to uncover the breasts or to emphasize their details through an effective transparency of the robe. In the fourth century the entire robe disappears, and the female nude emerges, but it is far from universal, for Aphrodite is the *only* goddess who is so revealed.

Greek classical sculpture begins after the Persian invasion, around 475, and continues until the death of Alexander the Great in 323. The classical sculptor moved away from the stiff frontal pose; he idealized images in stone; his figures were an imagined perfection. In order to achieve this there was a search for ideal numerical ratios. One of the great classical sculptors, Polycleitus, codified the rules of proportion and stated that the full figure should have the height of exactly seven and a half heads. Matter became form, form became art, and art in stone captured the simple nobility and restrained concept of beauty which embodied the Greek ideal.

Such was the genius of the great stonecutters of this period that the best of their work has seldom been equaled, and never surpassed, in the succeeding centuries. The Greeks saw the human form as the supreme embodiment of the ideal beauty; even their gods took the shapes of men. The Greek sculptor felt, therefore, that he must glorify the body, a temple of living splendor. Each classic statue represented all men, not a specific or individual man. The only exceptions were a few portrait busts commissioned by rich politicians.

When the Persians occupied Athens in 480 they smashed everything on the Acropolis, so almost nothing of the three or four decades prior to the invasion survived intact. A few statues from the nearby island of Aegina (circa 500) did escape but they have been overly "restored." They are in Munich. After defeating the Persians and on returning home the Athenians either buried their broken statues in trenches or used the pieces along with other rubble in expanding the city's walls. In such locations did later archaeologists find them. For this reason we have more Athenian Archaic statues today than statues of the Classic period.

The statue known as "The Critian Boy," which was carved just before 480, is one of the few surviving pieces which clearly indicate the transition stage from the stiff, block-enclosed Archaic figures to the much freer Classical style. In this figure the human body is conceived as an organism of flesh and bones, capable of both grace and movement. The weight is very carefully distributed and this is reflected in the position of the legs, the torso, and in the lines of flexed muscles.

Several classical pieces were dug up at Olympia, whose very site was buried and lost for centuries. By the middle of the fifth century (circa 450) a complete mastery of the material breathed new spirit and new beauty into the stonecutter's art. The Acropolis was rebuilt under Pericles and his successors, Phidias and his assistants completed the incomparable statues and reliefs of the templed area, and Greek sculpture reached its fullest flower.

Classical statuary is best represented by what has survived in bronze, for all the marble statues of this period are broken. Among the half dozen fine bronze pieces that we still have are the "Charioteer of Delphi," once part of a larger group including a chariot and horses, celebrating a victory in the Pythian Games of 474 B.C. The fixed majesty of this figure at the museum in Delphi is profoundly impressive.

Another fifth-century bronze, perhaps the finest single piece of Greek statuary in the world, is a powerful, greater-than-life-sized "Poseidon" (or Zeus), from about 460 B.C., which was pulled up from the sea minus its arms by some fishermen in 1926; the arms were found two years later and have been welded onto the figure which occupies a place of honor in the Athens Museum. The perfection of the outstretched arms and of the figure itself are unsurpassed. As there is no positive way to identify this statue some specialists have called it "Zeus," others "Poseidon." The majority view now favors Poseidon.

Charioteer at Delphi, circa 470 B.C. Only surviving figure of a once much larger piece consisting of a chariot and its horses. Early Classic bronze.

Harissiadis

Head of the charioteer. Museum of Delphi.

Later bronze pieces include a marvelous Athena in her plumed Attic helmet, 7 feet tall, excavated in Piraeus in 1959, and a smaller "Boy of Marathon," about two-thirds life size, dredged from the sea off Marathon, with eyes of inset limestone and glass pupils. This piece is sometimes called the "Boy of Praxiteles," as it strongly suggests the style of that famous artist who brought the Golden Age of Greek sculpture to an end. The date of this piece is somewhere between 340 and 300 B.C. Another bronze hauled out of the sea off Antikýthera is of a young man (sometimes he is called "Paris"), which is dated from circa 340 B.C.

Bronze Poseidon (*or Zeus*) *circa* 460 B.C. *The figure is 6 feet, 10 inches high. Arms were found after the statue had been dredged from the sea and were welded on later.*

Harissiadis

Head of bronze statue of Poseidon. Athens, National Archaeological Museum.

Not a single statue by the great Phidias, master sculptor of the Periclean age, has survived, but what remains of the pedimental statuary and of the metopes and frieze on the Parthenon and on the small temple of Nike, done under his direction (some of it probably by his hand), may be the highest point that sculpture in marble has attained in the entire history of man. The best sections of these reliefs and of the pedimental statues, known as the "Elgin marbles," because Lord Elgin carried them back to London, are there today in the British Museum. Even Greeks admit that they are magnificently displayed.

No statues and few reliefs of consequence remain on the Parthenon itself, but a considerable display of the material is in the Acropolis museum. The finest caryatid (female figure) column from the Erechtheum, constructed at the end of the fifth century, is also in the British Museum. The other five caryatid columns remain in place, with the missing lady in concrete.

Boy of Marathon. Slightly more than four feet in height. Circa 330 B.C.

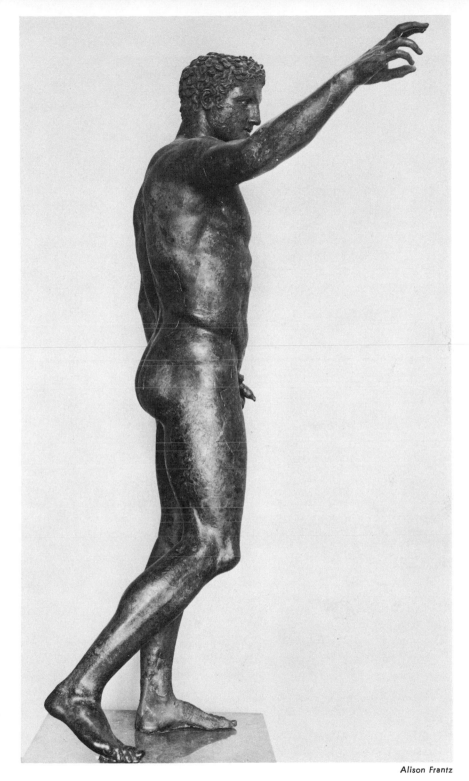

Bronze figure of a young Greek man, sometimes called Paris. Circa 340 B.C.

Statue of Apollo from center of west pediment of the Temple of Zeus at Olympia.

Pericles was responsible for putting Phidias in charge of all sculpturing on the rebuilt Acropolis, and the two men were good friends. Phidias sketched out the whole vast plan for the incomparable enterprise, but his apprentices and pupils probably executed most of it. The artist was most famous in antiquity for his enormous statues of gold and ivory (called chryselephantine), and for his large bronzes, but he was a marvelous stone-cutter as well.

The chryselephantine Athena that stood inside the Parthenon, of which no effective copy remains, was made at a cost of 850 talents, about $10 million in today's currency, and an incredible sum in the Athens of the fifth century. Phidias drove his large crew of workmen relentlessly, but he also inspired them and gave them a sense of dedication, so he seldom fired a man. The entire city felt a surge of pride as the great work took shape. The going daily wage was 2½ to 3 drachmas, around 50 cents, for the mass of laborers. Citizen inspectors examined the progress of the work frequently and prevented any padding or gouging in prices. Once when a workman fell from the scaffolding and lay at the point of death Athena appeared to Phidias in a dream and prescribed the cure.

The large amount of easily removable gold made theft a constant possibility, and even Phidias, who strove to account for every gram of the previous metal, was accused by his envious enemies of having taken some of it for himself. An even more serious accusation was made against his "impiety," for on the large bronze shield which stood beside the Parthenon Athena the artist had included the face of Pericles and his own balding head among the mythical heroes. Phidias was imprisoned for these offenses and while he was in jail he caught pneumonia and died.

Just after the middle of the following century (circa 350) Praxiteles, who rivaled Phidias in fame, brought the Classic period to a glorious close. Praxiteles put more realism into the marble than had his great predecessor, and in his feminine figures there is a deliberate voluptuousness. A single broken statue by Praxiteles (one not regarded by ancient critics as among his finest) has survived. It is the figure of Hermes holding the infant Dionysus; this statue was unearthed at Olympia in the southern Peloponnesus and is on display at the museum there.* Its surface has the very feel of human flesh. Praxiteles also carved the "Aphrodite of Cnidos" coming out of her bath with such sensuous realism that the statue was subject to an

* The much more ancient statue of Apollo from the temple of Zeus at Olympia represents the god in all his lofty magnificence. His shining countenance, all-seeing eyes, noble and delicate mouth reveal the spirit of "the divine amidst the desolation and confusion of this world." The sculptor is not known.

Hermes with the infant Dionysus by Praxiteles, circa 340 B.C. The only surviving statue by one of the great sculptors of the Classic period. Museum at Olympia.

indecency attack. Only a Roman copy of this work remains; Pliny called it "the finest statue in the whole world," and wrote that it was equally admired from all four sides.*

Another example of classical sculpture is the cult statue of Demeter, the Corn Goddess (circa 330), which is in the British Museum. The *Museo delle Terme* in Rome has a few priceless Greek originals of the Classic period (noteworthy is the "Daughter of Niobe" from some ancient pediment) and there are, of course, numerous Roman copies. Many a traveler makes no distinction between Roman copies and Greek originals, but to distinguish here is to know the body from the skeleton.

Unfortunately, even in Athens the museums display a vast array of broken bodies and headless torsos. There are enough of these to evoke a feeling of awe and wonder, but one must sadly admit that in so far as Greek classical sculpture is concerned it has to be judged from fragments, and the visitor who goes to Greece expecting to see in the museums there many near-perfect examples of ancient stone carving will come away with a broken heart. There were at least two dozen well-known sculptors of the Classic period whose work survives only in copies, or in fragments, or not at all. Myron, Kalamis, Pythagoras, Polycleitus, Kresilas, Alkamenes, Agorakritos, Kallimachos, Paionios, Strongylion, Skopas, Lysippus, and many others were profoundly admired in the fifth and fourth centuries.

The classical ideal was that man and the gods were at times so close together that they could be represented as one. The Greek artist was driven to try to find or to invent the cosmic harmony. The human intelligence was a microcosm of the absolute reality, and the creative fire of the human spirit was sparked by the universal flame. The classical sculptor, therefore, once he had mastered the secrets of anatomy, material, and motion, strove to chisel in stone figures of men embodying a perfect symmetry of form in which the historic particular disappeared and the universal poetic image emerged. Man was the divine equation which maintained the precarious balance between struggle and repose.

The Greek classical ideal was to capture and to preserve this ideal moment. Ephemeral human longing must be given an eternal look, anguish and doubt must be in proper balance with serenity. In classic sculpture the turbulence and pain of life are gone, only the dream remains, captured in imperishable form. The sculptors of the Golden Age thus represent in stone the perfectibility of the human potential, give to it an equilibrium,

---

* Even in the late Classic period most statues were painted, and this was considered so important that the best painters were paid as much as the sculptor. Praxiteles considered his masterpieces the statues painted by the great Nikias.

harmony, and serenity which have ever since been regarded as the most characteristic quality of Greek art.

The examples of Greek sculpture which are so well known in the Western world were all carved *after* the Classic period: the "Laocoön" in the Vatican, the "Venus de Milo" and the "Winged Victory of Samothrace" in the Louvre, etc. These are not classical works, but date from the middle of the Hellenistic period, well over a century later (200–150 B.C.). Thus, marvelous as they are, they represent the end and not the peak of the long tradition of stone carving in Greece. The "Apollo Belvedere" in the Vatican, once considered to be a Greek original, is now recognized by all authorities as a Roman copy. The National Museum in Athens has the male counterpart of the Louvre "Venus de Milo" in its "Poseidon from Melos," one of the few almost perfectly preserved marble figures in Greece which is neither Archaic nor a copy.

The "Laocoön" was dug up in Rome in 1506 and was at once recognized as the famous statue about which Pliny had written. It was carved on the island of Rhodes out of two blocks of marble, and shows Laocoön and his two sons struggling against the serpents. This piece of sculpture along with several other unearthed works of art became the nucleus of the Vatican collection. When Michelangelo heard of the find he rushed to see it and was so impressed that his own work in stone changed markedly as a result.

One of Laocoön's arms was missing, and Michelangelo attempted unsuccessfully to restore it. Perhaps he was too much of a perfectionist. In any case, the Italian sculptor Bernini of the seventeenth century had no such qualms and he did replace the lost arm, but in the wrong position. Bernini had the arm sticking out frontward and above the old man's head which destroys the tension and harmony of the struggling central figure. Critics and sculptors knew that something was wrong, but only very recently was the Bernini arm taken off and a correct restoration made with the hand behind the head. A careful examination of the lines of fracture and of the tensed muscles make it almost certain that the present restoration is accurate. Many viewers, however, have seen only the older Bernini restoration.

Laocoön was a Trojan priest who advised his compatriots not to allow the wooden horse of the Greeks to enter their city. He is reputed to have said, "I fear the Greeks even when they come bearing gifts." Athena, who had sided with the Greeks, was incensed by Laocoön's wisdom and sent two serpents to kill him. The serpents first attacked the sons of Laocoön, and their father hurried to the rescue. In the end all three were strangled.

In the sculpture itself the essence of pain and of struggle for survival are captured and preserved. Happiness passes, but pain and suffering endure, for both are present at the beginning and at the end of life. It is pain which makes joy possible and tranquillity a goal. The ancients knew that pain was inescapable, but if one faced it with dignity there was a nobility to the struggle which gave life a meaning.

The other two famous statues of the Hellenistic period, which are in the Louvre, the Aphrodite, or "Venus de Milo," and the "Winged Victory" from Samothrace, were excavated in Greece during the nineteenth century. The Venus was discovered by a Greek farmer who was digging a tree out of his field and unexpectedly unearthed a catacomb containing the statue. It was sent to France in 1821. Reports indicated that when she was found Venus held an apple in her left hand while her right held the sash that covers the lower part of the body. The arms were lost before the statue was loaded on its ship, either broken off as the figure was in process of being lifted on board or, according to another report, broken and lost in a fight between Greeks and French on the beach at Melos over possession of the marble. In any case, Venus reached Paris without arms. Very recently one hand was fished out of the harbor at Melos, but it is badly discolored and is of no use.

The "Winged Victory" was unearthed in several pieces and shipped to France in 1863, where it received scant attention. In 1879 twenty-six hitherto neglected fragments were gathered on Samothrace and sent to Paris, where they were pieced together to form the prow of a ship, the statue's original pedestal. The head of the figure was ground to powder in transit during a heavy storm. Preparing this statue for exhibit was a tremendous job, but the experts did not give up and finally were able to glue the many pieces together again in such an effective manner that today most viewers never even notice the various fractures which are clearly visible if one approaches close enough and examines the work carefully.

Another form of sculpture, the stone relief or stele, was used to mark graves and achieved great beauty and serenity. The Greeks did not list exaggerated deeds of the deceased to relieve their own guilt. The word *good-by* was the usual epitaph, and the relief figures represented simple farewell scenes. They expressed a restraint of emotion which still gives them an eternal freshness. In an art form saying good-by to something is one way to make it endure. The spectator of any epoch can realize his own particular feelings under the comprehensive types of these stelae which are the very finest distillation of human sorrow. No art could produce truer or more poignant pictures of grief.

Funeral stele of Ctesileos and Theano. Attic work of late fifth century B.C. *Husband and wife in simple parting scene. Wife, Theano, seated, is the deceased. Athens, National Museum.*

The Greeks have been singularly unfortunate in the survival rate of their finest pieces of sculpture, and this brings us again to the matter of copies. The Romans greatly admired Greek works of art and brought many fine works back with them to Rome. Hundreds of other Greek originals were copied by both Greek and Roman artists, some of them dozens of times. Praxiteles' nearly nude "Venus of Cnidos" was one of the most frequently copied. The Vatican Museum (with many improper fig leaves in place) is full of these copies, so are the Louvre and many other museums in the Western world.

How good are the copies? The best ones are extremely well done, but even these are clearly second best. There is, for example, a Roman copy of one of the caryatid female columns of the Erechtheum which was unearthed at Hadrian's villa at Tivoli, near Rome. A comparison of this piece with the originals immediately reveals a world of difference, but the copy must have been considered very good else the Emperor Hadrian, who was one of the most enlightened collectors of antiquity, would not have accepted it. The best copies were made by Greek artists commissioned by the Romans, and among these some are very beautiful.

Mathematically speaking, the Romans were able to produce very accurate copies by using the method called pointing. Scaffolds were placed around the figures to be copied, and exact measurements were made. The sculptor copying the work could use these measurements and the scaffold itself in order to cut and polish his own figure to exact proportions. However, those intangible and indefinable components of all great works of art—the angle of a smile, a look in the eyes, the very gloss on the marble itself, not to mention the kind and color of the marble, the angles of cutting it, etc.— were always different. Conclusion, no Roman copy was ever equal, or even nearly equal, to its Greek original. In the late Hellenistic and Roman periods when the art of sculpture went into a decline, there was a mass production of statues. The bodies were carved by the hundreds sans heads and arms, which were personalized and added later when the piece had a buyer.

ARCHITECTURE

The first Greek temples were constructed of wood, but none of these has survived. The Greeks began to build in stone in the seventh century, and these temples, like the earlier wooden ones, were based on the *megaron,* or hall, of the Mycenaean house which had a columned porch in front. The earliest stone temples copied those of wood exactly and reproduced the beams, pegs, rafters, and coffers of the ceilings in stone. The extensive use of columns probably was in imitation of Egyptian religious architecture, which was well known in Greece.

Never departing far from this very simple rectangular matchbox style, Greek architects were able to construct some of the most beautiful temples in the world by combining science with art and producing structures of marvelous proportions and symmetry. The Greek architect did not use the arch, which was well known in Asia, or the vault, or the dome. He was fascinated by the straight line, which as architecture progressed became the slightly curved line, suggesting the theory of relativity, which maintains that no line is absolutely straight.

Several Greek temples have survived in varying states of preservation, and it comes as somewhat of a surprise to many interested visitors that there are as many Greek temples in Italy as there are in Greece. There are three fine examples at Paestum, just south of Naples; another which is incomparably situated (and was never finished) at Segesta, not far from Palermo in Sicily; there are remains of several at Selinunte, and of two more at Agrigento, also in Sicily. All of these follow the Doric style of simple round columns with no base and an unadorned capital.

The Doric order appeared around the year 600, and in Greece most of the surviving temples follow this style. The Parthenon, of course, is the most notable example. Also on the Acropolis is the unique Ionic Erechtheum and the small Ionic temple of Athena Nike; down below where the marketplace was located in old Athens is the Theseum, or Temple of Hephaestus (Vulcan), the best preserved of all Greek temples, but not by any means the most impressive. Its frieze is still *in situ*.

On the nearby island of Aegina rises the beautifully situated Temple of Aphaia (circa 490), and in the mountain fastness of Arcadia is the Temple of Apollo at Bassae (circa 430) intact up to the roof; this temple had been lost to the Western world until it was rediscovered in 1765. The first Corinthian columns are found here, and the temple also had a beautiful stone frieze.

At both Corinth and Cape Sounian are the remains of two additional temples, but of these only a few lonely columns are still standing. The Temple of Apollo at Corinth (circa 550) is one of the oldest Greek temples of which any considerable part has survived, and the structure at Cape Sounian, dedicated to Poseidon, god of the sea, is contemporary with the Parthenon. It is certainly worth a trip to this southernmost point of Attica to view it, especially if one can take the trip in the afternoon and see the sun go down over the Aegean from the vantage point of the deserted

Harissiadis

*Temple of Hephaestus (Roman Vulcan), often called the Theseion or Theseum
because it also glorified the deeds of Theseus, mythical hero of Athens. Built
just before the Parthenon, this temple is the best preserved of all ancient
Greek temples. On the Agora in Athens. Circa 450 B.C.*

promontory on which the glorious white columns of this temple stand.
These graceful columns are still a beacon to the passing ships as they were
2,400 years ago.

Many of the Greek islands also boast of their ancient monuments. Corfu
and Thasos have their impressive Archaic remains, and Rhodes its citadel at
Lindos, poorly restored by the Italians. The sacred island of Delos displays
acres of ruins of great variety and in all stages of preservation. Delos was
the island most sacred to all the Greeks from whatever *polis*. Today it is an
abandoned and rocky sweep of ruins in the midst of the Cyclades, which
encircle it in the blue Aegean. Uninhabited until about 1000 B.C., Delos
embodied an aura of mystery and was a central and neutral spot where
Greek art and religion could meet and merge and be reborn. Sailors passing
by no doubt caught sight of the sun's reflection from its small lake and so
began the belief that Apollo, god of light, was born here.

According to the same legend, after Zeus had impregnated Leto he was
so afraid of his wife Hera's jealous rage that he abandoned Leto and she

was forced to wander among the islands seeking a spot to give birth to her child. Finally she stopped on Delos, which was then still floating about on the surface of the sea. Delos received Leto, four pillars rose up from the sea bed to anchor the island, and Delos became fixed in the water. Leto grabbed hold of the sacred palm which rose beside the sacred lake and straining heavily gave birth to twins, Apollo and Artemis. Temples sprouted up and Delos became in truth "the island built by heaven."

Apollo, the most Greek of all the gods, is often referred to as Delian Apollo, because of his birth on this island. Later, he is supposed to have ridden on the back of a dolphin to Delphi, where he killed the monstrous Pythian serpent and took over the headship of the religion there. On Delos there was once a colossal statue of Apollo in stone which was over thirty feet high. Only a fragment of it remains. The stone lions of Delos are famous because of their frequent appearance in photographs, but the island's mosaics, houses of prostitution along the water's edge, temples, homes, and cisterns which once served a large population are less well known.

On Delos too stood a temple to Dionysus, who was in conflict with Apollo for supremacy as the god most important in Greek daily life. Once there were over three hundred phallic symbols around this temple of Dionysus, of which now only two or three remain. Dionysus epitomized the biologic urge, the force of physical love, the life principle. As the ancient Greeks said, "Apollo was the head, but he needed a body." And modern Greeks add, "You don't need Apollo in the bedroom." Thus we see on Delos in conflict and in tenuous union the two main principles of ancient Greek life: the vital procreative energy, represented by Dionysus, and the symbol of light, artistic inspiration, and beauty, represented by Apollo. Delos, once the proud templed site of a thriving city and the center of Greek religion, is now only a vast maze of stony fragments, all that the pillagers have left behind.*

The Acropolis in Athens is still the heart and soul of what has survived of the Golden Age of Greek art. No traveler who visits Europe should return without seeing this sacred and incomparable hill with its complex of

---

* In human history, culture, and art Dionysus represents the impetuous, instinctive, subjective side of life. He is reckless will, blind and irrational. Apollo, on the other hand, is objective, calm, aloof, universal, unifying, and ordered. He is reason and harmony, while Dionysus is instinct. Nietzsche in *The Birth of Tragedy* describes the two polarities in detail. Apollo arouses "a delight in beautiful forms," while Dionysus gives to these forms a convincing significance, for he is the instrument of fertility in the cosmic pattern. In Apollo Dionysus is sublimated and given form. Often the two exchange characters and overlap in function, for their merging is man's best hope for immortality.

Temple of Athena Nike on the Acropolis. A perfect example of the Ionic order.

beautiful temples. The spectator is never disappointed, the imagination is never deceived, the anticipation is never dismayed. Every man deserves to look at least once upon this sight before he dies. He who does look is bound to be moved by a deep sense of the continuity of life; he will shed his individual skin and feel for a moment a part of all mankind. He will embrace his own roots and look into the bottomless well of his past and will feel that this experience is a window on all time. Here and here alone the Greek architectural ideal to capture in stone the art and nobility of mathematics was realized completely.

The treasury of the Delian League provided the funds and Pericles provided the spirit to rebuild the Acropolis, making it antiquity's most famous site. The splendid marble entrance, or Propylaea, which astonishes all visitors with its size and good state of preservation, is a majestic array of

Doric and Ionic columns topped with a roofing of huge indented marble slabs. It was never finished.

To the right of the entrance, on a little knoll, stands the tiny Temple of Athena Nike Apteros (Athena as Wingless Victory). It was often the Greek custom to deny to Nike (Victory) wings so that she could not fly away. This temple follows the Ionic order, and was beautifully decorated with a frieze of delicately carved figures, some of them perhaps by Phidias. The small slab of "Nike Untying Her Sandal" is one of the most admired pieces. The building was completely destroyed by the Turks, but after Greece won her freedom it was put together from the fragments. The work was not carefully done, however, and the temple had an awkward and lopsided appearance. About forty years ago it was completely taken apart and again put together after an exhaustive study of every fragment. It stands today as a monument to the talents of its restorers.

The Parthenon, which was dedicated to the patroness of Athens, Athena Parthenos, that is, Athena, the Virgin, was begun in 447 and was completed in 438, nine years later. Another six years passed before all the sculpture was done. The architects were Ictinus and his assistant Callicrates. Plutarch in his essay on Pericles comments on the construction:

> As the buildings rose on the Acropolis stately in size and incomparable in form and grace, the workmen vied with each other to see who could produce the most artistic work. Most marvelous of all was the rapidity of construction. Each one of these buildings, men thought, would require many successive generations to complete it, but all of them were finished in the heyday of a single administration.

The Parthenon is of white marble, veined with iron, and has 46 Doric columns, 8 in front, 8 at the rear, and 17 on each side. It measures 101 by 228 feet in size, and is about 65 feet high. Inside was the gold and ivory statue of Athena by Phidias, 42 feet in height. In the fifth century A.D. the temple was turned into a Christian church, with some destruction of its carvings, and in 1456 it became a Turkish mosque and a minaret was added but with very little damage to the building. Had it not been for these periodic religious conservations perhaps nothing at all would remain of the Parthenon today. Empires come and go but religion survives every political fragmentation.

In 1687 when the Parthenon was occupied by the Turks, who used it as a fortress against the invading Venetians, the temple was still mainly intact. The Venetians lobbed a shell inside which hit the Turkish powder magazine and at least half of the building was destroyed. Practically noth-

The Mourning Athena from the Acropolis, now in the Acropolis Museum.
Despite its small size this figure of circa 470–450 B.C. expresses great feeling.
Athena's peplos is gathered in a belt in the typical Attic style and has a
long overfall which balances the figure. Height 22 inches.

View of the Acropolis as one approaches it from the city below.

Acropolis of Athens. The Parthenon as seen from the propylaea, *or entrance.*

Acropolis of Athens. The Parthenon, 447–438 B.C.

ing remains of its ancient interior. After capturing the Acropolis the Venetian commander Morosini attempted to carry off the statues of the front pediment but his clumsy workmen dropped them on the stones below and most of them were smashed. In 1801 Lord Elgin took back to England 15 metopes (the outer stone panels), 56 slabs of frieze, and 12 statues, including nearly all of the remaining statues of the front and rear pediments, the spaces under the gables.

The outside portion of the temple, just above the columns, was decorated with 92 metopes, illustrating the struggle between the gods and the giants, between the forces of light and darkness, civilization and barbarism. They contained many figures of gods, centaurs, Greeks, Amazons, Trojans, and giants. The frieze, which ran for 525 feet around the top of the outer wall of the temple's interior shell displayed a procession of Athenians carrying gifts and bearing sacrifices to Athena in the great Panathenaeic Festival.

In the procession are young men mounted on noble horses, chariots, old men and maidens with olive branches and trays of food, women bearing the *peplos* for the goddess herself, servants carrying jugs of wine, animals being led to the sacrifice, and musicians playing their instruments. The

Alison Frantz

Panathenaeic procession on the Parthenon frieze.

relief of the frieze is only two and a quarter inches in height but the figures
are so carefully carved, modeled, and shaded that they produce the illusion
of depth and perspective. The procession consists of 400 figures of men
and women and 200 animals and suggests a long sweep without crowding.

The Parthenon temple structure itself is a miracle of the simple classic
style. There is not a single straight line in the entire building; all curvatures
are optical corrections to avoid the impression of sinking at the center or
leaning at the ends. The columns themselves are slightly bulged and tilted
in order to appear in perfect symmetry. Each column was constructed in
segments, bored in the center, and placed one on top of the other with an
olive beam passed through to hold them in place while they were turned
around and around one at a time until the joining spaces were ground to a
perfect fit and union. No mortar was used in the building.

All the statuary and parts of the building itself were painted in bright
blue, yellow, red, while the marble not so colored (mainly the columns)
was washed and polished with saffron and milk. The statues, before being
painted, were polished, oiled, and waxed again and again in order to make
them as lifelike as possible. Figures were beautifully draped in stone as if

the breeze had just caught them, their swirls and folds reflected the shadows, and a sense of life and motion was imparted to the individual reliefs as well as to the entire procession.

Nearly all of this is gone. All the color is lost. The interior of the temple is gutted, and most of the columns are broken. What we see today, marvelous as it is, is only a shell from which the warmth and breath have fled. In the noonday sun it is this skeleton which stands out gauntly against the blue sky, but by moonlight something of the ancient magic returns and the ghost may come to life again before man's believing eyes.

The third temple on the Acropolis, the Erechtheum, represents a conglomerate style. It consists of three separate chambers and in its original state suggested an Oriental structure. It had decorations of glass beads in four colors, gilt bronze, gold leaf, and figures in marble attached to slabs of black limestone. Inside was a golden lamp of acanthus leaves in which burned a sacred fire, never extinguished. All these embellishments are gone, but the lovely Ionic columns and the caryatids still make the building unique. There is nothing like it anywhere else in Greece.

This was the most sacred spot on the Acropolis, because according to legend it was here that Athena and Poseidon fought for the possession of Athens. Erechtheus was the grandfather of Theseus, who slew the Minotaur and was revered as a god. This lovely temple to him was the last to go up on the Acropolis, 421–405 B.C. Soon after it was completed Athens suffered her defeat at the hands of Sparta and lost both her wealth and her dominion.

Although the Acropolis still remains as the *sine qua non* of all sightseers of Greek antiquities, there were many other cities with similarly templed heights, and great monuments in stone were scattered all over the Hellenic world. Temples of which the remains are still visible stood at Olympia, Epidaurus, Delphi, Corinth, and Bassae on the Greek mainland, and Asia Minor was the site for many more. It was here in this transplanted Greece that the Ionic order flourished.

The Temple of Artemis (Diana) at Ephesus, constructed originally in 540–440, was destroyed in 356 by a paranoiac who deliberately set fire to the place so that his name might survive. The roof of cedar beams burned with a high intensity of heat and many of the columns toppled. This building was rebuilt in the decades after 356, following the original proportions (180 by 377 feet), but more harmonious in total effect, and was considered one of the Seven Wonders of the ancient world. Ephesus, now in Turkey, is a site that is still rewarding to see.

The Mausoleum of King Mausolus at Halicarnassus, another of the Seven Wonders, was built at about this same time and was so impressive

Alison Frantz

*View of the Erechtheum with its Ionic portico on the left and its caryatid
columns on the right.*

that it has given its name to all succeeding mausolea. A fragment of the
Carian king's un-Hellenic head, with his long wild hair faithfully copied,
has survived and is in the British Museum.

The great altar of Zeus and Athena at Pergamum, also in Asia Minor,
built around 180, was a structure of 225 by 250 feet decorated with a
spectacular frieze, at many places 90 inches in height, showing the battle
between giants and gods (as did the Parthenon). One surviving figure of a
giant caught in the coils of a snake strongly suggests the later Laocoön. The
altar frieze seethes with drama and action, and the facial expressions are
realistic in the best Hellenistic style.

The Pharos, or lighthouse, at Alexandria, another of the wonders of the
ancient world, was completed around 280 and reached a height of 400
feet; it consisted of great squares of diminishing size and was crowned
with a light (which carried 35 miles) and a 20-foot statue of Poseidon. Its
remains were toppled in an earthquake in the thirteenth century.

The marble for all the beautiful buildings of Athens' Golden Age came
from the quarries of Mount Pentelicus, northeast of the city, "a wooded

Temple of the Olympian Zeus, Athens. Note the Corinthian columns.

mountain with gurgling springs," which were first opened in 570 B.C. and are still visible from the Acropolis on a clear day. With the passage of time this white Pentelic marble becomes oxidized and takes on a warm gold patina which seems to breathe in the clear and warm Greek air. It was a worthy medium for architect and sculptor alike. Marble is still so plentiful in Greece that many a poor peasant's dwelling has a marble-topped kitchen table and sink.

The largest temple in Athens was the great temple of Olympian Zeus, a handful of whose rust-colored columns still stand in the heart of the city. The original temple was begun by the tyrant Peisistratus in the middle of the sixth century B.C., but was never finished. Around 175 B.C. a Roman architect took over, and work slowly progressed until the time of the Emperor Hadrian, who was responsible for the completion around A.D. 130.

The early Doric columns were all replaced and when completed this enormous structure originally had 104 Corinthian columns 90 feet high. These columns required 15,500 tons of marble, almost four times as much as the Parthenon. The dimensions of the temple were 135 by 353 feet. The few surviving columns, impressive as they are in their own right, rise like a cluster of strangers lost on Attic soil. The Athenians were more moderate in their taste and always placed classic restraint, perfection of detail, and harmony above size.

The stoa of Attalus (East Portico of the Agora) in Athens (150 B.C.) was a gift to the city by a Hellenistic king of Pergamum. Attalus had studied in Athens as a young man and took this way of expressing his gratitude for the education he had received there. The stoa consisted of a long colonnade which ran for 382 feet alongside the agora, or marketplace. It had a width of 64 feet. The colonnade was a place where people could meet sheltered from the rain and sun, and along its inner length was a row of shops. This stoa has recently been reconstructed with Rockefeller funds and is now a museum fronting the ruined agora.

There were many other temples and monuments in ancient Hellas, but a further listing would serve no useful purpose. The Hellenistic period was one of great building, and size for its own sake frequently became the goal. There was less attention to artistic detail. Slowly some of the old magic departed; the garden, however, did not die. Alexandria became the most flourishing city in the Greek world, Asia Minor continued to build impressive monuments in stone and to carve statues which were dramatic in their detail. But the grip of Rome slowly tightened on the Hellenic world and gradually the old culture and art melted away to be reborn in the new.

XII

Greek Humanism

Man is the measure of all things.

Protagoras

During the Dark Age (1100–800) the art of writing disappeared from Greece. The Linear B script of the Mycenaeans was forgotten when their civilization was destroyed by the Dorians. Perhaps this was a good thing, for when the Greeks found a new alphabet at the close of the Dark Age it was much simpler and more precise. This alphabet, which with minor changes is in use in Greece today, was borrowed from the Phoenicians around the year 850. It consisted of only 24 letters instead of the Linear B's 200 symbols.

The Greeks invented what the new alphabet lacked, a set of pure vowels. They took certain Phoenician consonants which represented sounds not occurring in Greek and used these to represent their vowels. Originally the Greeks read from right to left as was the Semitic practice, but during the sixth century they began to read from left to right and so some letters were turned around in order to face in the new direction. For example, ⊐ became E.

The Greeks also took over the Phoenician names for the letters: *alpha, beta, gamma, delta,* etc. These jingling names had no meaning at all in Greek, but in Phoenician they represented specific things: *āleph (alpha)* was bull, or ox; *beta* was house or tent, *gamma* was camel, *delta* was tent door, and so on. The original forms for these four letters were: ⊀ ⊲ ∧ △ which indicates their pictorial meanings. Add two dots as eyes for the bull, complete the square under the "b" ⊿ for the house, visualize a camel's most distinctive feature, his hump, for the "c" ∧ . The Greeks did not like the angles of the first three letters, so they straightened them; in English they became, A, b, c. It is also of symbolic importance that the first letter of the alphabet, which is also the first vowel, represented the bull, which was the symbol of fertility, the point of origin for any progression.

Initially a dozen variations of this Phoenician alphabet emerged in the different Greek city-states, each struggling for dominance. The one which finally won out was that which the enlightened Ionians used in their early literature. Homer was from Ionia and it is possible that he may have written down his poems in this new alphabet. In any case, the Homeric poems certainly helped to universalize this script. The Greeks from Chalcis in central Greece had a slightly different alphabet which they took with them when they established their colony at Cumae on the Bay of Naples around 750. The Romans adopted the Chalcidian letters and it is this "Latin" alphabet which we use in English today.

The Greeks wrote on tablets of clay, on wooden tablets covered with wax (easy to erase), on stone, lead, bronze, and especially on papyrus sheets which they learned to use from the Phoenicians, who had learned about them from the Egyptians. Our own word *paper* is derived from *papyrus.* The early papyrus sheets were from 20 to 30 feet in length and were rolled around a stick, which made unrolling easy. There was neither punctuation nor even a separation of the words in the early manuscripts and it took several papyrus rolls to make a "book" of moderate length. These ancient papyrus rolls soon rotted away in Greece, but several of them survived in the much-drier climate of Egypt, and it is from these and from inscriptions on stone that we have obtained our direct knowledge of ancient Greek writing.

The Greeks also used the letters of the alphabet in their system of numbers. The first ten letters represented the numbers from one through ten. The eleventh letter represented twenty, the twelfth was thirty, et cetera. Occasionally a more primitive method of strokes was used; a vertical stroke was one, two vertical strokes were two, and so on. A horizontal stroke in many parts of Hellas was equal to ten. More common still was the rude picture of a hand for five, V, and two such symbols joined together, X, represented ten, as in Rome.

Another way to indicate numbers was by having the first letter of the word for that number stand for the number itself. For example, the Greek word for *ten* was *deka,* so the letter "d" (which in Greek was $\triangle$) was often used to indicate ten. There was no symbol for zero; this concept, which was brought into Europe by the Arabs from India, simplified mathematics considerably. Yet with the aid of their abacus the ancient Greeks could add, subtract, and multiply sums in even less space than it would take us today with our superior numerical system. On the left side of the abacus each unit was multiplied by 5, and moving upward each slot meant a multiplication by 10. Thus, the number 648 was represented as follows:

		— thousands
0	0	— hundreds
	0 0 0 0	— tens
0	0 0 0	— ones

The Greek calendar began with year 776 B.C., legendary date of the first Olympian Games; the yearly calendar was based on the sun and the moon, but varied greatly from city to city. The Athenian year began on the day of the first full moon after the spring solstice of June 21. Hence, the Athenian year commenced toward the end of the month of June. The twelve months symbolized religious festivals, and it was in the ninth, at the end of our March and the beginning of April, that the greatest festival of all was held, the Greater Dionysia, during which the Panathenaeic procession, the presentation of drama, and the recitations of Homer all took place.

Out of these meager materials, and with the aid of a brilliant imagination, the Greek mind created a great literature, a system of mathematics, a great philosophy, a great art, concepts in ethics and politics which still prevail, scientific and aesthetic principles which are still basic to our thinking. All this was possible because man was the center and heart of the Greek cosmos; he was himself a *microcosmos,* a universe in miniature. Man was the measure of everything. Only the gods were immortal, but man was godlike in his striving and in his dignity. He exulted in the wild joy of life, but at the same moment he was aware of the immutable laws of the universe.

The dynamic tension between these two forces: a joyous delight in life, on the one hand, and the recognition of an unalterable order, on the other, released in these ancient Greeks all the dynamic energy of which individual man is capable. We all must live and die in the prison house of this earth, but what a great boon to be given such a wondrous prison! In this view of life there was full acceptance, but there was no resignation, no humility. The *Iliad* tells us, as Kitto so graphically pointed out:

> The lives of men are like leaves that flourish and grow warm with life feeding upon the earth, then fade away and die. But the tree will put forth new shoots in the spring season.

Here we feel the breath of continuous creativity along with continuous death. The nobility of striving is never forgotten. The days of man are not like the grasses, nor is man a flower of the field which flourishes only to die as in the Old Testament where the writer adds: "For the wind passes over it, and it is gone, and the place thereof shall know it no more." In this passage from the Hebrew Scriptures, God is great, man is nothing.

It would be inaccurate to say that the Greeks turned this around and thought, "Man is great, God is nothing," but it would be accurate to say that Homer painted the gods so very much like querulous, violent, and jealous men that the following generations of Greeks must have concluded that gods like these could not have been too important. In other words, they must have been taken mainly as symbols. One thing was certain: the Greek universe exalted the nobility of man rather than the glory of the gods, who were made in man's image.

Hector in the *Iliad* expresses poignantly the desire of the human spirit to endure, and he finds his own immortality as the bright warrior:

> *Some day a man who is yet unborn will say*
> *As on his ship he sails the wine-dark sea,*
> *"There is the mound of one who died in ancient times*
> *Slain at the peak of his might by glorious Hector!"*
> *So will it then be said; and my glory will live forever.*

The Greeks were the creators of philosophy, and all of Western philosophy is derived from theirs. Never has a people probed with greater impartiality its own psyche and its own institutions. Never has a people sought more brilliantly to plumb and to clarify the abstract or to give order to the unorderable.

The cradle of Greek philosophy was Ionia, which was also the cradle of Greek literature. Greek philosophy began with the attempt to define reality; it developed into a statement of and a search for the ideal, and finally, expanding the bases of its own orientally inclined Orphism, under the influence of Christianity it became mystical and religious. One of the first philosophers to look reality in the face was Heraclitus, called the obscure, who was born around 540 B.C. Like many others before and after him, Heraclitus retired from society and formal religion (he was a high priest) and in this period of isolation thought out his philosophy, which was also almost a religion.

It is worth noting that such fundamental probings of the human condition, its origin, purpose, and destiny, have always been nonsocial experiences. Moses alone on Mount Sinai felt that he had heard the voice of God and came forth with the Ten Commandments; Buddha abandoned his wife and child and after six years of isolation he returned and delivered his famous speech at Benares which became the basis of Buddhism; after forty days Christ came out of the wilderness and delivered his Sermon on the Mount, the essence of Christian principles.

Heraclitus saw the universe and life as eternal change. Everything was a becoming, nothing *is*. "You can never step twice into the same river," he said. This eternal ebb and flow of reality was its very essence. All reality, said Heraclitus, manifests itself in apparent opposites: night and day, life and death, good and evil, love and hate, but these opposites are not real, each completes the other, both are fused in an ambivalent one. Life is eternal, but not individual life. Matter is eternal, but not particularized matter. In the eternal clash of opposites neither ever wins, but this clash is the constant of the eternal becoming, which is constant change.

Virtue lies in obedience to Nature's laws and human energy should express itself in reasonable action. "Heed not me, but hearken to the *Logos*," said Heraclitus. The *logos* was the spiritual essence of the world, the Word, the wisdom of the absolute. Someday the universe would be destroyed by fire in order to begin itself all over again. Man embodies reality as the drop of sea water embodies the sea, as the dewdrop reflects all light, as a tiny flame has the qualities of all fire. After death the individual soul returns to the absolute just as the drop of sea water is lost again in the sea, just as the tiny flame returns to the cosmic and universal fire.

The Greek philosophers, though they were numerous and brilliant, were not in the early centuries the teachers of men. "We poets are the teachers of men," says Aeschylus as a character in one of the plays of Aristophanes. He could have said it in real life just as well. Homer was the first teacher and the great master. Education was humanistic education all the way down the line, that is, it implied familiarity with a traditional library of books. It was what was later called "a classical education," and its basic elements continued to be those of Western learning up to this century.

It was not education for a trade or craft, the father of the family gave that; it was not theoretical education, the philosophers gave that. It was familiarity with one's own roots. Perhaps that is why the Greeks knew so completely their identity, while we are not at all sure of ours. Any Greek could truthfully say, "I know who I am. I know what I am. I know where I belong." Since both his individual identity and his involvement with the community were clearly known and recognized, the Greek citizen did not expend his energies in a search for identity or in the restless anxiety of not belonging which characterizes contemporary society all over the world.

Conclusion ↓

"Man is the measure of all things, of those that are, that they are so, of those that are not, that they are not." This statement by Protagoras of Thrace, who came to Athens in the time of Pericles, was the base of Greek humanism. Plato interprets the meaning of the sentence by saying that (a) it included both concrete and abstract "things" and (b) it meant that each man must ascertain his own truth, i.e., what was true for one man might well not be true for another. Character and wisdom produced an individualized truth, and each man was his own measure.

Protagoras was a Sophist, which originally meant "a teacher of wisdom"; the word evoked no disparaging tone until religion later turned against pagan philosophy. But the Sophists were skeptics as well as teachers, and Protagoras himself got into deep trouble because he had said that he did not know whether the gods existed or not, because the subject was too obscure and human life was too short. Real higher learning began in Greece with the Sophists, who were wandering scholars who rented halls, taught their courses, then moved on to another city to repeat them. They were the "university professors" of the fifth century.

Central to the Greek ideal of education was the cultivation of the *logos*. Literally, this meant "the word," but in a broader sense it meant also the art of thinking and of discourse. Socrates, who never wrote a word, was an admirable example of a man who used the *logos* with telling effect. Indeed, learning through discourse was the very heart of Greek education. Students did not necessarily read very much, but they did listen while others read or talked.

Logos in a social sense came to mean the art of general conversation, and at any gathering of educated men such conversation was the primary aim. Man's superiority over the animal kingdom was manifested in the *logos*, which made civilization possible, and the more words and discourses (*logoi*) a man knew the more respected was his intellectual stature. At these social gatherings dice would often be thrown in order to decide who the lead-off man and chairman would be. The conversation was *always* general conversation, never small talk, that is, talk broken up into groups of twos and threes. While one man spoke, all the others listened. It is an art, unfortunately, which has all but disappeared from American life, where small talk has become the normal form of social expression.

We do have something akin to Greek conversation in our small advanced university classes, especially in our seminars, but in social gatherings Americans seldom converse seriously about serious subjects. On the contrary, we talk seriously about frivolous things and frivolously about serious things. To the Greeks serious discourse on a variety of important topics was the essence of being human, and a richer and broader humanism was always the goal.

There were exceptions. Some rich citizens provided music and entertainment by jugglers for their guests. These guests enjoyed dallying with the "flute girls" both during the meal and after it. Xenophon in his *Symposium* recalls a feast at the home of the rich Callias in which the host provided a group of jugglers and the party turned into a conflict between Socrates, whose talk distracted attention from the show, and the Syracusan whose group had been hired for the entertainment of the guests.

The men dined as they reclined on couches with head rests while the women used straight chairs and small tables. The *pièce de résistance* was generally some kind of fish; eels and shark meat were especially popular. There was also dried fish from the Black Sea and other areas far removed from the Greek mainland. Beef, lamb, and pork were not nearly as important items of the diet as they had been in Homeric days. Cheese, bread, olives, and watered wine were, of course, a constant of the daily fare.

Cultivation of the *logos* was only one of the primary aims of Greek education. If for the moment we put aside physical training, cultivation of *arete* was the other. The Greek word *arete* has often wrongly been translated as *virtue,* which centuries ago in our tradition took on the coloration of goodness, or freedom from sin. *Arete* was something quite different. In the Homeric world it was equivalent to manliness; the noble and courageous warrior had *arete.* Later, the meaning of the word was broadened, and it came to mean *excellence,* but it was always a very special kind of excellence, and implied that which was characteristic of the source. For example, the *arete* of a philosopher would be profound and right thinking, the *arete* of a poet would be sensitivity to beauty and powerful writing, the *arete* of a judge or lawgiver would be a strong sense of justice, the *arete* of a woman would be chastity and devotion, the *arete* of a dog, if *arete* could be applied to an animal, would be loyalty. Each separate being achieving its fullest potential, this was *arete.*

Plato in his *Protagoras* gives a complete outline of Greek education around 400 B.C. His remarks refer to boys because it was the Greek tradition that girls be educated in the home, and the kind of education they received was clearly inferior. Plato wrote:

> Education and admonition commence in the very first years of childhood, and continue to the very end of life. Mother, nurse, father and tutor are all quarrelling about the improvement of the child as soon as he is able to

understand them. He cannot say or do anything without their setting forth to him that this is just and that is unjust; that this is honorable, and that is dishonorable; this is good, that is not good; do this, and abstain from that. And if he obeys, well and good; if not, he is straightened out by threats and blows, like a piece of warped wood.

Later the child went to school and had professional teachers. In order to make sure that the boys got to school without loitering they were accompanied by a *pedagogue,* which in Greek meant "an adult who walked along." This pedagogue was merely a slave who had charge of accompanying the master's sons safely to and from school, protecting them along the way. He did not teach anything. This slave "was often old and trusty, often old and useless, always ignorant, and never respected." The young boys invariably tried to take advantage of him.

At school one teacher was generally responsible for all subjects, at least in the early grades. After the boy had learned his alphabet and could read he was given the works of the great poets, especially those parts which contained admonitions or praise of the respected heroes of the race. The boy was also taught music, how to play the lyre, how to make the most of gymnastics, and how to dance.

The master of gymnastics occupied a very important place in the curriculum, because the Greeks firmly believed that only a strong body could produce a sharp and cultivated mind. By building up strong and well-trained bodies the schools also taught Greek boys never to play the coward in war or on any other occasion. When they were older still they all learned the laws, not only the specific statutes but also the philosophical and moral backgrounds on which all law rested. The importance of the entire educational system was that right mental attitudes, proper behavior, and the acquisition of knowledge could all be taught and were not the result of mere natural predisposition or divine grace. The right of men of genius to be above the law was also an axiom of Greek political and educational theory.

In the gymnasium and in all athletic games and contests young men participated in the nude. Some writers of those days make mention of boys eager to show off their bodies, and it is also reported that older men often gathered at the gymnasium in order to watch the exercises, although this was against the law. At Sparta an end was quickly put to the presence of hangers-on by adopting the rule: "Strip or get out!" The older men had no wish to humble themselves before the boys.

Up until the time of Aristotle, Greek education consisted of three parts: *letters,* which included reading, writing, learning the poets, and arithmetic;

music, which meant primarily learning how to play on the lyre; and *gymnastics,* which included specialized athletic training and dancing. Aristotle added a fourth division: *drawing;* which enabled a man to judge properly the great works of art. The Greeks did not study foreign languages for they felt that everybody else should learn Greek.

In gymnastics they were interested primarily in learning the proper *form,* even in the athletic contests; form meant being able to maintain a graceful and rhythmic action not only in dancing and ballplaying but even in the most violent physical exertion. After such violent exercise the athletes would rub their bodies with oil and then scrape off the excess with an instrument made for this express purpose. In prosperous times they also took a bath, but this was not the norm, for water was not abundantly available.

With this basic curriculum the ancient Greeks, especially the Athenians, produced a well-educated citizenry. A distinguished British classicist, J. P. Mahaffy, who wrote a book on the subject, said: "The Greeks were far behind us in the mechanical aids to human progress, but in spite of this, the Greek public was far better educated than we are—nay, to some extent, because of this it was better educated." The same authority points out that in ancient Greece the whole man was educated, and every man the same, in order to bring out his quality of humanness. There was thorough intellectual, political, moral, social, physical, and artistic training. This identical curriculum for all did not create a race of identical citizens to whom the notion of conformity was the norm; on the contrary, it served to bring out the quality of uniqueness which makes all individuals different, stimulating each to aspire to his own highest potential. In our own educational system, which proudly boasts of dozens upon dozens of school subjects and dozens upon dozens of departments in which specialization is the rule, this is something to think about.

"We hear it often repeated that human nature is the same at all times and in all places; and this is urged at times and places where it is so manifestly false that we feel disposed peremptorily to deny it when paraded to us as a general truth."* Human nature is indeed alike in its lower activities; when men act like animals there is a remarkable uniformity among them. But in what we might call the higher developments mankind varies greatly at all times and places. No two individuals are exactly alike and no two societies show any more similarity between them. The assumption, even in our own time, that the way of life, the moral

* J. P. Mahaffy, *Old Greek Education.*

principles of civil liberties and democratic government, the constitution, let us say, successfully worked out by one people can be transferred to another either by force or by wishful thinking is probably the most stupid blunder of our age.

Contemporary man takes pride in his humanity and justice, but in our time one of the most civilized of nations murdered in cold blood over five million persons because they represented another religion or were dissenters politically. In warfare nations today wipe out hundreds of thousands, including women and children, with a blink of the eye and a shrug of the shoulders. Even in the most civilized countries what is not seen is either felt not to have taken place or is said to be perfectly justified in view of the circumstances. Moral principles are preached from the pulpits but they do not prevail in the national or international life. The tragic human dilemma is that man can conceive of a better life than the one he seems capable of living.

It is necessary to make these comments before going on to those areas in which the Greeks acted in ways which we would call inhuman. One such practice was that of infanticide. In Sparta each baby was examined by a council of elders, and those found to be too weak or deformed were thrown off a cliff onto the rocks below. In Athens the father of a family, if he so wished, was allowed to "expose" an unwanted baby in order to get rid of it.

The babies of slaves seldom were allowed to survive, and many other infants were "exposed" if the father felt that his family was growing too large. Female infants were especially liable to this cruelty. The process was to place the baby in a large earthen vessel, a kind of rude cradle, and to leave it in the neighborhood of a temple or some other public place. There was at least some hope that another person might find and adopt the abandoned child.

Even Plato in his ideal state sanctions infanticide in the cases of babies who are weaklings or are deformed. How widespread infanticide was in actual practice we do not know, but we do know that Greek families were strictly limited. There is no reference in the literature or in the legal documents to very large families. Four children was about the absolute maximum; two was the norm, and very frequently these two did not survive beyond young adulthood.

Abortion was widely practiced, although it was against the law. Greek midwives were adept in getting rid of an unwanted fetus, and probably with no greater likelihood of infection or death on the part of the mother than pertains today with our own two or three million illegal abortions yearly. The citizenry of Attica declined by 50 percent in the first few decades that followed the outbreak of war with Sparta. Polybius, writing in the year 150 B.C., commented that many cities and fields of Hellas were becoming so deserted that in vast areas the land was yielding little fruit and human industries few products. In Macedonia a stringent law was passed forbidding infanticide and in a single generation the population jumped by 50 percent.

The Greeks continued to be "cruel" to their prisoners of war; killing or making slaves of them was the norm, and Thucydides reports one instance in which one thousand ringleaders of a revolt on Lesbos were executed by the Athenians. True, this was not a common practice in Athens. On the other hand, torture was a regular feature of the courts. The Greeks believed implicitly that by torturing a man they could force the truth out of him. Only state torturers were allowed to perform this job, and as might be expected in a slave society, accused slaves suffered most of the torment.

The execution of a condemned criminal, however, was much more "humane" than that which prevails in America today. The condemned person was allowed to have his family and friends visit him nightly, and on the day of the execution the jailer gave him a cup of hemlock (which by trial had been found to be the most humane way to execute a man), and he was told to take it by a certain hour. The jailer then left the condemned man with his family and friends, who remained with him chatting as life ebbed away, and finally closed his eyes when he was dead.

Women, alas, were second-class citizens in most of ancient Greece. They were taught reading, writing, and domestic science in the home, but few learned much beyond this. They seldom walked on the streets unless at a religious festival or at a funeral. Country women were freer, but doubtless led harder lives from the physical standpoint. Both Plato and Socrates admitted that women had the same faculties and capacities as men, but affirmed that they possessed them in lesser degree. Thucydides stated categorically: "That woman is best who is least spoken of among men, whether for good or for evil." The Spartans had a different attitude. Aristotle says it was the freedom of women that ruined Sparta.

Men, of course, were expected to have concubines for the health of their bodies. If they had none among the slaves at home, there were plenty of prostitutes available. Marriage was always arranged by the older members of the family who acted as matchmakers, much as they do in Greece today. Each side boasted of the fine qualities of its prospective groom or bride, a dowry was arranged, and when everything was settled the wedding took place. Marriage was mandatory even in Athens by the age of thirty in order to ensure the continuance of the race. (After Pericles this law became a dead letter.)

People seldom married for love, but a deep devotion between husband

and wife often appears in Greek literature: Odysseus and Penelope, Hector and Andromache, Orpheus and Eurydice, even Helen and Menelaus, if we are to believe Euripides. The miraculous transformation of a man or woman's character through romantic love, however, does not form a part of the Greek tradition.

Getting married in ancient Greece was both a solemn and a joyous occasion. Before the wedding the young bride would cut off a lock of her hair to give as an offering to Artemis, goddess of virginity, along with her toys and her girdle. On the day of the ceremony there was a ritual bathing of the bride, who then put on her veil and brightly colored bridal gown. At her home an animal was sacrificed and prayers were offered for her happiness and for her husband's future. The animal's gall bladder was taken out so that its bitterness would not influence the marriage. Then there was a great wedding feast after which bride and groom retired to their home, followed by their noisy friends, much as today. These friends remained for some time outside the dwelling to make teasing remarks and to sing bawdy songs. On the following day the bride took off her veil of virginity, and friends brought her gifts.

If the couple had a baby boy the father would place an olive branch above the threshold; if the baby was a girl, tufts of wool were used instead. Five days after the birth a female member of the family took the child in her arms and with the family following walked rapidly around the hearth, thus placing the infant under the protection of the household gods. Five days later the father formally accepted the child as his, and bound himself to provide for its care and education. When the mother's milk gave out, a clay bottle with a clay nipple was used to feed the baby. After this the nurse or some female family member first chewed the baby's food.

Greek children had many toys: humming tops, rattles, swings, seesaws, hobbyhorses, dolls, hoops, balls, stilts. Archytas, the philosopher, is credited with inventing the rattle, thus saving wear and tear on thumb and household articles. Children played hiding games, tossed up pebbles and caught them on the back of the hand, shot dried beans as marbles and animal knucklebones as dice, played a kind of soccer and also handball. They often tied a beetle to a thread and let it fly around. Leapfrog and blanket tossing were popular when the children got a little older.

There was a special class among the women of Greece known as "companions," or *hetairai*. These women usually belonged to the citizenry, but had for some reason fallen from social grace or else had willfully retired from it, and thus lived away from their families in places of their own. Such independence allowed the *hetairai* to have lovers, but they were not promiscuous. They took love seriously. Aspasia, who ran a school, was one of the most famous of the *hetairai,* for she later became the consort of Pericles and the uncrowned queen of Athens. Aspasia was a foreigner from Miletus, so Pericles could not marry her according to his own law. But when his wife fell in love with another man Pericles looked on it with favor, gladly gave her a divorce, and took Aspasia home with him. Aspasia left her school, which had become famous in Athens, and turned his house into a salon like those of the French Enlightenment. Her conversation and knowledge were noteworthy; Socrates praised her eloquence and intelligence and even remarked that she probably wrote some of Pericles' most famous discourses. Her golden hair and silvery voice were admired as much as her cultivated mind.

The *hetairai* were generally women of more than average intellect, but it was in the art of love that they all excelled. Many of them dyed their hair yellow, and they all wore robes decorated with flowers. The charm and beauty of Phryne of Athens sent many artists into a frenzy; she posed for the Aphrodites of both Praxiteles and the painter Apelles, Alexander's favorite.

Athenaeus reported that in the festival of the Eleusinians and in the festival of Poseidon Phryne took off her robes in view of all the Greeks, unbound her hair, and went into the sea. When she died the local people had a gold statue made of her and set it on a beautiful marble column at Delphi. It stood next to the statue of a Spartan king. Lais of Corinth was another equally famous model for painters and sculptors. Myron, Demosthenes, and Diogenes all adored her; she turned a cold shoulder toward the first two, but yielded to Diogenes for a mere token because it pleased her to have the love of a philosopher. When Lais died she was given a tomb worthy of a queen.

The women of Greece took a leaf from these *hetairai* when it came to artificial improvements of their own persons. High-heeled shoes became popular, and false hair, dyed hair, rouge, and pearl powder were all used in a woman's makeup. Many husbands, of course, objected to these things on their wives with the same warmth with which they had applauded them on others. In any case, if a man's wife lacked breeding or culture he was to blame. Socrates put it very bluntly: "If a sheep is in bad condition, we blame the shepherd, if a horse is mean, we abuse his rider; so if a husband neglects to teach his wife, is the fault not his?"

The greatest test of Greek humanism came with the bloody and long war between Athens and Sparta. Culture flowered in adversity, for during the war Athens continued to produce a great literature and art. Socrates, the noblest Athenian of them all, pursued his relentless search for truth. Sophocles probed into the destiny of man and never mentioned the war, Euripides meditated upon human character and warned of any trust in victory or revenge, Aristophanes openly ridiculed those who governed the state, preached vigorously against war, and satirized the Sicilian expedition of 415–413 which assured the defeat of Athens. These men were never gagged, and humanism, despite the war, enjoyed its most glorious moment.

But there was Alcibiades. He was at first the most brilliant general of the war on the side of the Athenians. He was inordinately handsome, vain, intelligent, proud, and utterly lacking in moral scruples. He was one of Socrates' most intimate friends and students. When he heard the admonitions of Socrates he was moved and ashamed, and the tears came to his eyes. He swore that he would improve himself. But his resolution was always short-lived, and invariably he returned to his shameless way of life.

Alcibiades more than anyone else was responsible for talking the Athenians into the war against Syracuse, for he appeared to believe that in Sicily Athens would find manpower, fertile lands, abundant food, and wealth. He was made co-commander of the expedition, but after the great convoy had already sailed, Alcibiades was indicted for having mercilessly mocked the sacred Eleusinian mysteries and a speedy ship was sent to bring him back for trial. He got on board, but when the vessel stopped at a port en route Alcibiades escaped and fled to Sparta.

On hearing that he had been condemned to death in his absence he passed over to the Spartan side and gave his hosts much sage advice about the prosecution of the war against his own city. While in Sparta he forsook his hedonistic way of life and lived like a good Spartan. The queen fell in love with him and by her he had a son; Alcibiades made sure that the whole town knew the boy was his. Perhaps he hoped that the child might be legitimized and that he would thus be father to a prince. But when the king returned to Sparta (he had been away for *ten* months) he was in a frenzy despite the old Spartan tradition of sexual freedom for wives, and Alcibiades fled to Ionia and joined the Persians.

He also gave them good advice about the weaknesses of his native *polis*. After a few years, however, he became disillusioned with his life in exile and by stages reingratiated himself with those who had come into control of the government in Athens. He was appointed as regional commander in the area of the Hellespont and defeated the Spartan fleet in 411. Four years later, in 407, he returned to Athens, where he was welcomed with enthusiasm. He was made a general of the army, but the Athenians still distrusted him and were never able to take full advantage of his incomparable military genius.

The disastrous Peloponnesian War ended in 404 with the capitulation of Athens. Spartan terms were unexpectedly generous, but fanned by the victors there was a clear change in the political wind and a conservative dictatorial government was installed by the defeated Athenians. Many thousands of democrats were exiled, most of them fleeing to Thebes. Fifteen hundred opponents of the tyrannical regime were executed. Critias, another intimate friend and student of Socrates, was one of the tyrants. After a few bloody months of the mailed fist, the democratic exiles mustered an army and swooped down on Athens; the tyrants met them with a miserably small body of men and were overwhelmed. Democracy was restored in the city.

Given a new lease on life politically, Athens was still in dire straits in every other regard. The city was almost bankrupt, her colonies were all gone, her army and navy were vanquished, she had lost a third of her population in the war either in battle or during the two violent outbreaks of plague, her wheat fields had been devastated. (Athens never recovered from this), and there was scarcely anything to eat. Conditions were in this critical state when Socrates was brought to trial in 399.

The old philosopher, then seventy, was accused of not believing in the gods in which the *polis* believed, of introducing into the city new gods, and of corrupting the youth. The penalty proposed was death. Instrumental in formulating this indictment was a man whose son had allegedly been "corrupted" by Socrates, that is, turned into a good-for-nothing drunkard. The jury of 501 men heard all the testimony in a single day and by a vote of 281 to 220, the death sentence was approved.

It is clear that a majority of the jury members linked Socrates with Alcibiades, the traitor, and with Critias, the tyrant, although in fact the philosopher was probably responsible for the only decent moments that either of these men lived. But when a people suffer greatly there is nothing like a scapegoat to relieve their sense of defeat, inadequacy, and frustration. Socrates, unfortunately, was the scapegoat.

He need not have died, but he chose to die with dignity rather than to accept exile or to flee in a cowardly fashion. The defense had the right of proposing an alternative sentence, and exile might have been proposed, and would probably have been accepted. Socrates refused. It was also the hope of some that the philosopher would at least repent officially and promise to be more careful in the future. But Socrates would not even consider that possibility. He said to the jury, "Men of Athens, I love and honor you, but

I shall obey God rather than you. If you kill such a one as I am, you will do far greater hurt to yourselves than to me. I will never cease to inquire and speculate about the condition of man and of all reality as long as I have life and strength. I am, to use a rather grotesque phrase, the gadfly of the state. You will not soon find another man like me."

Plato and other friends arranged bribes with the jailers and were all set to have the old man escape and flee, but Socrates would have none of it. He examined the possibility calmly, logically, as he had examined everything else in his life calmly and logically, and he refused to leave. When the jailer brought the cup of hemlock he drank it slowly, still chatting with his friends. Plato has recorded in his beautiful and dramatic prose the scenes at the court and Socrates' last days in his cell.

No ignorant and willful mob had condemned Socrates to death. Athens was then a city of defeated and suspicious men who had seen friends and relatives die because of the treacherous meanness of Alcibiades and the bloody hand of Critias. If there had been a Gallup Poll among the Athenians of that day Socrates would probably have been found guilty. Since the real god *polis* had collapsed, the one great god or spirit of the *polis* must have been betrayed. Socrates was regarded as the betrayer. Under similar circumstances he would probably be found guilty in many well-educated countries in our own time. One distinguished classical scholar, Kitto, says that the death of Socrates was a terrible Greek tragedy in which both sides were right. Has not every generation in history crucified its noblest men?

Socrates never wrote a sentence, but he was master of the *logos,* the spoken word, and his stimulating discourses made Plato, his pupil, possible. Plato, in his turn, made Aristotle possible. And perhaps we have here in immediate succession the three best-known and most worthy philosophers of the Western world. One scholar writes, "Among classical authors Plato is second in importance to Homer only, if even to him." The Greeks themselves evidently thought so because so many copies of Plato's works were made that his output has survived almost intact. Plato fled from Athens, however, when Socrates was killed, and he did not return for many years. It was clear to him that his *polis* was passing through a very ugly crisis.

Around the year 385 he did come back and established his famous Academy in a grove of trees sacred to the god Academus where a well-known gymnasium had been before. Some historians have called his Academy the world's first university, but it was more of an institute for advanced study than a university. In any case, it was Greece's first center of higher education, and it lasted until all institutions of "pagan" learning were closed by the Emperor Justinian in A.D. 529, nine hundred years later.

First Greeks, then great numbers of Romans came to the Academy to receive the benefits of a classical training. Many others attended the second famous institution of learning in Athens, the school founded by Isocrates, in which rhetoric and the *logos* composed the supreme and all-absorbing subject. This school provided a broader humanistic education than Plato's and from it emerged most of the literary writing of the following century. The Academy was more specialized and perhaps more personal, because Plato believed that true learning passed to the pupil from the master as a spark from a flame.

The curriculum of the Academy embodied the tenets of Plato's ideal education, which rested on an intense study of mathematics and the pursuit of justice and virtue. It was the furthest thing imaginable from a trade school. Mathematics was instruction in the order of the universe, as well as in shapes and numbers. The only realities were the "universals," the "abstracted ideas" back of the particularized physical. Strongly influenced by Greek Orphism, Plato scoffed at the Homeric gods and their scandalous conduct but he was a strong believer in one God and in the good; he also (like his mentor Socrates) believed in the immortality of the soul and was a clear precursor of Christianity. Throughout his life he was obsessed by the desire to abstract human experience and to restate it as philosophical essence. The physical universe (Socrates called it "the rabble of the senses") was a delusion; behind it stood the real truths, which were ideas. "Goodness," "justice," "beauty"—these are the only enduring realities. They are not touched by time or change. They make possible human knowledge, all of which is particularized. Without them and their reality knowledge and the world itself are but chimeras.

In his *Republic* Plato compares life on this earth to that of prisoners chained in an immobile position in a cave so that all they can see of what goes on outside consists of shadows. If after years of such living these prisoners were suddenly released, would they not still regard the shadows as the reality and the newly disclosed realities as the shadows? The true philosopher has gone through both experiences, is convinced that the second is the more real, and returns to the cave where the mass of men still live in order to convince them that they should come out of the shadows. Medieval Scholasticism accepted many of Plato's concepts as bases for its own Catholic philosophy. Only the soul was real.

Plato's ideal commonwealth was a highly regimented state, a kind of aristocratic communism, in which was maintained a correct equilibrium between physical and spiritual needs. Family life and private property almost disappeared, every citizen was to be educated to his capacity and at this point the inequalities of intellect and of will would begin to appear. Women and men must have equal opportunities to be educated and to hold positions.

A small group of older citizens whose intelligence, wisdom, and character had already been amply proved would govern the state. They would have neither property nor wives. There would be no laws because laws bound justice to precedent. While every citizen would be guaranteed an equal opportunity for instruction, all would be compelled to fall ultimately into those classes and kinds of work which were appropriate to their abilities as judged in a series of tests.

Philosophy would control this ideal state, direct its education, and guide its thought. Life would be made as simple and as selfless as possible so that the welfare of all would be the constant goal. Books which might lead to corrupt or wrong thinking would be prohibited; Plato even disliked Homer because he had made Achilles too self-willed and violent. Personal rights must be subordinate to community rights, for only the state had absolute validity; it must be dominated by "the idea of the good," what we moderns would call justice, and this good was fused with the state's religion. Therefore, antireligious thinking was not to be tolerated.

Plato's ideas sounded much like the teachings of the early Christian Church. They also recall the avowed aims of the Spanish church-state of the sixteenth century and many of the pronouncements of twentieth-century fascism under which the most fit were supposed to rule and the ministers of education rigidly controlled thought. Plato himself would doubtless have decried all of these parallels.

He might have found more amenable to his taste the virtuous zeal of the Puritans in the United States, but he was very careful to point out that he did not expect any state ever to become his ideal commonwealth. He was writing about an intangible limit toward which mankind might strive, and that was all. To Plato knowledge and virtue were inseparable and properly instilled would lead to his ideal of voluntary rule over voluntary subjects.

When Plato was about sixty there came to his Academy a young man of seventeen who studied with the master for the next twenty years, and when Plato died at the ripe age of eighty-one this disciple, Aristotle, raised an altar to his beloved master and on it wrote some beautiful words. Soon he was recognized as a philosopher in his own right and was invited to the court of Philip of Macedon to instruct the king's son, Alexander, then a boy of thirteen. For four years Aristotle held this position and taught the young prince what he could. When Alexander, at the age of twenty, fell heir to his father's expanded kingdom he was a thoroughly Hellenized young monarch.

So great was the young king's admiration for Homer that when he embarked on the military campaigns which led to his conquest of a good part of the then known world he carried along with him, in a special jewel-studded case taken from the defeated Persian king, a copy of the *Iliad*, annotated by Aristotle. In his tent at night Alexander frequently inspired himself by reading passages from this famous epic. When he went to bed he slept with it beside him.

Plato's great dream had been that statehood would take a leap forward when philosophers became kings or when kings became philosophers. He had his chance at making this dream a reality as tutor to the son of King Dionysius I of Syracuse, in Sicily, but he had not succeeded. Plato's disciple, Aristotle, in his turn enjoyed only a modicum of success with Alexander, but this was enough to make it possible for his impetuous young charge to Hellenize the world. Alexander always showed a profound respect for philosophy. In a letter he wrote to Aristotle: "I would far rather surpass others in the knowledge of what is excellent than in the extent and power of my dominion."

Alexander, who was not himself a Greek, was destined to achieve both goals for Hellas. Under him Egypt became a Greek colony, Alexandria (which he had founded) became the most populous, most cosmopolitan, and wealthiest Greek-speaking city of the Hellenistic world, and Greek culture soon thoroughly permeated the fabric of Roman civilization. When Alexander died Hellas was at her peak; soon afterward began the decline, at first imperceptible, then increasing in pace, until at last the lifeblood was all but drained away.

The idea of a united Greece forming one great nation was not, of course, original with Alexander. Isocrates of Athens had vociferously espoused a union of the Greek states and a war on Persia. When Alexander's father, Philip, had embarked on this course, Isocrates felt that his dream was on the way to becoming a reality. Philip, indeed, had many supporters among the disunited Greeks, one group always hoping with his aid to unseat another.

But there were also among the Greeks many who opposed any kind of union and harked back to the good old days after Marathon and Salamis when the independent *polis* had stood supreme and glorious. Demosthenes, the Athenian, was one such superpatriot. The star that guided his life was to uphold the old values and to defy Philip of Macedon. While his colleagues argued for collaboration with Philip, Demosthenes denounced the Macedonian king in a series of great orations so filled with invective and acrimony that any such speech has ever since been called a *Philippic*.

Demosthenes was the last of the great orators, and he used methods which some of the older hands would not have sanctioned. He moved his arms about when he spoke, he sawed the air, he contorted his face to achieve the proper expression, and he used his voice like a musical instrument. He practiced speaking with pebbles in his mouth in order to perfect his enunciation, and he also ran until out of breath and then forced his words out loud and clear. He rehearsed before the mirror in order to perfect his pose, his expression, his gestures, and his delivery. When at last Philip swooped down upon Athens, Demosthenes thought his last day had come, but Philip was extremely generous toward the defeated Athenians, whose culture he greatly admired.

Demosthenes not only survived, he lived to repeat his anti-Macedonian tirades against Alexander and was not finally condemned and hunted down until Alexander's successor took over Greece. Demosthenes had fled from Athens and was on a nearby island when the pursuers closed in on him; he cheated them by committing suicide. It was one year after the death of Alexander, 322, the same year that saw the death of Aristotle. The great days of Athens were ended.

The Greeks invented philosophy, which means literally "a loving of wisdom." Their wisest men attempted to give rational explanations of the origin and nature of the universe and of the operation of its various laws. Matter, energy, spirit, justice, virtue, and order were but a few of the things that intrigued Greek philosophers and still intrigue us today, because they raise questions which have no final answers. Socrates, Plato, and Aristotle, whose lives followed in sequence, were probably the greatest philosophers the world has ever produced, and they all came from a tiny city-state with a total population of not more than 300,000. Does not our century appear dark by comparison?

Socrates was the original inquirer. By questioning he led men down all the mind's dark corridors to think and to search for truth even at the cost of life. Plato was of a more mystical turn of mind; he probed into the depths of the human condition, he abstracted essence, he eschewed the physical world, he was in love with justice and with virtue. He was the philosopher par excellence, and all succeeding philosophies have used his works as a starting point. Aristotle was primarily a scientist; he established the basis of the scientific method. But science in those days, of course, was not a vast accumulation of empiric knowledge. It was conjecture and experimentation on a very thin basis of observed reality.

Aristotle made hundreds of mistakes, but his inquiring mind hit the nail on the head as many times as he missed it. The over-all average is not bad, even for a scientist today. In the latter years of his life Aristotle founded and directed studies in the third of ancient Greece's famous schools. He called his institution the Lyceum and in it provided a variety of courses for those of a scientific turn of mind. His scholarly ideals were later transplanted to Egypt and flowed even more profusely in the generations of scholars connected with the famous library at Alexandria.

There were no limits to Aristotle's curiosity; he was an eclectic who studied everything: physics, biology, astronomy, philosophy, mathematics, mechanics, metaphysics, psychology, ethics, politics, aesthetics. He wrote what is probably the most heart-rendingly human statement of all time: "Probably every art and every philosophy has been repeatedly developed to the utmost and has perished again."

He also established logical reasoning by using condensed syllogisms, an approach which fascinated St. Thomas Aquinas, who used the same method to prove his own Christian beliefs sixteen centuries later. But Aristotle was no Greek St. Thomas; he believed in working for the development of man's highest potential of intellect, not for the improvement of his virtue or for the salvation of his soul. His twenty-seven popular dialogues, which Cicero considered as beautifully written as Plato's, have all been lost. The Aristotle we know is revealed to us by his dullest technical essays and a few fragments.

In spite of all their respect for intellectualism, philosophy, and humanism the Greeks knew nothing of individual liberty. The state was always more important than freedom of conscience. If a man showed too much disregard for the gods of the state or was too free in his speech he was in for trouble, as the death of Socrates plainly tells us. Separation of religion and state was unthinkable; they had been one since the very beginning. It was inconceivable that the state could survive without the gods who were its especial guardians. It was the *polis* that mattered, not the individual. Diogenes, who is reported to have said, "I am a citizen of the world," was a voice crying in the wilderness.

Plato wrote that "the children belong less to their parents than to the *polis*." And even Plato in his *Laws* (a product of his old age) stipulated that in his ideal state it is obligatory to believe in a virtuous divinity. Those who dissent, Plato wrote, must be persuaded to the *right thinking,* and a man found twice guilty of "impiety" would be regarded as incorrigible and condemned to death because of the danger he represented to the state.

Greek civilization recognized no "inalienable rights" given to man by his Creator. It was the state which granted man all his rights, reserving to itself the prescription of beliefs as well as of duties. True, with the passing of time many of the more rigid laws of an earlier age became dead letters, but it is well to remember that no Greek state ever regarded itself as the guardian of individual liberty.

This ideal of Western man, not always observed in practice but in all good times still held inviolable by our dreaming, is a precious distillation of all the centuries of human history which have gone before us. It is the last best fruit of civilization, made possible only by aeons of struggle and of suffering. On the other hand, the naked isolation of the individual in today's world, tossed about as he is between aspiration, chance, and nothingness, was something that no ancient Greek ever had to endure. He was an integral part of his society and culture; he always *belonged* completely; his life was the measure of all values.

The citizen of Athens at its heyday might proudly say to himself: "Greece is the center of the world, Attica is the center of Greece, Athens is the center of Attica, the Acropolis is the center of Athens. When I stand upon the Acropolis I am at the center of everything."

XIII

The Universal State:
Roman Greece—The Byzantine Empire

Captive Greece made captive her rude conqueror.

Horace

The ancient Greeks had all the accouterments of creativity: an insatiable zeal for life, a stupendous curiosity, a concept of what was beautiful, the will to give it form, a love of the idea above the physical reality, a profound belief in the glory of man. The Greeks thought and felt life itself as a form of art. Their two ideals were *polis* and culture. They had no wish to sacrifice for collective Hellas. They never formed a nation. Their cosmos was all ego. Their political and social organisms were sound philosophically but had no roots in the popular fancy and no way to grow. Culture and community were more important than expansion of the *polis*.

When the Romans conquered Greece they reversed many of the above statements. Their universal state, followed by its universal church, was a miracle of organization. They were not without culture, but they believed that the state was the most important element in their lives because it was the state that they had created, and not the culture, which they had taken from the Greeks. And, after all, were not the Greeks now the slaves of the Romans? This judgment, as is usual in history, was deduced from their exhilarating success. New sets of values inevitably follow in the footsteps of victory.

The Roman conquest of Greece was a gradual thing and extended over half a century. The Romans captured Syracuse, the last important Greek colony in Sicily, in 212 and soon thereafter were engaged in large-scale warfare in Greece. They were eager to even the score with the Greeks, who under Pyrrhus of Epirus had invaded Italy in 280 B.C., driving to within twenty miles of Rome. In the Second Macedonian War (200–196) a Roman army, with considerable Greek help, conquered Hannibal's ally, Philip V of Macedon. This time the Romans played the role of "liberators" of Greece from Macedonian rule. It was a misnomer, as the Greeks soon learned, but for a time they were taken in because the Roman general, Flamininus, appeared at the Isthmian Games at Corinth and loudly proclaimed the independence of Greece. The assembled multitude hailed him as savior. Flamininus, an avid philhellenist, was probably sincere, but the Romans who followed him were not much interested in Greek independence.

A Third Macedonian War broke out in 171, and after four more years of fighting Rome suppressed the Achaean League, sacked seventy cities of Epirus, made slaves of 150,000 of their inhabitants, and sent a thousand noble Greeks back to Rome as hostages. Among these was the famous historian Polybius, who went to the home of the Scipios. He became a great admirer of Rome and the most notable apologist for the extension of her sway, which he regarded as a boon.

Not all Greeks concurred. The city of Corinth chafed under the Roman bit and finally rebelled. The consul Lucius Mummius, whose name has gone down in infamy, was sent to quell the revolt. He took the city, burned it mercilessly, enslaved its inhabitants, and sent its art treasures back to Rome (146 B.C.), the same year that Carthage fell leaving Rome unchallenged in the Mediterranean. Mummius was such an uncultivated clod that when he contracted for the transportation to Italy of these Greek masterpieces of paintings and sculpture he made the condition that if any of the items were lost the carriers would have to supply new ones!

Romans now began coming to Greece in droves in order to be educated, and Greek slaves formed a countercurrent which flowed toward Rome carrying Greek culture like a great tide. For all intents and purposes the two cultures were blended to form the Greco-Hellenic heritage which became the basis of Western civilization.

Athens was the great university and center of art to many Romans. In 86 B.C. Sulla entered the city with his soldiers, killing and plundering as he went. The Athenians pointed to the Acropolis and Sulla is reputed to have said, "I spare the many for the sake of the few, the living for the sake of the dead." Later, in 48 B.C., Athens sided with Pompey, who lost to Caesar, and Caesar spared the city saying, "How many times will the glory of your ancestors save you from your own mistakes?" In 42 B.C. the Athenians again took the wrong side with Brutus and Cassius against Mark Anthony, but Anthony, instead of punishing them, brought gifts. Octavian did the same a decade later. In A.D. 66 Nero plundered Athens and all Greece of works of art to rebuild Rome after the great fire, but by this time Greece and Rome were merged in one.

Christianity, the new religion which displaced the old, was the activating heart of this process. It was an amalgam itself, a fusion of ancient pagan and Hebrew beliefs with those of the followers of Christ, or, shall we say, with the contemporary beliefs of a dynamic Jewish minority within the Roman Empire. Greek religion, Greek philosophy, Greek literature, Greek art—the entire corpus of Hellenic culture now emptied into the Christian melting pot. The pagan world of Greek antiquity was completely recast by the new religion. Greece became Christian before Rome, and the Greeks were ready to receive the words of Christ long before Paul brought them to Greece. These words were a blend of Greek philosophy and Oriental mysticism, and the soil and mind of Hellas had long since been plowed for the new harvest.

The ancient Greek parallel of Christian doctrine was the Orphic mystery religion, which had its roots in Asia and Egypt, and which continued very much alive in Greece in the rituals of the Eleusinian Mysteries, the Dionysian festivals, the esoteric cults of Corinth, etc. According to this Orphic belief, the body was "unclean, transient, contemptible," while the human soul was "eternal and indestructible." Plato's philosophy embraced this element of Orphism, which had come into Greece from the Near East.

It is no wonder that Plato became the greatest agent of Hellenization among the leaders of Greek thought, for his basic approach to life was already an appealing blend of Greek and non-Greek elements. The very cornerstone of his *Republic* was the duality of life, the earthy body versus the eternal soul, and Plato's gaze was fixed absolutely on the eternal world, which to him was the real world, while the one that we know is only a shadow.

A century later, after Greece had been overwhelmed by Philip and Alexander and had begun to lose her old independent spirit, conditions were ripe for the rise of an "otherworldly" kind of philosophy of an even more drastic nature. Zeno provided this in Stoicism, which advocated the suppression of the body appetites as a way toward perfection of soul, whose final stage, even on earth, might be to achieve union with the divine. Stoicism brought together many of the best ideas of previous Greek philosophies. It was the last effort of the pagan mind to formulate a system of moral values and spiritual goodness for those who had already abandoned the old gods.

Around 314 Zeno (who was himself half Semitic) came to Athens from Cyprus and for forty years preached about the Supreme Intangible God and the brotherhood of all men. He made no distinction between rich and poor, freemen and slaves, and spoke of the one God who dwells in every man. This was not a God apart, but a God within. Zeno led such an admirable life in Athens that the city presented him with a golden crown and built him a tomb at public expense. St. Paul, 350 years later, also speaking to the Athenians, affirmed that his God was not to be found "in temples made with human hands," but that He was at the side of every man, "for in him we live and move and have our being." The similarity between the two doctrines is obvious.

The Stoic philosophy also caught on in Rome. Edith Hamilton in *The Roman Way* states that "a second-rate Greek philosophy developed into a first-rate Roman religion." The Romans were not interested in the abstract; what they wanted was something practical for the betterment of mankind. They found it first in Stoicism, and later in Christianity, which was Stoicism plus the charisma of the early evangelists who interpreted the life of Christ.

To the Stoics, man, caught in the midst of the imperial mire, maintained an invulnerable dignity and serenity. Through sheer will he was the architect of his destiny. The Stoic believed in controlling the lusts of the flesh and in pursuing right action regardless of consequences. "Virtue," wrote Seneca, "is its own reward." He also said, "God does not leave a good man in prosperity. He tries him, He strengthens him. He prepares him for Himself . . . I do not obey God—I agree with Him."

And Epictetus, the slave, affirmed that he had embraced freedom, which no power on earth could take from him. When others taunted, "But the emperor has the power to put you to death . . ." Epictetus answered, "He cannot imprison my spirit. He has only the power to cut off my head." To Epictetus dying in one's faith was the final freedom and meant eternal victory over one's executioner. Was this not also the Christian belief?

But there was another swing of the pendulum. The old values of Homer still survived in Greece, and these found their noblest exponent in Epicurus, who had attended Plato's Academy at the age of nineteen (around 321 B.C.), and drew up his philosophy as a specific protest against that of Platonism. Epicurus himself wished above all else to live unobtrusively and happily. He thought that in order to achieve happiness, which was the highest goal, man must be freed from fear, and fear of the gods was perhaps the greatest fear of all. Certainly this was the case if one followed the admonitions of Plato.

Epicurus did not deny the existence of the gods, but he did affirm that they had no interest in the affairs of men, that they could not be reached by prayer, and that man should live *as if* they did not exist. The human soul, he preached, was inseparable from the body, and when the body died the soul died with it, just as thought, which is a function of the brain, dies with the brain. Philosophy could never explain the world, Epicurus thought, but it could serve as a guide to wise behavior. If man would live naturally, taking all things in moderation, he could conquer every dread, even the dread of death, and he would find happiness, goodness, and tranquillity.

Epicurus and Epicureanism were close to the feeling of the Book of Ecclesiastes in the Old Testament:

> For the living know that they shall die: but the dead know not any thing
> . . . There is nothing better for a man, than that he should eat and drink,
> and that he should make his soul enjoy good in his labour . . . For there
> is no work, nor device, nor knowledge, nor wisdom, in the grave, whither
> thou goest. . . . I have seen all the works that are done under the sun;
> and, behold, all is vanity and a striving after wind. That which is crooked
> cannot be made straight, and that which is wanting cannot be numbered . . .
>
>> *To everything there is a season,*
>> *And a time to every purpose under the heaven:*
>> *A time to be born, and a time to die;*
>> *A time to plant, and a time to pluck up that which is planted;*
>> *A time to kill, and a time to heal . . .*

The Book of Ecclesiastes, by an unknown author of the second century before Christ, is so heretical that had it not been erroneously ascribed to Solomon it would never have been preserved among the Sacred Jewish Scriptures or been included in the Christian Bible. It echoes profoundly the Greek Epicurean way of life.

Epicurus himself was a kindly, generous, loving, and moderate man. He did not believe in regaling the body appetites as the way to happiness, despite what many of his followers claimed in later years. But he was a joyous skeptic, and when Christianity came into vogue bringing its early puritanism into Greek and Roman life Epicureanism was one of its natural targets.

The Romans also regarded Epicureanism as a subversive doctrine because they needed fear of the gods in order to keep the populace in its place. Consequently, the only reports which have survived concerning Epicurus are by his enemies and can hardly be considered objective. In any case, it very soon did not matter, for the new mystery religion from the East which took root in Rome when Peter became its rock eventually swept everything before it, and in the end became the universal (catholic) Roman church.

Despite the magnitude of Alexander's conquests, when the young general died at the age of thirty-three his empire fell apart as his lieutenants squabbled over the remains of the imperial feast. But the bond of a common language and a common Hellenic culture preserved the cultural unity of the Greek-speaking world for many centuries to come. In Egypt a dynasty of Macedonian Ptolemies ruled that country for three hundred years. Cleopatra, last of the line, was a direct descendant of the first King Ptolemy. She still observed the Macedonian court etiquette and her language was Greek.

Cleopatra was probably a blonde; she was not beautiful but she possessed a wanton grace and intelligence which made men lose their hearts. Both Julius Caesar and Mark Anthony went crazy over her. She and Mark Anthony were defeated by Octavian (Augustus Caesar) at the naval battle of Actium just off the western coast of Greece on September 2, 31 B.C., in one of the most decisive encounters of history. The following year both Cleopatra and Anthony committed suicide in Egypt and Octavian took control of the entire Mediterranean world. The Hellenistic age was ended. Egypt, however, remained Greek in culture for another six centuries until A.D. 643, when it was conquered by the Arabs.

Alexandria, Cleopatra's capital, was the second largest city (after Rome itself) and the most cosmopolitan metropolis of the empire. Immediately after its founding in 332 B.C. it had become a thriving and populous center of the Hellenistic world. In industry, commerce, and culture it soon occupied the first place. Its famous library, its museum and university, and its lighthouse were among the great achievements of the ancients. Egyptians, people from the Near East, Jews, Arabs, Persians, Greeks, and Macedonians all flocked to the emporium of the Mediterranean.

There was an extremely large Jewish colony in the city, and at least one authority, Philo, himself a Jew, claimed that 40 percent of the total population was Jewish. It was probably about half that much. The Jews were restricted to a certain section of the town, and anti-Semitism existed in those early days just as it did later. The Jewish historian Josephus gives a full account of it. In this case it was the pagan population which manifested its prejudice against the more puritanical and theistic Jews, who looked down their noses at the many gods and "the flesh-pots" of Egypt.

These Egyptian Jews were proud of their immense synagogue, whose hall was so large that special signals had to be instituted so that those in the rear would know when to respond, for hearing the rabbi was out of the question. The sacred readings were originally in Hebrew or Aramaic, but after a generation or two the Alexandrian Jews forgot both of these languages completely, and the congregation had no idea what was being said in the services. The only language they knew was Greek.

As a consequence, at the special request of Ptolemy II and the high priest Eleazar a group of Jewish scholars who knew both Greek and Hebrew was sent from Jerusalem to Alexandria in order to translate the Old Testament into Greek. Actually, there were seventy-two translators in the group, but the number seventy stuck in the popular mind, and the translation they made (288–247 B.C.) was known as the Septuagint, from the Latin *septuaginta*, seventy.

The Greeks in Alexandria assembled the finest library of antiquity. Manuscripts were collected from all over the ancient world and sent to the city where they were housed in a special building. Most of Plato's library wound up here. Around the Alexandrian collection arose a group of scholars who not only utilized the manuscripts but also formed the basis of a great "university." During the same period that the Old Testament was being translated several of the scholars headed by Zenodotus made a careful study of the Homeric poems.

A century later, around 150 B.C., the renowned Aristarchus of Samothrace, head of the library, set himself the task of editing a definitive text of Homer. With the aid of other Alexandrian scholars he examined all the available manuscripts, threw out spurious passages, made critical notes on words of uncertain meaning, and finally "published" his edition from which was derived the text of the Homer that we have today. He knew a great deal more about the ancient Homeric idiom than Zenodotus, so his interpretive as well as editorial work was much superior.

Greek was the language of culture throughout the Mediterranean world despite the dominion of Rome. Greek works of art adorned Rome and other cities of the empire. Greek philosophers lectured in Rome and were regarded as the leaders of thought. The Emperor Hadrian spoke Greek fluently and spent many years in Athens, where he held court, built the library, the great arch, and completed the colossal Temple of the Olympian Zeus. Hadrian dressed like a Greek, had Greek advisers, and worshiped Greek gods. The wealthy Attic rhetorician, merchant and politician, Herodes Atticus (A.D. 101–177), welcomed Hadrian to Athens, and he was also the teacher and friend of the Emperor Marcus Aurelius, who later wrote his famous *Meditations* in Greek.

When Paul preached the gospel in Greece he of course spoke Greek, and Hellas was the first country to accept Christianity. Speaking to the Athenians (circa A.D. 50) Paul accused them of being too superstitious, then pointed at their altar TO THE UNKNOWN GOD, saying, "Whom therefore ye ignorantly worship, him declare I unto you. God that made the world and all things therein, seeing that he is Lord of heaven and earth, dwelleth not in temples made with hands."

The entire New Testament was written in Greek, and all the early bishops of Rome (thus began the Papacy) were Greek and conducted services in that language. Many of the early Church Fathers were also Greek: Origen of Alexandria, Clement, Basil, Gregory, Polycarp, and Athanasius. They blended Hellenism with Christianity, and transformed a Jewish sect (some say a Jewish heresy) into a dynamic Greco-Roman church.

Greek literature was well known in Rome, and Roman literature imitated but never equaled it. Homer was profoundly revered. The Stoic philosophy permeated Rome and made many converts, among them the great Marcus Aurelius. Greek art was the basis for Roman art. The poet Horace, who lived at the time of Octavian (just before Christ) summarized what was taking place in his famous line: *"Captive Greece made captive her rude conqueror."*

The population of the Roman Empire at its peak around A.D. 100 totaled perhaps 70 millions, of whom 45 million spoke Greek. The other principal elements in the empire were some 20 million Gauls and Spaniards, and from 5 to 8 million Italian Romans. Two centuries later the western part of the empire was clearly disintegrating. The Emperor Constantine in A.D. 330 transferred his capital from Rome to Byzantium on the Bosporus, which had been a Greek city for a thousand years.

The principal truth about Greek culture is that it was (and is) a continuous blending. Minoan merged into Mycenaean, Mycenaean into Dorian, Dorian into Archaic, Archaic into Classic, Classic into Hellenistic, Hellenistic into Roman, Roman into Byzantine, Greco-Roman Byzantine into the revival of learning known as the Renaissance, and finally the Renaissance into our complex modern Western European civilization. Similar parallels would apply to the evolution of European religion as it moved from paganism into Christianity. Its original earthy symbolism became increasingly complex and mystical in the hands of time. To the ancient Greeks, for example, the dove was sacred to Aphrodite. Perhaps it was a symbol of the sex of the female human being. Doves were also the only birds used in Hebrew sacrifices; they stood for a flawless purity and were worthy of being a divine offering.

Vergil tells of two doves guiding Aeneas to the gloomy vale in which grew the Golden Bough (we might say "burning bush") which was the sacred vine of ancient mythology. This was supposed to be a divine plant which shone with a brilliant light and symbolized the sacred altar fire and the eternal spirit, eternal creativity. In actuality, it was probably the mistletoe caught in a ray of sunlight.

The followers of Christ saw a dove appear when their Master was baptized and considered it to be the Holy Ghost. Vessels holding the sacred oblations for the sacrament of the Last Supper were often made in the shape of a dove. Early Christians also believed that the soul left the body in the form of a dove or in the form of a phoenix, much as the ancient Greeks believed that it took the form of a butterfly.

We have already told in Chapter X about the slain, dismembered, eaten, and resurrected gods of Greece (Orpheus, Dionysus, Persephone) which symbolized the earthly seasons and the continuous renewal of life. In the springtime of civilization men saw the divine spirit as an ever-present, all-encompassing force which could easily be felt and seen. Nature and God were one. The creative principle of the universe was always visible in the ever-burning altar fire. Life was continuous, constantly renewed, an unbroken chain in which each individual was linked inseparably with his ancestors.

Plato and the Stoics refined this thinking in philosophical terms acceptable to the more enlightened Greeks. But it was Plotinus of Alexandria (born around A.D. 203) who gave the final summation to idealistic Greek philosophy just before it merged with Roman Christianity. Plotinus, known as the last of the great philosophers, was an Egyptian with a Latin name and a Greek education. He studied in Alexandria and then went to Rome, where his mature years were spent. Amid the revelry and pleasure-seeking of the Eternal City Plotinus lived a life of abstinence and was respected as a saint. His teachings were listened to with awe. He was the founder of Neoplatonism, and his stress on the spirit essence of human life made him a notable link between paganism and Christianity.

Plotinus regarded the body as a restraint; it confined and limited the soul. He refused to allow his portrait to be made and he would not indulge his body senses. The end purpose of life, he thought, was to establish a union with the transcendent creative principle, the *logos* of the universe. In this lay the great potential of man. The Christians regarded Christ as the manifestation of the *logos* in human form.

Plotinus prepared the minds of the Romans to accept this regenerating spirit of Christ which inspired men to lead good and beautiful lives. "Beauty is in the eye of the beholder," Plotinus said. "There is nothing in itself beautiful or ugly in the universe. It is a matter of soul. But what resemblance is there between things that are beautiful in this world and those that are beautiful in infinity? How are they alike? It is, we say, because they share in an eternal idea, an eternal form."

Plotinus and Greek philosophy helped to spread Christianity in Rome, but it was the Roman Emperor Constantine who made the empire Christian. Constantine was the illegitimate son of Constantius, emperor of the western part of the Roman Empire, which under Diocletian had already begun to split into two segments. Its eastern capital was at Nicomedia, near Greek Byzantium, while the western capital was moved from Rome to Milan in order to be nearer the northern frontier of Italy, which was menaced by the barbaric tribes.

When his father died in 306 Constantine replaced him as emperor of Britain and Gaul. In the year 312 he marched into Italy and defeated Maxentius, whose troops had proclaimed him emperor of Italy. On the eve of the battle between the two contenders Constantine reported that he had seen in the sky a cross of light on which appeared in Greek these words: *In this sign conquer*. That night Christ appeared to Constantine in a vision and instructed him to fashion a banner like this sign. The emperor followed this advice and won an overwhelming victory.

The following year (313) the famous Edict of Milan proclaimed religious freedom throughout Constantine's dominions, which meant primarily freedom for the Christians. A few years later (323) Constantine acknowledged that he himself had become a Christian, and exhorted his people to follow him. By this time he had defeated all adversaries and made himself emperor of the whole Roman Empire. He established himself at his capital Nicomedia in the east. The Greco-Roman world had a new religion, but it enjoyed no peace. In no time at all the Christian subjects of the Emperor Constantine were scrapping among themselves.

The first great split over church doctrine was caused around 325 by a priest in Egypt named Arius, who held that Christ was not of one substance with the Father. The son was divine in his great goodness, but he was not the same as God. He was only the *logos,* the most perfect of all created beings. Arius was not alone in this belief; he and his coreligionists soon constituted a strong minority clique within the Church. A terrible dispute arose over this point of doctrine and Arius was unfrocked by his bishop. The Emperor Constantine was disturbed by this. He had already seen the wisdom of utilizing the new Church as an instrument of state policy, for by announcing himself as a convert he had immediately won the support of millions of dedicated Christians and soldiers. (Quite the opposite of what was suggested by Stalin's irreverent quip: "How many soldiers does the Pope have?")

Constantine, therefore, recently entrenched in his position with Christian support, had no intention of now allowing his Church to splinter and thus lose its strength along with its unity. In a letter sent to both Arius and the bishop who had unfrocked him the emperor referred to the cause of the dispute as "trifling" and to the uproar it had caused as "the silly reactions of inexperienced children, and not of priests and reasonable men." The letter, unfortunately, fell on deaf ears.

The pagans, in the meantime, were having a field day making jokes about the squabbling Christians, at least some of whom appeared to have several gods, just as they had. So, in the year A.D. 325, Constantine called the Council of Nicaea, attended by 318 bishops of the faith, to discuss and to reach a decision in regard to Christian dogma. The emperor apparently cared little what was decided so long as a decision was reached.

The vote was overwhelmingly against Arius, for in the end only two of the bishops present voted against the statement that Christ and the Holy Spirit were both of one substance with the Father. Therefore, the Christians now really had three gods in One, as the Hindus had had before them. It was a strange way to avoid polytheism, but it had the mass support of the hierarchy and it stuck.

In less time than it takes to tell about it Christians were talking of the "Arian heresy," and from this it was but a step to silencing all those within the Church who were unwilling to accept the newly proclaimed Christian beliefs. The Arians, for their part, just as zealously persecuted the Roman Catholics whenever they had the chance.

It is amusing that the finicky and pernickety followers of Arius at the Council of Nicaea were willing to accept the Nicene Creed if they were allowed to add one single letter to one single word in that famous creed. They wanted to change the Greek word *homoousion* (of the same substance) to *homoiousion* (of a similar substance), that is, Christ was "like" his Father but was not consubstantial. The opponents of Arius, equally contumacious and pernickety, would not budge one inch, or, should we say, would not budge one "i," one "iota." Thus, a dispute over *one letter*, and the smallest letter in the alphabet at that, divided the Christian world for centuries!

One could not tell this at the time, for the Council's proclaimed creed was accepted by all but Arius and two of his partisans, who were promptly excommunicated. The Nicene Creed still forms the basis for most of the Christian dogma of today and is recited verbatim in many churches. Its acceptance appeared to be so complete just after the Council had met that the new Christian Church considered itself to be the "universal," that is, the "catholic," church, and thus assumed this name.

But beliefs die hard, and beliefs that are subject to compulsion die hardest of all. The Arian interpretation persisted in the underground Byzantine Church throughout the following centuries. It was also widespread among the Romanized Nordic tribes and its shadow was one of the main causes of the final split between the Eastern (Greek Orthodox Church) and the Roman Catholic Church in the year 1054.

The French Visigoths were fervid Arians, as were the Lombards who invaded Italy in the sixth century and the Vandals who had preceded them. Also, when the Visigoths conquered Spain in the sixth century they brought Arianism into that country. These Visigothic Arians vigorously persecuted the Roman Catholics of Spain as they had previously persecuted those of France.

In its early years Christianity was a dynamic, virtuous, and morally persuasive religion. Its adherents lived purer and more honest lives than did its pagan adversaries. Christians were willing to die but not to kill for their beliefs. Their early martyrs were often examples rightly held up for the admiration of mankind. But when the Christians changed their position from minority to majority, they also changed from persecuted to persecutors.

The single fixed doctrine became essential to the universal church. There had to be one God only, one *kind* of God, and one church as His instrument, hence the old polytheism, in whatever shape, manner, or form should not be tolerated. Christians, therefore, were clearly not believers in religious freedom once they had achieved freedom for their own beliefs. A glorious beginning had everywhere become fanatical. This is the way history goes, from tolerance to intolerance, from inspiring nobility of faith to compulsion of dissidents. It is little wonder that contemporary man feels he cannot be truly free until he has killed the last god.

When the pagan epoch of religious tolerance ended, with it disappeared for centuries philosophy, nonreligious literature, and inspiring art. The language of the Byzantine Empire was Greek, its cultural and artistic heritage also were Greek, but all the ancient Greek gods were dead. A Jewish heresy now reigned supreme in the Roman empire. The ancient world was shattered and ancient civilization was no more. But rooted in the new religion a new culture soon emerged to shed compassionate petals over a tomb. The Middle Ages were thus conceived.

Constantine not only made Rome officially Christian, but he decided to establish a new and permanent capital of the empire in the East (A.D. 330). The place chosen was Byzantium, an old Greek settlement named after Byzas, the Greek who had founded it in the eleventh century B.C. Constantine refounded and renamed the city after himself, Constantinople. The new capital occupied a magnificent situation on the Golden Horn and was a perfect gateway between Europe and Asia. The emperor constructed great walls around the city and built himself a luxurious palace.

Constantine also put up many other beautiful buildings and adorned his capital with great works of art from all over the Greek world: the colossal Athena Promachos from Athens, the giant statue of Zeus by Praxiteles from Olympia, statues from the Pergamene school, pieces of sculpture from Rhodes and many other islands. Later, the famous bronze horses (wrongly attributed to Lysippus) were brought to Constantinople. Of all these works only the Hellenistic bronze horses now remain. They decorate the Cathedral of St. Mark in Venice, having been plundered from Constantinople in 1204.

The Greek world had been despoiled in order to embellish the new capital, which soon outshone both Rome and Alexandria in size and splendor. As time passed, Constantinople became less and less Roman and more and more Hellenic. Latin was replaced by Greek as its language, and the Eastern Greek Orthodox Church gradually drew away from that of Rome.

But Constantinople was never a truly Greek city. There were too many cosmopolitan elements in its makeup: Romans from Italy and the West, various peoples from Asia Minor, civilized barbarians, and Greeks from all over the Hellenic world. Oriental influences were especially strong, far stronger than they had ever been in Greece or in the Hellenic Near East in previous centuries. The new capital fused all of these diverse elements and soon became the center of a new culture: *the Byzantine.*

This Byzantine culture was wedded to the Eastern Church, which perforce rejected what was clearly pagan, i.e., Greek philosophy and Greek religion. The Emperor Theodosius in the year 394 closed most of the pagan (Greek) schools and temples in the empire, and stopped the Olympian Games after more than a thousand years. Yet he married the daughter of a Greek philosopher, Leontius, and this lady persuaded the faculty of the new university at Constantinople to provide a curriculum heavily weighted with Greek subjects. Fifteen of the thirty professors who made up its initial faculty taught some aspect of Greek culture.

Theodosius unified and held together the empire while he lived, but after his death in 395 it fell apart. Alaric and his Visigoths invaded Greece in 395 and devastated the land. The Vandals poured through the peninsula in 466 and again in 475, and were followed by the Ostrogoths in 482. The Huns invaded Greece in 540 and reached as far south as the Isthmus of Corinth. Greece shuddered but her new religion survived every depredation. The glorious Parthenon was turned into a Christian church.

Literature in Greek continued to flourish throughout these and the following centuries. But the new shoots were producing most of the fruit; the old vine was moribund. Nine tenths of the writers who wrote in Greek were from the Asiatic and North African provinces and scarcely one tenth from Greece proper. Although the influence of the soil that nourished it was reflected in this literature, Christianity was its primary and continuous source of inspiration.

One last great effort was made to relink Byzantium with Rome and thus to restore the glory of the ancient Roman Empire. The Eastern Emperor Justinian (527–565) headed this crusade. Justinian was steeped in the Roman tradition and had the Roman genius for conquest, law, and government. His crusade was initially successful. He won some brilliant military victories, took back much of the territory that had been lost, and expanded the frontiers of his domain far to the west. He reconquered northern Africa and Italy, established himself firmly at Ravenna, which remained in Byzantine possession for two centuries, and even rewon a strip on the coast of Spain.

Justinian also drew up a code of laws on the Roman model, which was one of the great legal monuments of all time, and he was responsible for the building of the great temple of Santa Sophia (Hagia Sophia) which was consecrated on Christmas Day in 538. It was the first "wonder" of the Middle Ages. This unique church with its tremendous dome, its glowing mosaics, rich carvings, and columns brought from Ephesus, Pergamum, and other centers of the ancient Hellenic world, was a unique fusion of Eastern and Roman architecture. It became the model for hundreds of Byzantine churches which followed. Greece was dotted with them from one end to the other. St. Mark's in Venice clearly reveals that Hagia Sophia was its inspiration, and in Ravenna many priceless temples reflect its lavish use of Byzantine mosaics.

As Constantinople grew in wealth and importance Greece sank into insignificance. Two years after his accession (529) Justinian closed the

Academy in Athens which had been established by Plato, and which had continued to function as an important institution of learning for over nine centuries. The direct continuity of the Greek educational system was thus finally broken and supplanted by Byzantine Christian ideals. This act of Justinian, more than any other, marked the end of antiquity and the beginning of a new order.

There is a special poignancy to the story of the displaced scholars. They had heard about the superior polity of Persia and set off in exile for that land in search of the idealized philosopher-king. The reality that they found was quite different. The Persians were swollen with pride, had little respect for philosophy, and their government and social life were rotten to the core. Disenchanted at what they saw, the weary scholars, at least those of them who had survived, returned to the ordered but closed society of the Eastern Empire.

Justinian was the last flicker, the final breath of Rome. For a time it had appeared that he might even revive the supine Roman Empire and give it a new lease on life. His victories ran like a flash flood over the exhausted territories which Rome had once so proudly ruled. But the seeds of destruction were growing faster still, and when Justinian died his empire collapsed "like a pricked bladder." His successors kept a toehold on Sicily, and Ravenna remained in Byzantine hands until 751, but a long night fell over the rest of Italy.

The sanitation, agricultural, and urban works of the Romans fell into ruin, and when the Lombards invaded Italy three years after Justinian's death (568) they found the countryside depopulated, the farms overgrown with weeds, the economy stagnant, and the political organization completely ineffectual. Rome was dead never to be revived, but its alter ego, Constantinople, had already become the most populous and richest city of the world.

The period of great migrations continued and Greece, like France, Italy, and Spain, suffered from one invasion after another. The Avars and Slavs overran the Greek peninsula early in the seventh century and many Slavs remained to mingle their blood with those who were native to the land. The Bulgars flowed into Greece like locusts in the ninth and tenth centuries, the Normans of Sicily sent invading armies in the 1040's, in 1082, and again in 1147.

During these same centuries two things happened which altered forever the focus and spirit of the whole Christian world: first, the Moslem Arab invasions of Europe and, second, the European counterinvasions of Moslem territories in the Crusades. The Moslem Arab expansion began in 622 when Mohammed established Islam as a permanent factor in world politics and human culture. Islam was not only a religion but a dynamics of action for a hungry warrior people. Fired with zeal for their new religion and eager to convert all nonbelievers, the Arabs closed ranks and formed themselves into a militant union. Their vigorous military operations went hand in hand with an equally vigorous Arab cultural renaissance, a great part of which was Hellenic in inspiration.

Byzantines and Arabs shared the same dwelling place, which was not large enough for both. The Arabs twice besieged Constantinople, once for six years (672–678), before they were finally repulsed by "Greek fire," a new weapon composed of flaming naphtha and quicklime. They captured many Byzantine towns and monasteries, became enamored of their works of art, avidly collected books from their libraries, and quickly appropriated to themselves as much of their superior culture as they could assimilate. Their mosques imitated the architecture of the Byzantine churches, their minarets were inspired by the famous Pharos (Lighthouse) of Alexandria, their long flowing robes copied the Greek *chlamys,* and they often hired Greek artists to decorate the interiors of their buildings with brilliant mosaics.

The Arab hosts spread like wildfire across North Africa, took Alexandria in 640, and moved on to Spain, which they invaded in 711. Within a decade they had occupied the entire Iberian Peninsula from which they were not finally ejected until 1492, almost eight centuries later. In 827 the Arabs also invaded Greek-speaking Sicily, which was still in Byzantine hands. The Moslem culture remained supreme on the island for two and a half centuries.

The Arabs were particularly fascinated by the works of the Greek philosophers Plato and Aristotle, whose works they translated into Arabic and introduced into Western Europe. Scholars from many lands traveled to Sicily and to Spain to make copies in Latin of these and other Greek manuscripts. Usually a Sicilian Latinist or Spanish Jew who knew both Arabic and Latin was the key man in this process. He translated the manuscript orally into Latin as the visiting scholar copied it down. Many of the translations thus sounded very strange indeed.

The first European crusade against the Moslems, and the only completely successful one, was the crusade to free Spain of its Moorish invaders. This struggle began early in the eighth century and did not end until 1492, when the war was won. Strangely, it is never called a "Crusade" in the history books. What historians refer to as "The Crusades" were attempts by European armies (often they were more like mobs) to capture Christendom's most holy shrine, Jerusalem.

Christian pilgrims had been free to come and go from Jerusalem without molestation as long as it was in Arab hands, but when the Asiatic Turks took the city in 1071 things quickly changed. The Turks were the newly converted fanatics of the Moslem world. They swept over the remaining Asiatic territories of the Byzantine Empire and threw a mighty scare into Constantinople itself, which thought its final hour had come. The Emperor Alexius appealed urgently to the West for aid. The time was now ripe for expanding feudal Europe to take up the torch of civilization and embark on a crusade to rescue the East. To this pious ideal was added the freebooting instinct of the Normans, who were already seeking new and richer worlds to conquer.

The East had long been a kind of promised land for the more venturesome Christians of the West. It had the attractions of a great gold or diamond field. Constantinople was the richest city in the world; its streets teemed with people babbling a hundred languages. It was the center of art and the center of trade. The wealth of centuries was concentrated in this new Rome.

In 1095 Peter the Hermit, a monk famous in history, returned from his pilgrimage to the Holy Land with many terrible tales to tell. Barefooted, clad in a coarse robe, riding on an ass, and bearing a huge cross, he traveled over France and Germany haranguing great crowds in church or marketplace. He told how the Turks had wantonly destroyed many holy relics in Jerusalem and how brutally they were treating the Christian pilgrims in that city. His words stirred up a veritable hornet's nest among the European masses.

Pope Urban II decided that the Holy Sepulchre should not be allowed to remain in unclean Turkish hands. The idea of turning the Christian Church into a weapon for Christ quickly took fire, and thousands of "Crusaders" (takers of the cross) volunteered to "fight for Christ" until Jerusalem was reconquered. Thus began the First Crusade (1096), which used Constantinople as a take-off point for its campaign down the Arabian peninsula. Before it had ended, these "Christian soldiers" had stormed Jerusalem, slaughtered Saracens by the hundreds, and then sobbing for excess of joy lifted their bloody hands in prayers of thanksgiving. The Holy City was held as Christian territory from 1099 to 1187, almost a century.

The Byzantines in Constantinople at first regarded the Crusaders as allies who might help them regain lost territories, but the soldiers from the West known collectively as Franks and the Norman knights soon dispelled that idea. Unruly, arrogant, and predatory, they acted as if they owned the city. The emperor could not get rid of them quickly enough. The Frankish peasants who had reached Constantinople first were urged on their way and perished at the hands of the Turks; piles of their white bones greeted succeeding Crusaders. The hard core of Norman knights, supported by other knights from all over Europe, were the conquerors of Jerusalem.

The Fourth Crusade was even worse for Constantinople and the Greek peninsula. By this time the Italian city-states, Venice and Genoa, had awakened to the economic opportunity of transporting the Crusaders and their equipment in their large fleets. In 1203, with the planning of the Fourth Crusade, Venice agreed to transport 29,000 men and 4,500 horses and to provide provisions for these for one year, for 85,000 silver marks and half of all conquests. The army was ready to embark but as payment had not been made the Venetians refused to set sail.

The Doge then cannily decided to cancel payment altogether if the Frankish Crusaders would agree to help Venice win back some of her own lost territories. The Franks agreed and the army departed, but then instead of proceeding according to the original plan they assaulted and took Constantinople itself (1204). The city was savagely looted and the booty made Venice tremendously wealthy. The great Hellenic bronze horses which now stand atop St. Mark's were a part of this plunder. Constantinople remained in the hands of the Franks and Venetians until 1261, and Byzantine Christians have not yet forgotten the atrocities committed upon them by their supposed brothers of the West.

To make matters worse, the Crusaders and those who followed them also snatched large portions of Greece. The Franks built a series of defense towers which still dot the landscape, and set about developing the land along feudalistic lines. They controlled Athens for a hundred years (1205–1311) and remained in the Peloponnesus for over two centuries. They reestablished the Roman Church in their colonies.

The so-called Grand Catalan Company, an army of freebooters composed of Catalan, Aragonese, and Navarrese troops who had entered the Byzantine service as mercenaries, took control of the Duchy of Athens in 1311 and held it until 1388. Spanish replaced French as the language of government, and the regime was even more oppressive than that of the Franks. The Florentines were the next contingent to occupy Athens, and under the enlightened bankers of that flourishing city of the Renaissance there was a revival of culture in this part of Greece. The Florentines were proud of their Greek ward and its glorious history which was the inspiration for many of their own finest writers (Petrarch, Boccaccio, Bruni); they learned the Greek language, married Greek girls, and in general left a pleasant memory behind.

The Republic of Genoa occupied a few choice Greek islands off Asia Minor, and the Venetians, the greatest Italian conquerors of those days, grabbed a large portion of the eastern Greek mainland, the Ionian and other islands, including Crete, and in the Peloponnesus they took Nauplia and Argos, where their stern fortresses still stand guard on many a hill. They remained in Crete from 1204 to 1669, long after the Turks had taken the rest of Greece. They also established the feudal system in their domains.

With all of these foreign intrusions the Byzantine hold on Greece was very tenuous. The only continuing Byzantine institution was the Greek Orthodox Church. The goings and comings of so many different cultural and linguistic groups kept the land in a disorganized and chaotic state except for a few areas where foreign rule was strong and effective. Almost everywhere the natives of the land became feudal vassals of unwanted outside overlords. Their fragmented and miserable political and economic condition made it impossible for them to fight back in any unified fashion, so they fell into a pattern of isolated village living. It was much like the early days of Greek history, but with none of its promise and none of the glory.

The strongest man in each village was the Greek Orthodox priest, for he was the only element that represented any sense of continuity or over-all unity. As early as the fourth century these Greek priests began to occupy a position of unique importance in village life, and by the time of Justinian this place was secure.

It was not merely as religious leaders of the flock that they became important. The village priest was the community's most influential man in every sphere: he was the intellectual and business leader, the organizer of the village's political and social life, the moral guide and censor, the community's representative before the larger regional or imperial government, mentor to the young people, legal adviser, arbitrator, and judge. The importance of Archbishop (President) Makarios of Cyprus in our own time is but a continuation of something which began fifteen centuries ago. When all is said and done, this welding of church and community life was perhaps the strongest legacy which Byzantine rule left in Greece.

XIV

The Greek Renaissance:
The Turkish Occupation and
Fight for Freedom

> *One is not rich through one's possessions, but through that which
> one can with dignity do without.*

Epicurus

Contacts between the Hellenized East and the Latinized West were never broken, and while Europe rested in the shadow of its Dark Ages as its once great Roman cities dwindled to insignificant towns and villages, Constantinople continued to be the great center of culture, population, and wealth. Around the year 1000 it had a population of nearly a million. It was the hub of the caravans of the East, and its wharves were loaded with silks, spices, ebony, and other products which the fleets of the Italian city-states carried to Europe.

Many Venetian doges visited Constantinople, and in 991 Venice was granted preferential low tariffs in the Eastern Empire. In 1085 as a reward for their aid to the Byzantine emperor in his struggle against the Normans, the Venetians were granted a quarter of their own in Constantinople. The Crusades increased the tempo of contacts between East and West, and the Crusaders held the city from 1204 to 1261. In 1259 the famous Polo brothers of Venice departed from Constantinople on their journey to the kingdom of Kublai Khan of China.

As the size, wealth, and culture of Constantinople increased, the Byzantines became more and more interested in their glorious Greek heritage. This revival of Hellenism commenced in the 800's when the Byzantine scholars began to seek out, study, and copy the ancient manuscripts. From this time until the capture of Constantinople by the Turks in 1453 Byzantine culture was a bridge that led back to Greek antiquity.

Europe had the characteristics of an open society in the twelfth and early thirteenth centuries, and the blending of cultures was its most notable attribute. Wandering scholars traveled freely across frontiers which were not fixed. The concept of the national state, based on national languages and national churches, had not yet emerged. Latin was the language of a universal culture, and the Roman Church was the universal religion. Universities arose and began to flourish. Civilization burgeoned with a fresh meaning and there was a reawakened interest in the Hellenic past. The cradle of this revival of learning was Sicily.

Sicily had remained in Byzantine hands until the ninth century when the Arabs occupied the island whose language and culture had been Greek for fifteen hundred years. Greek continued to be widely spoken for many centuries after the Moslem conquest. In the eleventh century the Norman knights overcame the Arabs and established an aristocracy which ruled the island with remarkable success. In the eleven hundreds the Norman court at Palermo became one of Europe's most important crossroads and cultural centers. English-born Richard Palmer rubbed elbows with Greek-born George of Antioch, the Arab geographer Edrisi, and the Hungarian bishop of Agrigento.

The last great king of Sicily, Frederick II (1215–1250), who was half Norman and half German, continued the intellectual pursuits of his Norman forebears. Frederick was also emperor of the Holy Roman Empire, but Sicily was to him the promised land, and from Palermo his thundering statements shook the earth. One historian called him "the first modern," while his contemporaries referred to him as the *Stupor mundi*, "the amazement of the world." Frederick spoke Greek, Arabic, and four other languages; he was also a notable political philosopher and a poet of distinction. According to Dante, Italian poetry was born at Frederick's court; it was here that the philosopher Michael Scott translated portions of Aristotle and from here that the Arabic numerals were first introduced into Italy.

Frederick II was called the "Antichrist" because of his strong opposition to the Pope, and because he believed that all religions were impostures. The Pope excommunicated him for not observing a vow that he had made to go on a Crusade. Frederick deeply admired the ancient Greek literature, and in 1224 he held an exhibition of Greek classics in Naples. He died in southern Italy in 1250, and the revival of learning moved north to find its new home in Tuscany.

In the twelfth and thirteenth centuries men began to view the world in a new light, in all its promise, all its brilliance, all its vastness, all its peril. The individual acquired a transcendent importance. Arab, Christian, heretic, Byzantine, and Jew swapped ideas and felt the warm stir of a different life. All tried to penetrate the mystery of the universe, of the world of spirit, of nature. It was a germinal epoch in which differing philosophies compared themselves critically in the unending search for truth. The old, the new, and the different all had their place in the universalism of this turning point in history.

The East came west, and the West went east. Pisa was described in some chronicles as an "Oriental" city. Its cathedral and that of Siena strongly reflect Eastern influences, and the incomparable stone pulpits carved by Niccolò Pisano at Pisa and Siena were the first medieval works to reflect the clear inspiration of classical form and proportions. The intellect of medieval man was aflame, and art was an exotic flower brightly burning.

By the 1300's the Renaissance had begun in Florence, interest in the ancient Greek and Latin authors became a fever, and European humanists ransacked the libraries of Italy, Constantinople, the abbeys of Germany, Switzerland, and France in search of precious manuscripts. Boccaccio and Petrarch were fascinated and inspired by the classics, and many European scholars traveled to Constantinople to study.

Boccaccio tells of his visit to Monte Cassino, where he found a collection of these priceless books lying in the dust, often with pages, covers, and decorated margins missing because these had been ripped out by the poor monks and sold as charms or psalters. He and the other great writers of the Renaissance put a quick end to that. Collecting old manuscripts became of more value and status than possessing great wealth.

One European scholar who had gone to Constantinople to study Greek in the early 1400's brought back 238 manuscripts, among them the works of Aeschylus and Sophocles. Another returned loaded with texts of Euripides, Herodotus, Polybius, Thucydides, and Demosthenes. As the Turks tightened their stranglehold on Constantinople many Byzantine scholars left that city and emigrated westward. After 1453 this exodus became a flood.

The Italian Renaissance found its inspiration in the Golden Age of Greece and Rome. Writers, sculptors, painters, architects emulated the great classical artists in this rebirth of culture and learning. Florence was the cradle of the Renaissance, and from this small Tuscan valley the movement spread all over Europe. Florence was a city unique in the history of the world, an Athens born anew to close the Middle Ages and open the Renaissance.

Every branch of human knowledge and artistic creativity blossomed in the City of the Flower. Dante, Petrarch, Boccaccio, the Medici, Michelangelo, Leonardo da Vinci—all these and many more famous figures of the Renaissance were Florentines by birth or by adoption.

The seed germ of the Renaissance was a reawakening of the belief in the dignity and infinite potential of man; not man in the aggregate, but individual man who embodied the vital energy of the gods. This idea, of course, came straight from the Greeks.

To the Renaissance artist Nature took on a value of her own, and shared with God and man the divinity of the universe. As in the Golden Age of Greece, the undraped human figure was again considered the most beautiful subject for art. Man, who had hitherto been only a coin on which reality was stamped, now embodied reality and became a point of departure for a knowledge of the universe. Later he became a microcosm of the universe, for in his mind a miniature world spun out its dream in art and thought, emotion, imagination, and remembrance, recapturing and recreating the absolute reality. This was the *humanism* of the Renaissance.

Humanism was not only a respect for the dignity and worth of individual man, it was also a love for the ancient writers, because they are civilization's roots, and a wish to make them a part of one's life, and of the lives of others. Humanism was a zeal to rediscover and make known again the old values which had been lost in time. If the roots were found and watered, the plant would grow. Humanism was a veneration for books, because in books the dead live again through each successive reader. Humanism was a dedication to literature and to art based on all these precepts. The humanist, therefore, was both scholar and creative artist. He saw no separation between the two. The one discovered, preserved, made known the old; the other created on this base the new, and gave that value too.

Man was no longer a straw in the wind, a sound of the waves unanswered, a cry in the dark whose only hope was God. He was part dust, part deity, the noblest of creatures; he embodied the divine essence and shared with Nature and God the reality of the universe. His dignity and spirit were everlasting. His strugglings were not sound and smoke. Man was an imprisoned splendor which man must learn to set free.

The other side of the picture, alas, is not so bright. Constantinople, proud queen of the East, had a Turkish noose around her neck and the noose was drawn tighter with each passing year. The Turks were recent intruders in this part of the world. The first great migration westward of these Asiatic people had been in the eleventh century. A second wave was pushed out of Asia by the eruption of the Mongol horde under Genghis

Khan in the thirteenth century. The Turks were a primitive, barbaric people, who found their main outlet in war. Their conquest of the Arabian peninsula marked the death knell of Arabic culture. Under them Bagdad and other cities of Arabia ceased to be centers of a thriving Saracenic civilization. Neither did the Turks show any consideration for Greek, Byzantine, Persian, or Syrian culture; they came like a whirlwind, looting and killing as they advanced. They had been converted to Islam but seemed impervious to all aspects of Islamic civilization.

The Crusades were originally directed against the first wave of Turks who had taken Jerusalem, and the Frankish mob had for a while quelled the Turkish advance. But only for a while. By the 1400's the once mighty Byzantine Empire had greatly shrunk as the Turks chewed off piece after piece. In 1439 the Byzantine emperor, John VIII Palaeologus, promoted a meeting between Eastern and Western European leaders at Florence. His hope was to produce a united Christian front which could stave off the Turkish threat to Constantinople and to Europe itself.

The emperor attended the Council of Florence accompanied by dozens of Greek scholars and churchmen. Many of these scholars remained in Italy after the meeting was over and contributed to the growth of the Renaissance. A proposal to reunite the Roman and Greek Catholic churches was accepted at Florence and temporarily put into effect, but the West offered no military aid to save Constantinople.

Fourteen lean and hungry years went by. The emperor at Constantinople was now Constantine XI Palaeologus. He saw that a fight to the death was coming with the Turks and did his best to prepare his city for the assault. The leader of the Ottoman Turks, Mohammed II, determined to make the conquest of Constantinople the steppingstone to further Turkish expansion in Europe. His preparations were massive. He surrounded the city with 200,000 soldiers, and after a five weeks' siege his army stormed one of the gates and overwhelmed the heroic defenders in one of the most important battles of history. The emperor himself died sword in hand, and the Turkish soldiers ran wild for three days of pillage and rape.

Constantinople fell into Turkish hands on May 29, 1453, and the more than one thousand years of Byzantine history thus came to an end. With it died also the even more ancient Hellenism which had nurtured Byzantine culture for so many centuries. Athens was occupied by the Turks in 1456, and before long the Ottoman Empire had spread as far westward as Vienna. Greece now moved into the darkest period of its history; its people were to live in servitude for almost four centuries. Both Santa Sophia and the Parthenon were decorated with minarets and converted into Turkish mosques.

At least the Greeks were given a stable government and an improved fiscal system, and their religion, though often demeaned, was not suppressed. But the price paid for even these limited favors was unmercifully high. The prettiest Greek girls were frequently impressed into Turkish harems, and for two centuries every four years one fifth of all Greek boys from the rural areas were taken from their parents, forced to accept Islam, and became Janissaries of the Sultan. Intellectual life almost ceased within Turkish-occupied Greece but did continue strongly in Italy among the Greek exiles who had fled from Turkish rule.

In the Greek territories still occupied by Venice the Byzantine tradition was also kept alive. One of the West's greatest painters, known as El Greco (The Greek), was from the Venetian-ruled island of Crete, which was not lost to the Turks until 1669. El Greco went to Venice as a young man (around 1560), probably studied at the studio of Titian, and later emigrated to Spain where he finally established himself at Toledo. He might have become Philip II's court painter if he had been willing to sacrifice his artistic integrity for the kind of art that was in vogue at the moment. At the Benaki Museum in Athens are two paintings by El Greco; one of them in the Byzantine manner was painted before he left Crete.

Elsewhere in Greece what was left of Greek culture retreated to the monasteries or was passed along from one generation to the next by the Church and a few Greek schools in which classes often had to be held in secret. Church buildings were made small and unobtrusive with low doors at the sides so that the Turks could not ride into them on horseback. On the island of Mykonos and in many other regions tiny secluded Byzantine chapels, barely the size of a small house, but brightly domed and painted, were maintained to take care of a mere handful of worshipers. They were hidden among the dwellings so as to attract as little attention as possible.

Greeks who stuck to their faith generally remained second-class citizens and public religious ceremonies exposed them to the ridicule of their Turkish overlords. The Greek Orthodox village priest gave courage, nutriment and hope to the undercurrent of Greek feeling which struggled continuously to preserve itself. There was very little intermarriage between the two opposing religious groups, so the population at large did not absorb much Turkish blood. Her progress stifled, her liberties taken away, her culture run underground, Greece lived in chains of fear and misery, but in spite of all this she was able to preserve her identity.

Throughout the Turkish occupation the numerous isolated monastic communities of the Greek Orthodox Church preserved the Greek language and culture as well as the traditions of the Church. They also kept alive the dream of eventual liberation from the oppressors. Anchorites even established themselves on Mount Pentelicus just out of Athens. There were two main regions, however, where monasteries were clustered: the Meteora area of Thessaly, about a hundred miles directly north of Delphi, and the Athos peninsula, which juts out into the Aegean Sea southeast of Salonika, in the north.

The Meteora district is noted for its series of isolated stone columns which stick up from the surrounding plains like gigantic tusks. On top of these tusks, which were accessible only by hoisting rope and basket or by perpendicular ladders, the monks lived out their precarious lives. Tradition tells us that in some of the communities the hoisting ropes were not replaced until they had broken, for it was believed that it was proper for a monk to live always facing the possibility of imminent death.

The Athos peninsula is a long finger of land 40 miles long and 4 to 7 miles wide, all of which was (and is) covered with monastic communities, although today most of them are in a state of neglect. Mount Athos, which gives the peninsula its name, occupies the end of the finger; its pyramid-like marble peak soars 6,670 feet above the sea. On a clear day it is visible from both Salonika and Troy. When the Turks overcame Salonika in 1430, twenty-three years before they took Constantinople, the monks of Athos (despite their armed citadels) submitted without resistance, and the Turks in return did not disturb their pattern of existence in the ensuing years.

Mount Athos itself is the site of dozens of monastic buildings which dot the promontories and pockets of the great mountain and can be clearly seen from passing ships today. This is the holy of holies of the Greek Orthodox Church. The whole peninsula is green and rugged, thick with trees and flowing streams, devoid of flocks but alive with birds. For hundreds of years it has been the tradition of these communities to allow no female among them, not even as a visitor. Indeed, the restriction is carried to an extreme: no female being of any kind—cow, mare, dog, goat or cat—is allowed to invade the masculine serenity of the Athos monks.

Vatopedi Bay, on the tamer side of the mountain, is where most ships anchor, but it is on the other side that the striking effect of Mount Athos is seen to best advantage. Here the great peak rises quickly to dizzying heights from the sea, its head lost in the clouds. It may well be the most impressive headland in all of Europe. Within three or four hours a person can climb from groves of orange, lemon, fig, and olive trees, up through clustering arbutus, myrtle, cytisus, heath, carpets of forget-me-not, anemone, iris, and wild orchid, to a region of primroses and violets, and after these to the still higher belt of stunted birch and fir which encircle the apex of perpetual snow.

Both sides of the great ridge which forms the backbone of the peninsula are veined with sparkling glens and ravines which nourish a luxuriant vegetation. Nightingales and other singing birds, not subject to the monks' restrictive law, multiply happily and unmolested and flood the air with song. The Athos monasteries today, their mission long since completed, are only thinly populated with monks, scarcely enough to prevent their slow death. Young Greek men of our generation are reluctant to dedicate their lives to such a rigorous order in a world where other values seem to them of greater importance.

In medieval times these monastic communities of Greece consisted of many thousands of consecrated monks. They assembled ancient manuscripts, studied and copied them, and were a strong influence in keeping the Hellenic tradition alive. But in later years, as the monks themselves became less and less well educated, the libraries were neglected, manuscripts became mildewed and fell apart, and it was reported that on some occasions the less literate fathers used pieces of parchment as fishing bait. When the Greek War for Independence broke out in the early nineteenth century the Turks destroyed these ancient books even more massively by utilizing their parchment as wads for their cartridges.

The Turkish occupation of Greece lasted for 360 years, and despite the over-all primitivism and gloom that pervades the Ottoman period, there were occasional bright spots and periods of progress. Many well-to-do Greek families, merchants, and churchmen remained in Constantinople after its surrender to the Turks. They lived in the Phanar district of the city, clustered around the headquarters of the patriarch of their Church, and so were known as the Phanariots.

Two centuries after the Turkish occupation (around 1650) the rapid expansion of many Western European countries forced the Ottoman Turks, who were almost totally ignorant of European languages, customs, and institutions, to enter into diplomatic relations with the West. The sultans were obliged to seek help from their Western-oriented Greek subjects. The education and influence of the Greek Phanariots thus enabled them to move into important posts in the Ottoman government. For many years they were the only link between the Ottoman Empire and Western Europe.

Several Phanariots became the chief "official" interpreter (grand dragoman) of the sultan. The first Greek appointed to this key office (1656) was Panayiotis Nikousios, a distinguished Phanariot who was a graduate of the University of Padua. In this apparently innocuous position he became in fact privy counselor in the Ministry of Foreign Affairs of the Ottoman government. When Nikousios died in 1673 his position was occupied by a succession of influential Phanariots.

Other key posts in the government were also held by the Phanariots, and the Ottoman grip that had stifled Greek cultural life was slowly loosened through the labors of these men. The Greeks were finally allowed to establish their own public schools, and by the eighteenth century Greek intellectual life began very visibly to awaken.

During the hectic period of the French Revolution and the Napoleonic Wars that followed many French and British trading houses of the Mediterranean area were ruined or closed down and Greeks ships began to ply the sea again carrying essential goods. Greek shipowners and traders made sensational profits out of this trade, and by 1813 the Greek merchant fleet numbered over six hundred vessels. This improvement in the economic situation of the Greeks resulted in a feeling of greater strength and unity among them.

During the long years of Turkish occupation Athens had become an unimportant town, its wretched houses and shops huddled precariously around the Acropolis, which still rose gloriously above them. The Parthenon, having been turned into a Christian church, remained in almost perfect condition through the Middle Ages. The Turks used it as a mosque, added minarets, but did not damage the temple itself. They turned the Erechtheum into a seraglio, and so this building also survived almost intact.

In 1687 the Venetians, after they had been expelled from Crete, invaded Attica and laid siege to Athens. The Christian inhabitants of the city greeted them as saviors, but the greeting was premature, for the salvation was fleeting and the damage that the invaders left in their wake was permanent and irreparable. The Turks holed up in the Parthenon and stored their powder there. The Venetians lobbed a shell into the middle of this powder magazine and blew out the whole center of the building as well as destroying several columns. After capturing the citadel the Venetians constructed an ugly square tower of patched masonry at the right side of the entrance gate which was an eyesore for many years. By the time they were driven out of Athens the Acropolis was a shambles.

As the centuries passed Greeks became increasingly restive under Turkish rule, and Turkish rule became increasingly harsh and corrupt. Many local politicians broke away from the Ottoman Empire and proclaimed their independence. A new zest for nationalism was spreading all over Europe. Napoleon took advantage of this and by espousing regional "freedom" was able to conquer most of the Continent.

Greeks in many foreign countries were inflamed with the desire to see their homeland free again and conspired to bring this about. No group was more strategically placed than the Greeks who lived in Russia. This immense nation, linked to Greece through its Russian Orthodox Church, which Greek Byzantines had originally brought to them, welcomed many Greek exiles from Moslem Turkish rule. As far back as 1770, when Russia and Turkey were at war, Catherine the Great had actively encouraged the Greeks to revolt against their oppressors. There was a mass uprising in the Peloponnesus but no Russian help came and it was suppressed with great bloodshed by the barbarous Albanian forces of the sultan. For the next thirty years the Turks were firmly in control again; the Greeks had learned their lesson.

However, the world scene was changing rapidly. The old order was everywhere being challenged by the new. The successful American Revolution against Britain had inspired the oppressed peoples of Europe and the French Revolution (1789) universalized the ideals of liberty and equality in the Old World. The Greeks could not long remain untouched by the flame that was sweeping Europe.

The Ypsilanti family, a line of Phanariots who claimed descent from the old Byzantine rulers of Constantinople, were in the vanguard of the Greek revolutionary movement. Three generations of Ypsilantis dedicated themselves to the cause of Greek independence. Alexander Ypsilanti was executed by the sultan for treason; his son Constantine and his grandson fled to St. Petersburg.

Constantine headed an abortive rebellion in 1806 with several thousand Russian "volunteers." After his venture had failed he returned to Russia and died in Kiev. Constantine's son, also named Alexander, became an officer in the Imperial Russian Guard. In 1821 Alexander organized a Sacred Battalion of Greek and foreign patriots in the Danubian basin: on March 6 of that year he proclaimed the independence of Greece and crossed the Pruth River into Greek territory, stating that "a great power supported him." His motley army suffered a series of humiliating defeats, and Alexander fled to Vienna, where he died in 1828 after a long imprisonment. His brother Demetrius fought in the Greek War for Independence and eventually became a general in the revolutionary forces.

Alexander, in spite of his failure, is still regarded as the Morning Star of the Greek Revolution. In the very year of his defeat (1821) a group of highly placed churchmen of the Peloponnesus, ignoring an urgent Turkish summons, gathered secretly at the monastery of Hagia Lavra,* and after deliberations their leader, Archbishop Germanos, raised the banner of rebellion. It was the banner of the Cross. A horde of Greek peasants gathered around Germanos, and the War for Independence was under way. It had no plan, it followed no strategy, it espoused no particular political philosophy. It was simply the spontaneous and reckless eruption of a people who wanted to rule themselves.

One of the most important factors in the war was Greek sea power. General Wellington had remarked that because of Greece's long and sharply indented coast line, her mountainous terrain and few roads, victory would be achieved by the side that held control of the sea. The seafaring Greeks had a sizable merchant marine of small vessels, and as the fever of independence mounted Greek sailors, who also formed the hard core of the Turkish navy, deserted in droves in order to man their own smaller craft. The Turkish fleet was soon left "adrift in the Mediterranean," as the British Admiralty so colorfully put it. Certainly with its newly impressed seamen it was no match for the more experienced Greeks, who thus won command of the sea early in the war.

Back on the mainland the undisciplined swarm of peasants around Archbishop Germanos, armed mainly with scythes, clubs, and slings, advanced rapidly across the Peloponnesus and within three weeks not a Turk was left in the open country. Several Turkish strongholds were captured, and with each victory the same scenes of butchery were repeated. After the fall of Tripolitsa 2,000 prisoners of both sexes, including many old people and children, were slaughtered in cold blood.

Turkish reprisals were equally brutal. The Turks massacred many Greeks on the island of Chios, executed the patriarch of the Greek Orthodox Church in Constantinople, and thus infuriated the Russian czar, who regarded himself as the protector of the Greek Christians under Turkish rule. Russia again declared war on Turkey. Britain and France, fearing the expansion of Russia into the Balkan area, did all they could to help the Greeks. For eight years the bloody conflict continued, but by 1829 the Turks were defeated and in 1830 Britain, France, and Russia guaranteed the independence of the new Greek state.

* Built by the tragic emperor Nicephorus II (963–969), who yearned to surrender his crown and retire to this refuge as a monk. But his other yearning—for women—was even stronger, so he kept putting his retirement date off. His dearest nephew cut off his head while he was sleeping and succeeded him. His golden crown with its green and red jewels is at the monastery.

The Greek struggle for freedom aroused sympathy throughout the Western world. Greek colonies in European and North American cities sent both funds and volunteers. Many famous non-Greeks also took part in the struggle. Lord Byron bought and equipped a ship, named it the *Hercules,* and took off for Greece in the year 1823. He was accompanied by E. J. Trelawney, an Italian doctor, a small crew, and a retinue of eight servants. On board was medicine for 1,000 men. When the ship reached Greece Byron equipped a group of 600 mountaineers at his own expense and became their captain. The discipline of these men was deplorable. Byron did what he could to mitigate the ferocity of the war and was able to save the lives of many persons who would otherwise have been slaughtered in cold blood. However, Byron had been in Greece less than a year when he became ill and died.

Other foreigners in the Greek forces were Lord Thomas Cochrane, admiral of the Greek navy, who had won fame in the South American wars for independence; Sir Richard Church, who became commander in chief of the Greek army; and the North American Samuel Gridley Howe, a medical doctor, who served as surgeon general in the Greek armed services. Howe's even more famous wife, Julia Ward Howe, won considerable renown as an abolitionist and as author of "The Battle Hymn of the Republic." Her husband left an interesting account of the war in his book *Historical Sketch of the Greek Revolution, 1828,* and in his journals and letters edited by his daughter.

The disorganized, inefficient, and undisciplined character of the Greek forces is made clear in an entry in Howe's journal dated October 23, 1825:

> A Greek soldier is quite a man at ease; a gentleman, in fact, who does and says what he will, and goes where he wots. When he enters the army, as it is called, he goes to some captain and agrees with him to be paid two and a half dollars per month and shoe leather. The captain perhaps writes his name down on a piece of paper, and the affair is settled. Once in two or three days, perhaps, he calls on his captain, squats down on the floor, and witnesses his bravery, displayed by cursing the Turks. If they are on the march the soldier goes ahead, behind, or strolls to one side, according to his will. Arrived at night in a village they can fend for themselves, leaving the captain's immediate attendants to shift for him. If the inhabitants of a house refuse to open their door, the soldiers break it open; if good fare is not produced, they beat the family.
>
> A soldier obeys the order of his captain or not, just as he chooses. If ordered to march on such and such a day to such a place, he goes, or says

he will not go so soon, or perhaps not at all. When he wishes to leave his captain he generally goes and picks a quarrel with him upon some trifle, and then goes off in a pretended rage, or he goes and joins another captain without any ceremony at all. He finds his own musquets and pistols, and draws cartridges from the government. When in a town he draws rations of bread and meat, and perhaps a few little pickled fish. When in the village, he lives on the villagers. There is no baggage-wagon, and seldom a horse. A soldier carries with him his bed, his table, his chair, his all, in his capote. His knife is to him daggar, fork, and spoon. He carries no change of clothes, nor will he lay off his dress, perhaps, once in three months. At night he never thinks of getting more than a dry place and a smooth stone for a pillow. As for this way of life, one soon gets used to it. It is now two months since I took off my clothes at night or have had any other bed than the floor and a blanket, yet I sleep as sound as ever I did on a feather bed with clean linen sheets, and my head is as easy, with only my handkerchief between it and a flat rock, as it was on down pillows.

The North American public was so sympathetic to the Greek cause that several towns in this country were named or renamed for famous Greek cities or heroes. This is the origin of our Syracuse, Ithaca, Ypsilanti, our several towns named Athens, Sparta, Thebes, and Corinth. When Greek independence finally came Great Britain, who regarded the Mediterranean as a British lake, was the power behind the treaty that acknowledged it.

The war left the Greek people in a state of economic collapse and political chaos. The total population of Greece at the start of the war in 1821 was 875,150 Greek Christians and 63,614 Moslems. After the eight years of fighting this population was reduced to 741,930 Greek Christians and 11,450 Moslems. In 1834 the capital was moved from Nauplia to Athens, which was a more central location with greater historic appeal. But Athens in 1834 was a miserable little town of only 8,000 inhabitants and filthy, rubble-filled streets. Seldom has a nation begun its life with such paltry resources.

Even before the war had ended there was a brief attempt at a Greek republic. Count Ioannes Capodistrias (Capo d'Istria), who belonged to a well-known family on the island of Corfu, was elected provisional president by the National Assembly in April, 1827. The count was in Russia at the time of his election, where he had risen to become the foreign minister of the czar. He had won considerable recognition at the Congress of Vienna, where he skillfully represented Russian interests. Capodistrias arrived in Greece in 1828 and attacked his job with vigor and devotion. He conducted the foreign affairs of the emerging state with notable acumen, but his attitude concerning domestic problems was often dictatorial, and he appeared to regard himself as indispensable. Many powerful Greek families soon came to hate him, and in 1831 he was assassinated at Nauplia, then the capital, at the instigation of two of these aristocrats. The country reverted immediately to a state of anarchy.

Great Britain, France, and Russia decided to impose a king on the Greeks without further delay, guaranteeing him the independence of his country. King Louis of Bavaria was offered and accepted the throne in the name of his son, Otto, who was then a boy of seventeen. Otto arrived in Greece in 1833, and immediately made a hit with the Hellenes by adopting the national costume and by changing the spelling of his name to the Greek Otho. But the honeymoon did not last long. Otto's Bavarians monopolized the government, cornering all the important positions for themselves. At the first sign of resistance the press was muzzled. Economy and finances remained in a state of shock. Otto repeatedly gave evidence of his ineptitude as ruler, and finally in 1862 the Greeks rose up and expelled the Bavarian dynasty.

The country went through another time of troubles before another king was found. The protecting powers had agreed that he could not be a member of one of their own royal houses. This time the choice fell on Prince William George of Denmark, who was then also a young man of only seventeen. He became King George I of Greece and reigned for fifty years until 1913, when he was assassinated. Under his reign Greece got back the Ionian Islands, which had been under the British. Large areas of Thessaly and Epirus further increased the size of the country, and in 1913 Crete, too, became officially a part of Greece. This large island had been buffeted about since the Greek War for Independence, being given first to Egypt, next to Turkey, then it became autonomous, and finally its territory was added to that of the kingdom of Greece.

The most famous Greek premier during the reign of George I was Charilaos Trikoupes, who was appointed to this office in 1875 and dominated Greek politics for twenty years. He helped the country to become a constitutional monarchy and built up the transportation system, linking the shattered regions. The Greeks were now almost masters of their own political destiny, but the economic conditions of the country were still deplorable. The standard of living was below that of Spain or Portugal, illiteracy was fantastically high, and industry was almost nonexistent. In such a state did Greece enter the twentieth century.

The life of a nation, like the life of an individual, is a compromise between lost opportunities and future hopes. Man always hurries; God moves slowly. All the beautiful things that man has made are ephemeral, because, like Dionysus, man creates only to destroy. Apollo has no sanctuary among us, no sacred spring, and he was the most sublime of all the gods. There is a line in a Greek poem which says, "On Rhodes there are many roses," which means that beauty has many faces. Greece has discovered almost all of them. There is no single way to the final harmony that is God.

Greece entered contemporary life like a tree whose leaves are all dying, whose trunk is broken, whose roots are gone. With the cyclic return of spring can a nation, too, resurrect itself? Or do the laws of nature not apply, or apply only once, to the story of a people? Perhaps it is given to no nation to twice occupy the zenith. Today it is the United States and not Greece which has the absolute duty to be great.

From chaos to the Parthenon, and from the Parthenon back to chaos, as Nikos Kazantzakis has pointed out. Art is the tenuous poetization of being. Its object is to create a new reality with a soul, and to breathe hope. The Greek word for art is $\tau \acute{\epsilon} \chi \nu \eta$ (techni), which indicates the unity of creator and thing created. Realism was and always is the death of a culture, the beginning of man's descent. Achilles and Odysseus are dead. There is no Troy, no Ithaca. There is only the sea, the highway to every adventure. We call it civilization. The rosebush calls it a rose.

XV

Greece Today:
The Imprisoned Splendor

Inferiors revolt that they may become equal, and equals that they may become superior. Such is the state of mind that creates revolutions.

Aristotle

Greekness is a word dear to us Greeks. It means our goal, the liberty we wish to have in our country but never have completely. We have savored of democracy intermittently. It is a safety valve they open briefly from time to time, every two or three years, no more.

Vassilis Vassilikos,
contemporary Greek novelist

In her general contours Greece is like a cluster of grapes dangling in the Mediterranean. Her heavily broken coastline is 9,385 miles in length. The peninsula is ringed with islands, 166 of which are inhabited. Hundreds of others jut from the mythical sea without any permanent population. The Pindus mountain range rams its irregular saw down the spine of Greece fragmenting the country by nature. More than three fourths of the land is mountainous, and Mount Olympus in the north soars to almost 10,000 feet. It is guarded still by storm clouds and the eerie cry of the eagle.

The climate of Greece is Mediterranean, mild and dry, with two crops a year possible in most regions. Scattered among the hills are cattle, pigs, burros, goats, horses, and there are more sheep than people. Cheese is the staple in the rural diet as it always has been, but when possible lamb with rice or wheat pilaff becomes the main dish. A Greek herder can go for days on a crust of bread and a few olives. Eggplant, fish, stuffed grape leaves, rose-petal jelly, and *retsina,* a wine with a faint taste of turpentine, add a touch of variety to the Greek cuisine. *Moussaka,* made of eggplant, ground meat, and cheese, is one of the most popular composite concoctions. Turkish coffee and flaky pastries flavored with nuts and honey top off the meal on the more pretentious tables.

Greek farmers grow olives, grapes, figs, tobacco, barley, wheat, rice, oats, cotton, citrus, but the Greek by instinct is a shepherd. He lives in the open air with the earth and the sky as his constant companions. He is a telluric creature, and he loves freedom. With the sea always near, the Greeks are also daring fishermen and are among the world's finest sailors, just as they were in the days of Homer. Their homeland is hard, poor, and proud. They are aware of its great history and carry it like a broken flower in the heart.

The landscape of Greece, rising, flowing, undulating, makes its beauty unfold continuously, renew itself. It has a rhythm, a serenity, and a profound unity. The mountains, rivers, valleys, rocks, even the clouds take on a human quality, and become an extension of man. No great imagination is required to see Agamemnon stretched out on the mountains of Argos, to find the horses of Zeus prancing in the clouds above Olympus, to hear the sacred lyre of Orpheus in the olive groves that hug the slopes and valleys of Delphi. The face of Greece is rugged, wild, beautiful. Nature and time are in a perfect equilibrium; they harmonize the clashing forces of the gods that created them. And wherever one looks these gods have walked from time immemorial.

It would be picturesque to say that everywhere in Greece today the past overshadows the present, but it would not be true. Athens today is a great metropolis of over two million inhabitants and is one of the most dynamic capitals of Europe. Its teeming streets and cluttered buildings reach all the way to the denuded hills which were once so many miles from the ancient *polis.* Windstorms blow dust and sand into every window and cranny when the Lord of the Sky loses his temper. This is only one penalty the modern Greek must pay for the sins of his ancestors who centuries ago cut down the forests on these same hills.

The environs of Athens are crowded with industries: oil refineries, electric complexes, cement plants, distilleries, factories, shipyards, textile plants, and many others. At Eleusis, a few miles north of Athens, site of the ancient Eleusinian Mysteries, great steel mills blacken the sky with smoke. A huge aluminum plant has been constructed on the Gulf of Corinth. On the plains and hills of Attica and Thessaly electric-power lines are visible in every direction, tractors plow the fields (though the women still cover their faces as they work), long freight trains chug north and south, highways are filled with trucks and cars; the beaches, mountains, and ancient ruins boast 2,000 new hotels erected in the past ten years. Before the 1967 military coup over 700,000 foreign tourists were visiting Greece each year and spending millions.

The Skaramanga shipyards are producing trim steel vessels by the dozens, and Greece's merchant fleet, which now approaches twenty million gross tons, is third in the world. A very large proportion of these vessels are registered under other flags. Great ships come into the very heart of Piraeus and dock next to the downtown sidewalk. In 1834 this thriving port, today one of the busiest of the Mediterranean, was marked by a single building. It is now impossible to tell where Piraeus ends and Athens begins. One great megalopolis covers the whole area where in bygone times long twin walls linked ancient Athens to her port.

In 1830 the population of Greece was approximately 750,000; by 1914 this had grown to about 4.5 million, and today the total is close to 9 million. Per capita income is still among the lowest in Europe. In 1930 it was approximately $100 a year; in 1969 official statistics (padded a little) reported it at just above $700 a year. The purchasing power of the dollar has gone down so much since 1930 that this amount does not represent seven times as much purchasing power. It represents three or four times as much purchasing power, still no mean increase. But the improvement, sad to say, is even less than this, because the Greek economy, which has been firmly in the hands of conservatives for the past generation, has produced a crop of multimillionaires. The enormous incomes of these families brings the per capita income up in the statistical averages but fails to do so in hard cash for the immense majority of Greek citizens.

There is not enough land in Greece for the people who live there. One million acres of farmland are now under irrigation, but there is less than one and one-third acres of tillable soil per Greek, and production on this cropland is only about half as much as it is in Western Europe. The country does not produce enough food for its own needs. Only one fourth of the land is suitable for agriculture; the rest is rock or forest, but mostly rock. And yet approximately one half of the people still live from agriculture. The Greek National Anthem begins with the words: "I recognize you from the sharpness of your spade!"—a tribute to the earth of Hellas, which is man's true umbilical cord.

Hundreds of thousands of Greeks have emigrated during the past century. There are about two million persons of Greek descent living in the

United States. The funds they periodically send home to their relatives help greatly to keep the standard of living in the poorest regions above the subsistence level. Nearly two hundred thousand of these emigrants have returned to their homeland in recent years, taking back with them good American ideas and hard American cash. Even so, the rate of emigration has averaged almost 100,000 annually for the past decade, and in some years the population of the country has actually declined as a result. There are too many Greeks, and Greece is still a very poor country. However, in these postwar years progress has sent its arrows into the hinterland, and the country today is a far cry from the Greece of a generation ago.

Recently constructed electrical power plants have brought electricity to 2,000 villages which had none before. Illiteracy has been drastically decreased, but large numbers of children do not go beyond the third grade. Lack of medical service and low farm income still keep the rural Greek population poor, underfed, and oftentimes needlessly ill. The extremes of the very rich and the very poor are still characteristic of Greece in the twentieth century. The middle class is growing, but it is still very small.

Aristotle Onassis is only one of a trio of ship magnates whose fortunes make them multimillionaires. Onassis also controls Olympic Airways, which flies from Greece to all parts of the world. For years Onassis has been the leader of the European jet set; his recent marriage to Jacqueline Kennedy made his name a household word. Other less well-known Greeks perhaps merit more attention because of their outstanding achievements: George Seferis won the Nobel Prize for literature in 1963 for his lyrical poetry which so well expresses the heartbeat of Greek culture. Nikos Kazantzakis (author of *Zorba the Greek* and over thirty other works), who died in 1957, is one of contemporary literature's most admired authors. Elia Kazan, now an American citizen, is a famous theatrical director and was a cofounder of the Actors' Studio in New York.

Raphael Demos is a distinguished professor of philosophy at Harvard University. George Papanicolaou, professor of medicine at Cornell, was responsible for the famous "Pap" smear test for cervical cancer in women. Dmitri Mitropoulos was a famous orchestra director in the United States. Spyros Skouras was a powerful motion-picture magnate in this country, and George Pantahos was responsible for the "Pantages" theaters and Pantages vaudeville circuit all over America. Melina Mercouri and Maria Callas are too well known to require comment, Katina Paxinou and Irene Papas are equally famous inside Greece, and Michael Cacoyannis is a motion-picture director of international distinction.

Many foreign writers of our epoch have found inspiration in Greece for some of their best-known works: James Joyce in *Ulysses,* Lawrence Durrell, with his *Alexandria Quartet,* and Henry Miller, with his *Colossus of Maroussi,* are three of the most widely read. Edith Hamilton, Robert Graves, C. M. Woodhouse, and the sculptor Michael Ayrton are among the many, many others who have fed their roots in Greece. Greek music, as we all know, is as beautiful and as stirring as any in the whole wide world.

The Greeks themselves, despite the mass migrations that have inundated their land during the centuries, still preserve many of the qualities found in the Homeric poems. The "guest-friend" relationship is deeply rooted, especially in the country districts. The ritual is not only to welcome the arriving and speed the parting guest but also to prove one's hospitality with many gifts. The recipient is expected to bestow other gifts in return. The circle must be made complete. A simple "thank you" is not enough. Only a crude American would let it go at that.

The family in Greece still arranges many marriages, but young love, brooking no refusal, has also come of age. Sex is mandatory for the unmarried male, forbidden under the harshest penalties for the unmarried woman. The husband rules his house absolutely. Even in Athens a wife must wait until she gets her husband into the bedroom alone before she dares to lay him out. If a married man carries on with another woman, the people will say "poor wife." But if a wife carries on with another man, they will say "that slut."

Strange things still take place when a Greek gets angry. Twice during the last visit that I made to Athens the newspapers reported that a man had had his ear bitten off in a fight. Once it happened in a line of people waiting for a bus. One Greek pushed another aside in order to get ahead of him, and the man who was pushed hurled himself at the pusher and bit off his ear. The second incident involved two men who were in a violent dispute over the reputation of the sister of one of them. The paper duly reported that in each instance the de-eared men were speeded to the hospital where their ears were sewed back on, apparently as good as ever.

Another Greek habit is to smash the glasses and plates after a customer has had a few *ouzos* in a taverna. The party is thus enlivened and the taverna proprietor actually makes money on the breakage, often selling the crockery at twice what it cost him. Onassis is known to have paid as much as $700 for a few moments of fun, throwing the glassware at a taverna wall. Smashed plates and glasses are considered the strongest approval of the local *bouzouki* music and of the fare. Musicians have been known to measure the degree of their popularity with the thickness of the debris at their feet.

Under the present junta regime crockery tossing began to seem too tame so many customers took to removing and setting fire to their clothes. The junta quickly reacted and put an end to this "barbaric custom" and to the glass breaking as well. Breakers of the new law are threatened with a six months' jail sentence to cool off. Restaurant business has gone into an alarming decline as a result, despite the introduction of plastic crockery, which has taken all the fun away because it will not break. The whole thing is not so humorous as it may seem, for have not the Greeks been smashing up their political parties, their courts, and their parliaments for many generations?

THE RECENT YEARS

Greek history in this century has been marked by a growing sense of nationalism, an increase in the Greek middle class, industrialization of the cities, and a slow but steady improvement of the economic status of the Greek farmer and herder. Along with these positive factors the people have had to contend with deeply rooted political corruption, undisciplined political parties, court nepotism, an agonizingly slow rate of improvement in the country districts, and in more recent years a steady growth of the cantankerous extremes of the political right and left.

The outstanding Greek political leader of the first half of the twentieth century was a Cretan lawyer turned diplomat, Eleutherios Venizelos, who served several times as prime minister of his country. Venizelos, whose family had emigrated to Crete from Greece in the eighteenth century, first became prime minister in 1910. He was specifically called to power to allay the frustration and unrest of the people. During the next ten years he gave his country its first effective constitution and made Greece at last responsive to the rule of impersonal law. From 1910 until his death in 1936 Venizelos was the most important man in Greece. Under him the king gradually lost political stature as the prime ministry increased its strength and responsiveness to the popular will.

During its century and a half of independence Greece has had seven kings and two republics. Not one of the kings had any Greek blood in him; the royal family is notably Germanic. But this is nothing new in Europe; Britain also has a Germanic dynasty and Spain had both a long Hapsburg and a long Bourbon line. A chronological list of the kings of Greece follows:

Otto I (or Otho), from Bavaria	1833–1862
George I, from Denmark (assassinated)	1863–1913
Constantine I, his son, married Kaiser's sister, favored Germans in World War I, forced out by Allied powers	1913–1917
Alexander I, second son of Constantine I, became king; the crown prince was unacceptable to Allies. Alexander married a Greek girl and the monarchs became very popular. King died of blood poisoning when bitten by pet monkey	1917–1920
Constantine I, restored to throne, but was forced out again after disastrous defeat of Greeks by Turks	1920–1922
George II, his son, ruled briefly, forced out by military-led antiroyalists	1922–1923
Second Greek Republic, brief period of dictatorship, followed by productive ministry of Venizelos. Republic died when political parties became hopelessly deadlocked and depression hit Greece	1924–1935
George II, restored by plebiscite; after one year allowed Prime Minister Metaxas to become dictator	1935–1941
German occupation of Greece	1941–1944
George II, again restored by plebiscite	1946–1947
Paul I, his brother, became king when George II died	1947–1964
Constantine II, King Paul's son; forced out by military junta in 1967	1964–1967

The Greeks, like the Latins, have a plethora of political parties, that bane of Mediterranean individualism. Strong political passions make stable government extremely difficult. The country's foreign affairs in this century have further aggravated the situation; they have been anything but tranquil. Since 1910 Greece has been embroiled in two Balkan wars, in the first and the second World War, in a civil war which almost resulted in a Communist take-over after World War II, and on several occasions the country has been on the verge of a struggle to the death with Turkey, her prime despoiler in modern times.

As a result of the two Balkan wars (1912–1913) and Venizelos' astute diplomacy Greece's national territory and population were almost doubled within three years. Crete, Macedonia, Epirus, a considerable part of Thrace around Salonika, and all but a few of the Greek islands were brought into the national territory. The "Great Idea" of the Greeks scattered throughout the eastern Mediterranean was near realization. The kingdom of Greece now included most of the territories where a Greek-speaking population predominated.

During World War I Venizelos and King Constantine I favored opposite sides. The prime minister strongly supported the Allied cause, while the king, who was married to a sister of the German Kaiser, just as vigorously supported the Central Powers. The king, realizing that he was opposed by both the prime minister and most of the people, resorted to a policy of "strict neutrality." In 1917, however, the Allies compelled Constantine to abdicate, and Greece entered the war on the Allied side. In 1918 her troops, along with those of Britain and other Allied powers, entered Constantinople, where they were cheered by the more than 100,000 Greeks who still lived in that city. As a result of the war additional Turkish territory was given to Greece. Soon thereafter Turkish nationalism was aroused by the brilliant Mustafa Kemal (Atatürk) and in 1922 the Greek army was routed and many of the gains of World War I were lost. The Greek defeat was blamed on the royalist leaders, several of whom were executed when the opposition gained control of the government (1923). The following year Greece was proclaimed a republic.

At the Lausanne Conference of 1923 it was agreed that there would be a peaceful exchange of the 400,000 Turks still living in Greek territory for the approximately 1.3 million Greeks who lived in Turkish territories. After this had been done the vast majority of all Greek-speaking peoples were brought under one government, except for those in Rhodes and the Dodecanese islands which had gone to Italy after her war with Turkey in 1911, and those in Cyprus, which had been in British hands since 1878.

Both the Turks and the British refused to allow Greece to get hold of Cyprus, the Turks because 18 percent of the half million population was Turkish and the British because of the island's strategic value. The conflict was resolved politically in 1960 with Cyprus becoming a republic, but the island is still a powder keg and no real solution to the problem has yet been found. Rhodes and the other Dodecanese islands were finally returned to Greece by Italy in 1947, following World War II, after an occupation of thirty-six years.

From 1924 to 1935 Greece was a republic. In 1928, after several dictators had proved ineffectual, Venizelos was appointed premier for the seventh time. In the elections that followed his party was overwhelmingly endorsed by the people. But the bitterness of partisan politics still existed, and when the worldwide depression hit Greece Venizelos was replaced by a royalist (1933).

In 1935 George II was recalled to the throne. One year later General John Metaxas, the prime minister, became dictator of Greece, largely as a result of the fascist wave then sweeping Europe. "Fear of communism" was the rationalization of the new government, which despite its oppressive politics did carry out a program of drastic economic reforms embracing wages, working hours, health insurance, and other social benefits. The Greek armed services also were greatly improved.

Metaxas at first appeared to align himself with Hitler and Mussolini, but in 1940, when Il Duce demanded passage of Italian troops across Greek territory, Metaxas answered with a resounding "No," and ever since that time October 28 has been a national holiday known as "No Day." The Greeks were united by their opposition to Italy and surprised the world by defeating Mussolini's legions in the field, then driving them out of Greece and halfway across Albania.

Anticipating a full-scale invasion by Hitler, Greece allowed 60,000 British auxiliary troops to land on her soil, but when the German blitz hit the country both Greek and British forces were quickly beaten and the British took refuge on the island of Crete. In April, 1941, the swastika was hoisted over the Parthenon on the Acropolis.

The Germans were opposed by the guerrilla efforts of the Greek National Liberation Front, dominated by its hard core of well-organized Communists. In 1944 the British invaded Greece from the south and the Germans withdrew northward. Most of Greece then came under the control of the National Liberation Front, and the constitutional British-backed government of George Papandreou in Athens had no power outside the capital. Over 10,000 persons were killed in Athens when Papandreou and the British demanded the disarming of the soldiers of the National Liberation Front. The arrival of Winston Churchill and Anthony Eden in Greece averted a national disaster, and an end to the bitter conflict was arranged.

In 1946 a plebiscite endorsed King George, who was invited to return to his country. He was certainly not received by acclamation, for the people remembered that he had been responsible for the Metaxas dictatorship. Many Greeks would have preferred a republic instead of a monarchy in any case. George II faced an impossible task. Communist and other leftist elements in Greece opposed him with armed resistance and received considerable aid across the northern border from their brethren in Romania, Albania, and Yugoslavia.

In 1947 full-scale civil war broke out, and Britain was powerless either to avert or to stop it. The British people were finding unbearable the cost of supporting armies scattered all over the world. The Communists tenaciously but tenuously held control of most of Greece. A temporary power vacuum appeared in the country and the United States decided to intervene in Greek affairs. President Truman proclaimed the "Truman Doctrine," which meant simply that the United States would support governments based on the will of the majority operating in an atmosphere of freedom from political oppression. It would help any people who asked for help against subjugation by armed minorities or outside pressures.

In support of this policy American money and military aid began to pour into Greece, and finally the war against the leftists was won (1949). The defection of Yugoslavia in 1948, and the sealing of that border, was of key importance in the final success of the American venture. During the years of violence over half a million Greeks had been displaced, and 25,000 Greek children had been abducted from their families by armed groups from Romania, Albania, and Yugoslavia. After the fighting stopped a considerable number of these children were returned to their homes.

The upshot of it all was that the United States took over the dominant position in Greek affairs after more than a century during which Britain had played this role. A billion and a half dollars in military aid went to Greece, and another $2 billion of United States aid was expended in other areas of the national life. All this in a country smaller and with less population than the state of Illinois.

The economic and social situation in Greece became relatively stable and there was even a measure of actual prosperity in the cities. The country was fortunate in having a gifted, dynamic prime minister, Constantine Karamanlis, during the crucial years 1956–1964. Although he was the leader of the rich man's party, Karamanlis was a great benefactor to all Greeks. He launched and carried to a successful conclusion a five-year plan of economic reform which pulled the country together. John Gunther remarked that in order to achieve these results "we have the spectacle of a passionately non-Communist government employing procedures invented by the Soviet Union."

After almost a decade as prime minister Karamanlis and King Paul fell at odds over a projected state visit of the king and queen to Britain. Leftist groups in Britain opposed the visit, and so did Karamanlis. On a previous visit Queen Frederika had been pushed around rather roughly. Furthermore, animosity between left and right inside Greece had become highly inflamed when a Socialist deputy was assassinated in Salonika.* The king and queen went to Britain anyway, Karamanlis resigned, and Greece

* The story of this assassination was novelized by Vassilis Vassilikos in a documentary novel with the strange title Z. Four months after the extreme right murdered Gregory Lambrakis in Salonika on May 22, 1963, the letter "Z" (for *zei,* he lives) appeared on

entered a period of political instability from which the junta finally jerked her with a noose around her neck.

The Greek royal family has been particularly ill-advised and incapable of symbolic leadership during the postwar years. Perhaps the days of the monarchy are ended. King Paul died in March, 1964, and was succeeded by his twenty-three-year-old son, Constantine II (Constantine XIII, if the Byzantine line is followed), who is the present nominal king of Greece. Constantine married Princess Anne-Marie of Denmark in 1964, and they have three children, a girl and two sons. The first son, born in May, 1967, in Rome, is heir to the throne. The Greek royal family fled to Italy after the military coup of April, 1967.

A primary cause of the political deterioration which led to the coup was the lack of discipline of the Greek political parties, the splintering of the two main opposing groups, and the increasing bitterness between them which made a crisis of every succession. The involvement of the United States in Greek politics is a subject apart, and will be treated later. The coup itself followed the classic pattern of promising law and order at the cost of liberty.

In the elections of 1964 the coalition Center Union party, organized and headed by George Papandreou, won 171 of 300 seats in the parliament. It was the first time in thirty years that a relatively liberal party had a real majority. The experienced, moderate, and magnetic Papandreou, then seventy-five, had served as prime minister in 1944 after being imprisoned by the Nazis. He had always been a vigorous opponent of the Greek Communists, and once resigned from office rather than accept their support and remain in power. His 1964 program called for a drastic renovation of the Greek government. An air of optimism pervaded Greece. Papandreou's son, Andreas, who had been educated at Harvard and was an American citizen and a professor of political science at the University of California, Berkeley, also entered the government in order to strengthen the hand of his father.

Andreas Papandreou had been a professor in the United States for about twenty years and was new to Greek politics. He had originally returned to Greece on a Guggenheim Fellowship in 1960 and between 1960 and 1964 had been shuttling between Greece and Berkeley. In 1964 he was per-

---

walls in Greece. Vassilikos points out the analogy to the early Christians who wrote "X" on the walls of Rome. The assassination took place in the novelist's home town, and the story he tells rings true. In the novel he also expresses the resentments of the Greeks over NATO, the close tie-up of Greece with the Sixth Fleet, Polaris missiles, the CIA (Central Intelligence Agency), and the large Greek bureaucracy (including the military) "who look on peace as a threat leveled directly against themselves."*

* Robert J. Clements, "Prefiguring the Coup," *Saturday Review,* Nov. 16, 1968.

suaded by his father and friends in Athens to run for the Greek parliament, so he resigned his professorship, made the race, and was elected. When the new administration took office he became minister to the prime minister (his father), a patronage-controlling position.

The Papandreou government got off to a good start. There was unprecedented political freedom in the country and many social, educational, political, and agricultural reforms were initiated. For the first time in a generation a fresh breeze was blowing across Greece. But after a few months things began to bog down. The Papandreous were opposed by the army and the conservative elements in the country, and on more than one occasion by American representatives in Athens, particularly the head of the Central Intelligence Agency. A crisis arose when Greece and Turkey came to the brink of war over Cyprus, and the United States, alarmed lest this should leave NATO's bottom side very much exposed, strove to effect a compromise partitioning of the island. George and Andreas Papandreou were invited to Washington but could not be persuaded to adopt the American view. Indeed, to have done so would have meant political suicide for both men and the immediate fall of their government. The United States reaction to this visit was that Andreas was more recalcitrant, more "neutralist," more dubious of NATO and of the alignment of Greece with the West than was his father.

The elder Papandreou then made a politically unwise trip to Moscow in order to put the old political squeeze on the United States. When he returned to Athens the leaders of the right demanded his resignation. George Papandreou announced that he would purge the Greek army of its rightist officers, and the king, under strong conservative pressure, opposed this move on the ground that it would expose the country to Communist domination.

Andreas Papandreou had been placed in charge of the political handling of the Cyprus problem, and General Grivas, commander of the Cypriot army, struck back with a host of charges against him. According to General Grivas, Andreas was head of the "Aspida" (Shield) conspiracy of leftist army officers against the monarchy. The alleged aims of Aspida were to get rid of the monarchy, break off ties with the West, and establish a dictatorship of the left in Greece. Twenty-eight army officers were brought to trial, and fifteen of these were found guilty, but witnesses against them later admitted to having taken huge bribes to present testimony, and the whole Aspida episode may well have been deliberately trumped up in order to blacken the Papandreous in the public eye. Andreas enjoyed political immunity as a member of the government and was never brought to trial. The crisis of July, 1965, which led to the military coup of 1967, was now at hand.

The king, anxious to replace George Papandreou as prime minister, soon found an opportunity. The defense minister surreptitiously reported to the king that a purge of the Greek High Command was being planned by the cabinet. When this news got back to the prime minister he (with cabinet support) demanded that the defense minister resign. He refused to do so. George Papandreou himself then *threatened* to resign, and the king without further ado acted as if the resignation were a fact and summarily replaced him with another prime minister, Athanasiadis-Novas, president of the parliament. This man was literally laughed out of office. In his younger days he had been given to writing poetry, and one of his more noteworthy pieces was about the whiteness of women's breasts and the great kick he got out of tickling them. Every time the prime minister appeared in public the Athenians howled: "Tickle them, tickle them!" Novas was the first in a series of ineffectual prime ministers, and finally parliament was dissolved and elections were set for May, 1967.*

The crisis of July, 1965, and the fall of the Papandreou government made Andreas Papandreou a national figure. Up to this time he had been a rather unpopular outsider meddling in Greek politics. Now he began to stump the country and to write in glowing terms about a "new deal" for Greece. His envisioned program was a mixture of Franklin Roosevelt's, plus several additions from Kennedy and Johnson, plus a considerable amount of his own nationalistic charisma. He was attacked vigorously by the right, and these attacks helped to increase his popularity. He won many followers among the youth, the workers, and the intellectuals. A large number of deputies of his father's party switched their loyalty to him, and Andreas began to replace his father in the limelight. By this time father and son were rapidly moving apart politically, and at the end of 1966 they were no longer on speaking terms. All communication between them had to be through an intermediary. Andreas almost broke away completely in order to form his own party, but he did not go that far. Elections were just around the corner, and he hoped to gain much strength at the polls. The Greek army and conservatives looked on his meteoric rise with a jaundiced eye.

The elections set for May, 1967, which never took place, would undoubtedly have given a majority to the Center Union party of the Papandreous, and within that party the faction of Andreas would almost surely

---

* From *The Death of a Democracy,* by Stephen Rousseas.

have outweighed and opposed that of his father. The right's fear of this was one of the obvious reasons for the coup. But with the Center Union thus split it is highly dubious if it could have operated as an effective political entity. Political paralysis might well have been the result, or political chaos, at least until the elder Papandreou died.

The human question cannot escape us now. A son, who had been helped by his father to obtain a Harvard education and thus a good position in the United States, was asked by his father to lend a supporting hand in the Greek government. The son was to become a member of a team (the Center Union party) of which his father was founder, coach, and captain. The son accepted this position, but when his father was abruptly replaced as prime minister the young man began to build up support for himself at the old man's expense. His power play led to a modern Greek tragedy. In the judgment of many people this would be regarded as somewhat less than honorable behavior.

Andreas Papandreou, with all his intellect and charisma, with all his political science and probable good intentions toward the people of Greece, shattered the political edifice it had taken his father half a century to build, became a popular demagogue, and rashly aroused the passion of both his followers and his opponents. He was trying to apply to Greece a policy and a program which would work only in a disciplined political environment. His tragic flaw was faulty judgment. To this extent he was as much responsible for the coup as the Greek army or the king or the American meddlers in Greek affairs. Impatience explains but does not justify his behavior.

Political fragmentation has always been the bane of Greek politics, whereas compromise is the first essential of all democratic government. If Andreas represents the kind of undisciplined and unethical behavior which characterizes Greek political life at the top, it is frightening to imagine what must have been going on lower down the line. A further irony is that in less than two years the old man died and the son might have inherited everything.

In April, 1967, a group of lower-ranking army officers, with a single general among them, seized control of the government. The junta leaders belonged to a political organization of their own, the Sacred League of Greek Officers, a secret order inspired by the Byzantine monastic community tradition. They were well organized and well prepared, but had not expected the take-over to be so easy.

The king was caught unawares by the coup, which was carried out expertly and without violence. He had not expected things to go that far; protesting his enforced puppetry Constantine left Greece and went into exile. Both Papandreous were arrested, many other prominent deputies, journalists, writers, "leftists," and intellectuals were placed under rigid restrictions, and over 5,000 of the most important or outspoken of them were sent off to prison on the island of Yiaros. The junta then appointed an entire new set of political bosses, replacing even the minor officials and the mayors of many small towns.

All essential freedoms and political rights were annulled. The press was muzzled, public opposition was silenced, free speech became illegal, even the educational curriculum was recast in order to emphasize "Greek Christian" values and a strong sense of nationalism based on the "old virtues." A silly and ineffectual attempt to stamp out miniskirts, beards, long hair, and indecent motion pictures made the regime look ridiculous. A more effective prohibition against the presentation of certain Greek plays of the fifth century B.C. which spoke too persuasively of injustice, bad government, revolt, or freedom proved conclusively how dogmatic the junta was in fact.* Hundreds of private organizations were dissolved, the officers of many others were replaced, tenure in the Greek civil service was abolished, and the junta closed its iron grip on the Greek Orthodox Church, the bar associations, the agricultural cooperatives, and even small Jewish organizations. Greece, in a word, became a police state.

More recently—in September, 1968—the regime made an Indian gift to the people of Greece. It drew up and submitted to the electorate a new Greek constitution which was overwhelmingly endorsed in a meaningless election. The junta found it difficult to coax any honorable Greek intellectual to help draft this constitution, so it was hardly inspiring, in the first place. And, in the second, the junta made it clear that none of the civil guarantees mentioned in the document would go into effect until "the revolution" was complete. As no revolution is ever complete, the bait of constitutional government was out-and-out hypocrisy.

The biggest myth today in regard to Greece is that this state of affairs is supported by the majority of the people. No such support exists. No intellectual or political leader of stature has either endorsed or participated in the new totalitarian regime. Indeed, it is a tribute to the Greek intellectuals that even those who had shown little interest in politics have sat on their

---

* The junta decree banned all performances which might "disturb public order, promote subversive theories, discredit the Greek nation or tourism, offend the Christian faith, the King or the government, undermine the people's social traditions, or harm the esthetic advance of our citizenry—particularly our youth." Among the famous classic plays banned are *The Suppliants,* by Euripides, in which a free city triumphs over tyranny; Sophocles' *Ajax;* the bawdy political satires of Aristophanes: *The Birds, The Clouds,* and *The Frogs;* and Euripides' *Phoenician Women.*

hands rather than give even the slightest evidence of support to the junta government. Others are still in prison. Many have gone into exile, and all who remained in Greece are using the weapon of silence and noncooperation. The ordinary Greek citizen, finding himself deprived of every democratic and human right in the country where democracy itself was born, is not liable to endure the present state of oppression for very long, which brings us back to United States involvement in Greek affairs.

No small nation in today's "free world" is able to control its foreign policy unless its domestic policy is impeccably administered and its opposing political parties united in confronting all outside pressure. Such a state of affairs is difficult to come by, but in Sweden, Norway, Denmark, Holland, Switzerland, and a few other small countries with a long tradition of stable government we do find examples. The more underdeveloped countries, however, which must receive heavy financial aid from the outside or drop completely out of the procession, are obviously beholden to their benefactors. Greece certainly falls in this category, along with Portugal, Spain, the Arab world, and most of the countries of Asia and Africa. This outside aid implies an inevitable repayment, and even prepayment, which is as much political as it is financial.

Greece has never been the complete master of its own foreign policy. After its independence in 1830 the country fell into the British orbit and remained under strong British influence for over a century. In 1841 the British minister to Athens, Sir Arthur Lyons, stated the case very clearly: "A Greece truly independent is an absurdity. Greece is either Russian or she is English; and since she must not be Russian, it is necessary that she be English . . ." Strangely enough, Russia herself recognized this political reality up through World War II. The Soviet Union even acknowledges today that Greece is not within the strategic Soviet sphere of influence. It has, indeed, recognized and accredited the junta government.

But after the Second World War had ended and the Greek Civil War broke out, an exhausted Britain withdrew from Greece in favor of the United States (1947). American money, machines, supplies, military equipment, industrial know-how, and many agents of the CIA flooded Greece, which was clearly on our side. For twenty years prior to the military coup of April, 1967, these close relations continued. Was it, then, mere coincidence that the man who headed the coup and now heads the junta, Colonel George Papadopoulos, was the main liaison officer between the CIA and its Greek counterpart, the KYP? Was it mere coincidence that another of the three spiritual leaders of the junta, Nicholas Makarezos, was the key intelligence officer of the KYP? Was it mere coincidence that the

Greek KYP was financed by the American CIA rather than by the government in Athens?

This need not imply that America's representatives in Greece directly encouraged the coup, but it does imply that their estimate of the situation, the advice they gave, the reports they made, the policies they backed both in Washington and in Athens must have been far off base. The king, for his part, also received much erroneous and misleading advice. As a consequence, when the coup came he was powerless to avert it. The fact that a coup was so easily engineered indicates the inefficacy of American policy as well as the frailty of Greek politics.

Of course, it can reasonably be argued that the Greeks themselves, and particularly those in government positions, should have known better than anybody else what was going on in Greece. But American wisdom, American dollars, and American might add up to a powerful and most persuasive trinity, whose godhead was fear of communism. Many Greeks have accepted this new deity, particularly the military establishment.

Strangely enough, George Papadopoulos, present junta head, and Andreas Papandreou, son of the deposed and recently deceased liberal prime minister of Greece, now find themselves beating the same drum. Its unpleasant tune is that American policy (George says "helpfully," Andreas says "hurtfully") led directly to the present military regime in Greece. This drumbeating focuses Greek attention on the foreign meddler and "goat," and provides, of course, an easy escape from their own political irresponsibility. Unfortunately, the majority of Greek citizens are inclined to agree with these two leaders and also cast a great part of the blame for their present predicament on the United States. Becoming the unpopular goat is one of the inevitable results of an unenlightened American foreign policy.

Emotions play as strong a role in national and international affairs as any of the more concrete aspects of domestic or foreign policy, and emotions are extremely susceptible to swings in the political wind. In 1967, just prior to the coup in Greece, secret polls indicated that the Papandreou coalition would receive at least 60 percent of the total vote in the forthcoming elections. The Greek colonels ostensibly rebelled against this potential "leftist take-over" in Greece which, they feared, would topple the monarchy and put their country in the Soviet camp.

But the real enemy was not communism, as the colonels so loudly proclaimed. The real enemy was a bankrupt Western liberalism and Western democracy with its widespread contempt of authority, student unrest, violence in the streets, hippies, welfare philosophy, pornography, and escape in drugs. To the members of the junta that is what Andreas stood for. The colonels further felt that the United States and Great Britain (and France, of course) no longer represented an acceptable political ideal toward which the Greeks might advance. In fact, in their eyes the Western democracies epitomized a political philosophy that is devoid of meaning. Greece could not experience a parallel lapse in law and order and survive as a healthy national organism. The United States and Britain might be able to "muddle through"; Greece never. The colonels, therefore, following the pattern of military take-overs of the past, "seized control of the government in order to save their country from social and political disintegration." This was the prevailing emotion behind the coup, and this is the kind of feeling and thinking which maintains the present military government in Greece.

Having said this, the easy thing would be to dismiss the coup as just another annoying military take-over in a politically and economically unstable country. One might add the pious hope that the junta will not endure for long or affirm with certainty that it will inevitably fall and be replaced by a government of the people. But this would be sidestepping one of the most important realities of contemporary Greek life. As many other countries find themselves in the same predicament, this point calls for a more detailed scrutiny.

The recent putsch in Greece represents a basic maneuver in twentieth-century world politics: the middle-class military coup. The Greek take-over was not a coup of the upper class, or of the king, or even of the higher-placed generals. It was a middle-class military coup, pure and simple, which with a single stroke ousted both the conservative king of Greece and the potential leftist government of the Papandreous.

The same process of industrialization which in recent years has increased and strengthened the Greek middle class has also increased and strengthened the working class. The working class, because of its labor unions and relative solidarity politically, is better able to mobilize itself than is the middle class. In Greece and other economically backward countries the result has been that the working class tends to align itself somewhere left of center, i.e., left of the status quo.

When a worker strikes or demands higher wages and better working conditions he does not do so for himself alone, but for all the members of his union. When a middle-class employee asks for a higher wage or better working conditions he speaks only for himself. This is the basic weakness of the middle class in today's political and economic life. But the middle class is far from impotent, for it has created and nourished the middle-class army as its very effective voice.

The one distinctive feature of today's middle class in Greece and most other underdeveloped countries is that it refuses to stay in the middle. As Aristotle said many centuries ago, those who are unequals want to become equals and those who are equals want to become superior. This characterizes the contemporary Greek middle class precisely. However, the middle class has no feeling of solidarity and no civilian organization which can act or speak out in its behalf. It is composed of many shades of opinion, of many political groups and economic philosophies, and it cannot even function effectively in free elections, for it refuses to vote with anything like unanimity. Its members move freely from one party to another in the political spectrum; they call themselves "independent" voters, but they are in fact captive voters, for they vote mainly against their opponents and not for specific programs or ideologies.

In this mélange of diverse and often opposing elements the military establishment constitutes a well-organized and well-disciplined minority. It is not that the middle class as a whole endorses the military when it intervenes in politics, but rather that the military establishment itself has become a middle-class institution, the only middle-class institution of the world's poor countries which can operate effectively in today's complex political scene.

In this middle-class military setup, deprived and disoriented rural and urban workers are continuously turned into less deprived and more clearly oriented middle-class soldiers. They receive more benefits and more economic security in the military service than they would on the farm or in the unskilled labor ranks in the urban centers. They learn that in the army it is not necessary to make any decisions or to take any risks. They are not at the mercy of the weather or of a capricious marketplace. They no longer fear poverty, disease, malnutrition, or political impotence.

They begin to be "educated," although the word here should perhaps be "indoctrinated," because along with whatever education they receive these soldiers are primarily taught pride in their country, in its history, and unquestioning loyalty to this symbol. They are also taught discipline, the one quality which is almost completely lacking in all political parties, excepting only the Communists. This is particularly true of the Greek political parties, but the same could be said for those of Spain before the Civil War, for those of Argentina, or Portugal, or even France, before de Gaulle.

Discipline, pride, and loyalty constitute a powerful weapon when they are united "to uphold respect for law and order lest everything of value [middle-class value] go down the drain." But soldiers need something more than slogans and ideals in order to function effectively. In the military scheme of things this means that scantily educated soldiers must be taught to regard their officers as the embodiment of the values which they have learned to hold sacred. The officer corps, in a word, is the nation's guardian, the protector of its history, its order, its decency, its law, and its progress. And, strangely enough, the more highly professionalized the army has become the more closely linked it is with the rest of society, especially with the middle class of which it is the only unified and solidly operating part. In Greece this has been especially true because the constant crises with Turkey over Cyprus have served to sharpen the army's morale and to increase its identification with the nation as a whole.

The officers, for their part, are quite aware of their newly acquired status and feel a sense of mission, almost a "call" to defend the middle-class establishment, *their* establishment, whenever they feel that it is threatened, either by the lower-class left or the upper-class right. But generally the middle-class army counts on the right for support and cooperation. Only when this is not received does it oppose the right, and even then always with the hope of reaching an understanding, an understanding between equals. The left, on the other hand, is almost invariably its enemy, because the non-Communist left proverbially operates with a lack of discipline in an atmosphere of disorder, and this is the one thing which the military cannot tolerate. The hard-core Communist left, small in Greece, which strikes directly for positions of power, is even more intolerable.*

Any political or economic crisis can bring about a middle-class military coup. The upper class wants to preserve privilege, the lower class wants to destroy privilege, and the middle class wants to acquire privilege. Whenever a crucial decision has to be reached the *appel au soldat* becomes a strong possibility if the decision is either delayed too long or is taken without strong majority backing. At the first sign of a breakdown in political stability the army begins to feel uneasy and mobilizes itself for action.

Where there is a swing toward revolution and disorder—a swing which might destroy the precarious equilibrium of the state—the middle class and the middle-class army regard it as a direct threat to their own existence. They fear such a swing, they openly revile it, and they stand immediately ready to suppress it. The cards are stacked, because in order to succeed the

* The Communist party, illegal in Greece, operated through the EDA, United Democratic Left.

swing toward revolution (inevitably weak in political organization and poor in planning) would necessarily (a) operate without proper discipline, which the middle class instinctively deplores; (b) offend the upper class, symbol of the nation's history and holder of its wealth; (c) offend powerful foreign friends, thus frightening away foreign investments, tourists, and canceling out numerous well-paying jobs with foreign companies already within the country; (d) would thus disrupt the economy, injure the national image, and hurt the middle class itself.

In summarizing the Greek situation it could be said that the middle-class military coup was the revolt of equals who, by virtue of that revolt and its success, became immediately superior. Unfortunately, this is probably not the last time such a thing will take place in Greece. At this point the question might validly be raised: if the military represents such a small sector of the middle class, if the middle class itself is so divided in its attitudes toward the junta, and if the workers and intellectuals almost totally oppose the junta, how indeed can such a government maintain itself?

The answer, given facetiously by one of the few Greek intellectuals who do not blame the United States for what has happened, is simply that the junta stays up in a vacuum, just like the astronauts. Once in position, an invisible force sustains them both. But speaking more realistically the military is a compact and disciplined minority within a thoroughly disorganized and disoriented social system in which the majority has lost the capacity to function peacefully. Under these conditions the organized minority always holds the trump card.

In Greece the net result of the recent middle-class military coup has been that the colonels, who certainly had no wish to do so, succeeded in ousting the king, something which both George and Andreas Papandreou with all their votes were unable to accomplish. At the same time the colonels abruptly prevented a swing toward the left. It was clearly a case of hitting two birds with one stone. The present junta government, therefore, despite its burdensome strait jacket, stands politically at dead center, an impossible position to maintain for long, but a position, alas, toward which the middle-class army gravitates as if by second nature. The foregone conclusion, of course, is a gradual loss of support, even within its own ranks.

Premier George Papadopoulos, who heads the junta, is one of the more flexible leaders of the military government. He recently overruled his fellow officers by staying the execution of an army private who had attempted to assassinate him, and he has stated publicly that he is anxious to vacate his "throne" with all the dubious niceties it has entailed. At the same time he has made it plain that he will not tolerate any breakdown in order when the parliamentary process is resumed. His exact words were:

> Unfortunately, the perversion of our political life in the past was so profound that I personally am certain that our citizens are not yet mature. We Greeks have the weakness of acting not only from logic but from emotion, and the politicians of the past must be cured of this weakness before they can help start a healthy process toward the formation of political parties and the holding of elections.

But Premier Papadopoulos is too cagey a politician himself to be pinned down to any timetable, so when questioned on this point he remarked, "When will this time come? I cannot risk a prophecy."

Today the people of Greece suffer, hope, and wait. Their king is in exile, George Papandreou is dead (his funeral was attended by an incredible multitude),* his son, Andreas Papandreou, ex-professor at the University of California, lives in exile. The junta released him from prison and allowed him to leave the country. Without a doubt Andreas is the symbolic leader of those among his countrymen—and they constitute a majority—who plan and dream of a free Greece. About six weeks before the coup Andreas made the following statement, which represents his basic views:

> Greece refuses the status of a poor relative or of a satellite. It insists on its own right, while executing its obligations as an ally, to determine its own course. It affirms its right to expand its commercial, economic and cultural relations with all other nations, independently of the bloc to which they belong. It assigns special importance to developing good relations with its Balkan neighbors, the countries of the Near and Middle East and the new nations of Africa. It insists on its right to follow closely developments in the European area, where a reduction of tensions, a rapprochement among nations of the East and West, and a new approach to European solidarity are taking place. But above all, Greece insists that its allies cease interfering in its internal political affairs.†

It was precisely this view which set the rightist Greek colonels back on their heels and impelled, they say, the strong reaction that still prevails in Greece. But the fact remains that Andreas Papandreou is the unofficial

---

* At least 300,000 Greeks massed in the streets of Athens as the elder Papandreou's flag-draped coffin was borne from the city's cathedral. The crowd began to chant: "We want freedom!" and "Down with tyranny!" It was the first large-scale public protest against the junta government (Nov. 8, 1968).

† Papandreou's remarks are from an article by him which appeared in the *New York Times Magazine*, July 21, 1968.

leader of those who oppose the dictatorship. Writing from Paris he recently said, "The struggle for freedom will succeed because the alternative is not viable; the junta has no answers to the problems of Greece." He went on to add that "the Greek problem is really an American problem" and asked for a reappraisal of America's policy toward his country.

It is impossible to separate the coup in Greece from American foreign policy which has linked the two countries so closely for twenty years. When President Truman decided to intervene in Greece in 1947 he pointed out that there were two possible directions which that country might take: first, the way of political freedom and social reform, which should help to make Greece an effectively functioning part of the free world; or second, the way of political oppression and terror imposed by either inside minorities or outside pressures, or both. For two decades the United States labored and expended hundreds of millions of dollars in order to bring about the first of these alternatives, but now, in spite of repeated and almost unrestricted opportunities, we have wound up with the second.

Official United States reaction to the junta take-over was not at first a very happy one. The Administration was embarrassed to find itself fighting for freedom in Vietnam and to have tyranny in Greece suddenly thrown in its face. American aid, especially heavy military aid, was cut. But when the Soviet Union invaded Czechoslovakia in the summer of 1968 this policy was changed. The *New York Times* summed up the present American attitude in the following editorial comment:

> Washington has decided to do everything it can to provide the Athens junta with the prestige and respectability it has hungered after since its putsch of last April. The reasons given for this course are drearily familiar: The United States cannot risk a vacuum on NATO's southern flank at a time of expanding Soviet influence in the Mediterranean . . . the colonels are a fact of life . . .

The junta, of course, is friendly to American interests. It is also friendly to minority Greek interests. It uses American arms and money to keep its own people in subjugation. It represents a dictatorship of the most oppressive kind. It allows none of the basic human freedoms. It imprisons Greek citizens without due process. Indeed, without any process at all. It is the unpalatable proof of the failure of America's policy in Greece.

The Washington *Post* very aptly characterized American policy in these words: "In the name of defending the free world, Washington props up a government that withholds freedom from its own people." As a reaction to recent Soviet moves this may be a defensible choice but it is by no means a desirable choice. And in the long run it will not prove to be an intelligent choice, because by supporting now a military minority at the expense of the Greek people the United States is in the process of alienating those very people who have always had the greatest admiration for the United States.

In the end the people of Greece are bound to take over their government, and what will they think of us then? Governments change, parliaments crumble, but the people go on forever. It is to the people that an intelligent policy must address itself. The fatal arrogance of power has led us far from this obvious truth of international diplomacy. It is so much easier to deal with smaller groups. The death of freedom in Greece after twenty years of unchallenged American influence has weakened the United States image everywhere.

Greece symbolizes the painful dilemma of American foreign policy all over the world. The duplicity of preaching morality in one area and self-interest in another has aroused much of the widespread frustration, unrest, lack of faith, and lack of direction in America today. Until this dilemma is somehow reasonably resolved neither the United States nor Greece, nor indeed any of the countries of the "free world," will be able to inspire their citizenry again with those democratic ideals which had their genesis in ancient Greece five centuries before Christ.

We have made the complete circle and are now back at the beginning. The early Greeks, like all primitive peoples, lived in an ordered universe, but as man has become more "civilized" he has become progressively more fragmented. Modern man sees the fragmentation of all reality and feels that he has neither identity nor epoch. There is no easy pathway back to the magic spring. But the value of a culture outlasts all the vicissitudes of history and all the vexations of power. What Greece has given to the world no coat of mail can hide completely. At this juncture the members of the junta in Athens might strive to remember the four virtues of Plato: wisdom, justice, courage, temperance. They have so far followed only the philosopher's self-righteous dogmatism. An old Greek proverb says: *The slip of a giant leaves a race track for a dwarf.* This, in a nutshell, characterizes the Greece of today.

Nikos Kazantzakis has put it well:

Ours is a sacred and most bitter fate. At the end of my trip through Greece I was filled with tragic, unexpected questions. Starting with beauty, we had arrived at the agonies of our times and the present-day duty imposed on every Greek. Today, a man who is alive—who thinks, loves and struggles—is no longer able to amble along in a careless way, appreciating beauty. The struggle, today, is spreading like a conflagration, and no fire brigade can insure our safety. Every man is struggling and burning along with all humanity. And the Greek nation is struggling and burning more than all the rest. This is its fate . . . The circle closed. My eyes filled with Greece . . . I saw more clearly the historic mission of my country, placed as it is between East and West; I realized that her supreme achievement is not beauty but the struggle for liberty.*

Odysseus, speaking for all Greeks, uttered a glorious and eternal response:

> Ay, miserable me, now I am only a shadow
> Of the strong man that I once was! But if
> You look with care at this old stubble
> Then you may guess how straight and tall
> Once grew the corn.

* From *Report to Greco,* by Nikos Kazantzakis.

Appendix: Concerning Translations

How good are the English translations of ancient Greek literature? The answer is that some are excellent and will serve the reader of today very well, while others would be almost impossible to read. Particularly in the case of Homer considerable care should be taken before one begins either the *Iliad* or the *Odyssey*. Either work can be completely ruined by a poor or outdated translation. The Italians have a phrase *traduttore, traditore* (translator, betrayer), which means, of course, that no translation can accurately reproduce the flavor and reality of the original. Nevertheless, there is always the best possible translation for any given reader's purpose.

The further back in time the translator goes, the more difficult his task becomes. Archaic forms of speech, old word endings, idiomatic expressions, and outmoded phrasings lose poetic value when they are rendered literally; and when they are transposed into the archaic form of another language which represents a completely different cultural and linguistic pattern they require the hand of a genius. Archaic speech is acceptable in the King James Version of the Bible, but no Elizabethan translation of Homer is anywhere near that good. Nor indeed is any translation made in the seventeenth, eighteenth, or nineteenth century. For the contemporary reader they all strike false notes.

If the scholar-specialist is truthful (but stuffy) he will say that Greek literature, like any foreign literature, can be appreciated to the fullest only in the original. But how many people today can read Homer in old Greek? There are good and bad translations, and the best ones have real poetic and dramatic value. Each generation of translators has improved in some ways on the best preceding version. For one thing, our knowledge of the ancient Greek language has steadily increased with the passing centuries and our knowledge of the ancient ways of life is in many regards more accurate than that of Homer himself. Furthermore, in recent decades so many poets of real genius have applied themselves to the task of translating from the old Greek that it is only logical to find an artistic progression in their various renditions. Consequently, for today's reader no translation made more than twenty or thirty years ago would be acceptable in a *literary* sense.

George Chapman's version of Homer, made in 1612, and greatly admired by Keats two centuries later, now sounds hopelessly stilted. Alexander Pope's translation, made in 1715, falls in the same category. But in their day both these English Homers were regarded as classics. Chapman, Pope, Dryden, and nearly all the earlier translators of Homer jar today's more sophisticated reader with their monotonous rhymed couplets and their Roman (Latin) names of the Greek gods. Today when we read "Jove" instead of "Zeus," "Vulcan" in place of "Hephaestus," "Minerva" instead of "Athena," or even "Ulysses" instead of "Odysseus," the feeling of reality is gone.

The translators of Homer are legion and include W. C. Bryant, Leigh Hunt, Tennyson, William Morris, A. T. Murray, George Palmer, William Cowper, Richmond Lattimore, Robert Fitzgerald, and Ennis Rees. Samuel Butler made a translation in prose which is still read, and so did a famous group of translators, who also worked at the end of the past century: Andrew Lang, Walter Leaf, Ernest Myers, and S. H. Butcher. Their version of Homer, still widely available in the Modern Library series, in a giant one-volume edition containing both epics, is one of the most accurate ever made. For the historian such precision is certainly very important. As a noted historian writes, "The greater a translation is a work of art, the less likely it is to retain the precision the historian desires in what we may call the technical words and phrases."*

But, on the other hand, to translate a great work of poetry into prose is like taking the Parthenon apart in order to reconstruct it in a different form. All the stones are there but all the magic has departed. What is gained in accuracy and comprehension is lost in feeling, and feeling, not precision, is the heart of poetry. The goal of the translator should be to call forth the emotions expressed by the original, or to come as near to this as possible. If this judgment is correct, we must rule out all prose translations as having insufficient poetic value, and the recent very popular ones by E. V. Rieu would thus summarily be discarded. Admittedly the student of history might turn this evaluation the other way around.

Among the recent poetic translations of Homer the following are of high artistic quality: Richmond Lattimore and Ennis Rees have translated both epics beautifully into English and Robert Fitzgerald has made a fine translation of the *Odyssey*. The earliest of these (Lattimore's *Iliad*) was made in 1951. Ennis Rees, especially in his *Iliad,* has kept continuously in motion the warm stir of life. He occasionally shocks his readers with such graphic contemporary terms as "bitchhearted," "nagging," "griping," "gang up," etc. And he uses the word "sin" in his *Iliad* (9. 504–512) where Lattimore uses "ruin," thus suggesting a completely different emotional frame. ("Ruin" or "Sin" *outruns all Prayers, wins everywhere, and forces men to stray.*) But in Rees's lines Homer's story moves dramatically and poetically to its tragic end.

* M. I. Finley, *The World of Odysseus.*

Robert Fitzgerald's *Odyssey* is certainly a masterpiece by any standards, but as another fine translator from the Greek, Rex Warner, remarked in reviewing this work, when we read Fitzgerald's *Odyssey* it is difficult to know whether we are admiring Homer or admiring Fitzgerald. Lattimore's severe hexameter lines are closer to Homer's original and have a majestic ring, but they do not sparkle like those of Fitzgerald. His *Iliad* moves a little more somberly than that of Ennis Rees, but once within its web the reader is completely enthralled.

A few examples will point up the different approaches. In Book 6 of Lattimore's *Iliad* Helen says to Hector that he has borne the brunt of the war and hard work:

for the sake of dishonoured me and the blind act of Alexandros.

Ennis Rees translates the same line as follows:

for the sake of bitch-hearted me and the willful blindness of Paris.

Lattimore's Greek names are carried too far for the general reader. Alexandros for Paris, Aias for Ajax, and Achilleus for Achilles will jar on most of us.

In Book 9 of the *Odyssey* Fitzgerald has Odysseus sum up his joyful feeling at a feast given by King Alcinous in these words:

Here is the flower of life, it seems to me!

Lattimore writes:

This seems to my own mind to be the best of occasions.

Ennis Rees puts it:

This seems to me the finest thing in the world.

Lattimore has used understatement, while Fitzgerald has stepped the phrase up. There is no word for "flower" in the original. The literal translation would read: *This to my mind is the fairest (or finest) thing there is.* Homer's key noun is "thing"; Rees has added the phrase "in the world."

In Book 11 of the *Odyssey* when Agamemnon warns Odysseus that he should return to Ithaca and to Penelope unannounced, Fitzgerald's concluding words are:

The day of faithful wives is gone forever.

Lattimore writes:

There is no trusting woman.

Rees says:

For no longer can women be trusted.

In Book 19 of the *Odyssey* when Odysseus is telling Penelope about his travels, in the prose version of Butcher and Lang he says in that version's famous line:

There is a land called Crete in the midst of the wine-dark sea.

Lattimore translates the phrase:

There is a land called Crete in the middle of the wine-blue water.

Rees puts it as follows:

Out there in the midst of the wine-blue sea is the wonderful country of Crete.

Fitzgerald, in one of his less poetic moments, writes:

One of the great islands of the world in midsea, in the winedark sea, is Crete.

The key Greek word here is *oinopos,* which means *wine-colored,* without reference to either "dark" or "blue." But the word was also applied to oxen, so "dark" would appear to be the more accurate adjective, as Butcher and Lang have put it. An additional argument in favor of this translation is that when wine is mentioned in the *Iliad* it is often described as having a "very dark, almost black" color. The phrase "wine-blue sea," therefore, was evidently used by Lattimore and Rees because they saw this sea themselves, and found it blue, as most travelers would today. Perhaps Homer felt the presence of dark depths when he used his descriptive phrase "wine-colored." Perhaps, too, a ritualistic feeling was implied in a linking of wine and sea.

If asked to select the best translation of the Homeric epics not all readers would have the same favorite. But any one of the above-mentioned would be worth an examination before a final choice is made. When we shift our judgment to Greek tragedies the same process repeats itself. Suffice it to say that Paul Roche's translations of Aeschylus and Sophocles are among the finest. The grand old lady of classical scholarship, Edith Hamilton, called Roche's versions of Aeschylus "the best I have ever read." Other critics feel that Lattimore has done an even better job. Rex Warner's translations of Euripides are outstanding and have great poetic charm. Translations of works in prose, and this would include the philosophers and historians, do not present as much of a problem as poetry. In this area the older versions by Jowett, Rawlinson, Dryden, and others are entirely acceptable. Before reading any work of Greek literature the person interested should examine the translations available and then make up his own mind. If he does less than this he is likely to wind up with the wrong version, wrong for him, in any case. Reading a foreign masterpiece in translation is at best a hazardous adventure, and a little caution in advance might prevent a big disappointment in the end.

Bibliography

Aeschylus. *The Orestes Plays of Aeschylus.* Translated by Paul Roche. New York: The New American Library, 1963.

Alsop, Joseph. *From the Silent Earth.* New York: Harper & Row, 1964. (A study of the Greek Bronze Age.)

Aristotle, Horace and Longinus: Classical Literary Criticism. Translated by T. S. Dorsch. Baltimore: Penguin, 1965.

Aristotle. *Aristotle's Politics.* Translated by Benjamin Jowett. London: Macmillan, 1885.

Auden, W. H., ed. *The Portable Greek Reader.* New York: Viking, 1966.

Baldry, H. C. *Ancient Greek Literature in Its Living Context.* London: Thames and Hudson, 1968.

Boardman, John, *Greek Art.* New York: Frederick A. Praeger, 1966.

Burn, A. R. *A Traveller's History of Greece.* New York: Funk and Wagnalls, 1965.

Bury, J. B. *A History of Greece.* London, 1913. Reprint. New York: Modern Library, n.d.

Chadwick, John. *The Decipherment of Linear B.* New York: Vintage, 1960.

Coulanges, N. Fustel de. *The Ancient City.* New York: Doubleday, n.d. (An old classic, originally published in French as *La Cité Antique,* Paris, 1864, and translated into English by Willard Small in 1873. This edition is a reprinting of that translation.)

Euripides. *Euripides.* Seven dramas translated and edited by Gilbert Murray. 2 vols. London: George Allen, 1913–1914.

———. *Three Great Plays of Euripides; Medea, Hippolytus, Helen.* Translated by Rex Warner. New York: Mentor, 1958.

Finley, John H., Jr. Introduction to *The Complete Writings of Thucydides.* New York: Modern Library, 1951.

Finley, M. I. *The World of Odysseus.* New York: Viking, 1965.

———. *The Ancient Greeks.* New York: Viking, 1964.

———. *The Greek Historians.* New York: Viking, 1959.

Frazer, Sir James. *The Golden Bough.* New York: Macmillan, 1958.

Grant, Judith. *A Pillage of Art.* New York: Roy Publishers, 1966.

Greece and Rome, Builders of Our World. Washington, D.C.: National Geographic Society, 1968. (A de luxe book, beautifully illustrated.)

Grote, George. *A History of Greece.* New York: Harper & Brothers. 1st ed. 1846–1856. 12 vols. Reprint. New York: Everyman's Library.

Guthrie, W. K. C. *The Greek Philosophers.* New York: Harper & Row, 1960.

Hadas, Moses. *The Greek Ideal and Its Survival.* New York: Harper & Row, 1966.

——. *The Greek Poets.* New York: Modern Library, 1953.

Herodotus. *The History of Herodotus.* Translated by George Rawlinson. London, 1858. Reprint. New York: Tudor Publishing Co., 1932.

Homer. *The Iliad.* Translated by Andrew Lang, Walter Leaf and Ernest Myers, 1883. Reprint. New York: Modern Library, entitled *The Complete Works of Homer,* 1950; the volume also contains *The Odyssey,* translated by S. H. Butcher and Andrew Lang.

——. *The Iliad of Homer.* Translated by Richmond Lattimore. Chicago: University of Chicago Press, 1966.

——. *The Iliad of Homer.* Translated by Ennis Rees. New York: Modern Library, 1963.

——. *The Odyssey.* Translated by S. H. Butcher and Andrew Lang. London, 1879. Reprint. New York: Modern Library, *The Complete Works of Homer* 1950. In 1 vol. with the *Iliad,* translated by Lang, Leaf and Myers.

——. *The Odyssey.* Translated by Robert Fitzgerald. New York: Doubleday, 1961.

——. *The Odyssey of Homer.* Translated by Richmond Lattimore. New York: Harper & Row, 1967.

——. *The Odyssey of Homer.* Translated by Ennis Rees. New York: Modern Library, 1960.

Hooper, Finley. *Greek Realities.* New York: Scribner's, 1967.

Horizon Book of Ancient Greece. Edited by William Hale. New York: American Heritage, 1965. (Beautifully illustrated.)

Howe, S. G. *Letters and Journals of S. G. Howe.* Edited by Laura Richards. New York, 1910.

Kazantzakis, Nikos. *Report to Greco.* New York: Simon & Schuster, 1965.

Kitto, H. D. F. *Greek Tragedy.* New York: Doubleday, 1954.

——. *The Greeks.* Baltimore: Penguin, 1966.

Lessing, Erich (photographer). *The Voyages of Ulysses,* with critical commentary by Cornelia Kerényi et al. Freiburg im Breisgau, W. Germany: Herder, 1965. (Beautifully illustrated.)

Lloyd-Jones, Hugh, ed. *The Greek World.* Baltimore: Penguin, 1965.

Lucas, F. L. *Greek Tragedy and Comedy.* New York: Viking, 1967.

Mahaffy, J. P. *A History of Classical Greek Literature.* 2 vols. New York: Harper & Brothers, 1880.

——. *Old Greek Education.* New York: Harper & Brothers. 1881.

——. *Rambles and Studies in Greece.* New York: Macmillan, 1913.

——. *Social Life in Greece.* New York: Macmillan, 1892.

Michalopoulos, André. *Homer.* New York: Twayne, 1966.

Nilsson, Martin P. *Greek Folk Religion.* New York: Harper & Row, 1961.

Otto, Walter F. *Dionysus, Myth and Cult.* Translated by Robert Palmer. Bloomington: Indiana University Press, 1965.

——. *The Homeric Gods.* Translated by Moses Hadas. Boston: Beacon Press, 1954.

Plato. *Plato: Dialogues.* Translated by Benjamin Jowett. 4 vols. London, 1871.

Plutarch. *The Lives of the Noble Grecians and Romans.* Translated by John Dryden. New York: Modern Library, n.d.

Pollitt, J. J. *The Art of Greece.* Englewood Cliffs, N.J.: Prentice-Hall, 1965.

Reinach, Salomon. *Orpheus, a History of Religions.* New York: Liveright, 1932.

Rexroth, Kenneth. *Poems from the Greek Anthology.* Ann Arbor: University of Michigan Press, 1962.

Richter, G. M. A. *A Handbook of Greek Art.* London: Phaidon, 1963.

Rousseas, Stephen. *The Death of a Democracy.* New York: Grove Press, 1968.

Sophocles. *The Oedipus Plays of Sophocles.* Translated by Paul Roche. New York: Mentor, 1958.

Spelios, Thomas. *A Pictorial History of Greece.* New York: Crown, 1967.

Thucydides. *Thucydides: History of the Peloponnesian War.* Translated by Benjamin Jowett. 2 vols. London, 1881.

Xenophon. *Memorabilia and Oeconomicus.* Translated by E. C. Marchant. Cambridge, Mass.: Loeb Classical Library, Harvard University Press, 1965.

Zeller, Edward. *Outlines of the History of Greek Philosophy.* New York: World, 1950.

Index

Abortion, practice of, 206
Academy in Athens, the, 212–13, 222, 223
Acamas, 49
Achaean League, 220
Achaeans, 26, 36, 39, 44, 72, 73, 77, 86
Achilles, 13, 28, 36, 42, 47, 49–50, 51–53, 54, 55, 56–57, 68, 72, 73, 74, 76, 77, 159
Acropolis of Athens, 109, 128, 129, 157, 164, 169, 173, 177, 184, 186–93, 220, 246, 261
Adkins, A. W., 83
Aegean Sea, 1, 3
Aegina, 91, 169, 184
Aegisthus, 15
Aeneas, 42, 43
Aeolus, 71
Aeschylus, 1, 88, 96, 121, 139, 140, 143, 144, 146, 149, 150, 155, 201, 240, 282; *quoted,* 134
Agamemnon, 4, 13, 15, 22, 25, 39, 42, 44, 47, 49, 51, 54, 56, 61, 62, 72, 76, 88, 89
Agamemnon (Aeschylus), 150–53
Agorakritos, 179
Agriculture in Greece, 253–54
Ajax, 13, 48, 54, 72, 159
Alaric, 164 n., 232
Alcaeus, 160
Alcibiades, 210–11, 212
Alcinous, 58, 68, 75, 77, 78
Alcman, 111
Alexander the Great, 85, 86, 133, 157, 215, 216, 221, 224

Alexandria, 38, 194, 196, 215, 224, 225, 234
Alkamenes, 179
Alphabet, the, 197–98
American Revolution, 247
Anacreon, 109
Anatolia, 22
Andromache, 49, 57
Anna-Marie, Princess, 263
Anthony, Mark, 85, 220, 224
Antigone, 88
Apelles of Cos, 162, 209
Aphrodite, 42, 44–45, 46, 48, 64, 78, 95, 159
Apollo, xi, 9, 27, 28–30, 44, 53, 55, 78, 148, 186, 252
Aquinas, St. Thomas, 217
Archaic Period, Greek, 85, 156–57
Archimedes, 87
Architecture, Greek, 1, 2, 134, 183–96
Ares (Mars), 44, 45, 52, 64
Arete, 67, 68, 203
Argos, 13, 34, 48, 64, 84, 237
Ariadne, 6, 10
Arian heresy, 229
Aristarchus of Samothrace, 37, 38, 225
Aristophanes, 1, 140, 148–49, 155, 210
Aristotle, 15 n., 37, 39, 87, 108, 109, 140, 143, 147, 212, 214–15, 216, 217, 234, 239; *quoted,* 31, 84, 148, 156, 253
Arius and Arianism, 229, 230
Art, Greek, 15, 22, 24, 129, 134, 156–96, 199

Artemis, 45, 72
Artemisia, 123
Asia Minor, 73, 86, 96, 125, 162, 193, 196, 237
Asklepius, 27
Aspasia, 209
Assembly, Athenian, 106–07, 130, 132
Astyanax, 57
Athanasiadis-Novas, Prime Minister, 265
Athanasius, 226
Athena, 43, 44, 45, 46, 48, 52, 54, 59–60, 61, 64, 68, 69, 95, 110
Athenaeus, 209
Athens and the Athenians, 4, 6, 26, 34, 64, 68–70, 80, 86, 87, 92, 102–03, 106–10, 115, 117, 119, 122, 124, 125, 128–32, 137, 139, 149, 161, 169, 195–96, 206, 207, 209, 210, 211, 212, 218, 220–21, 225, 236, 246, 250, 254–55
Athos, Mount, 24
Athos peninsula, 244–45
Atlantis, 14
Atreus, 17
Attalus, 196
Atticus, Herodes, 225
Augustus Caesar (Octavian), 85, 220–21, 224
Aurelius, Marcus, 225, 226
Avars, 233
Ayrton, Michael, 257

Balkan wars, 259
Basil, 226
Bassae, 193
Bavarian dynasty, 251
Bellephon, 49
Bernini, Giovanni Lorenzo, 180
Birds, The (Aristophanes), 149–50
Blegen, Carl, 6, 14
Boccaccio, Giovanni, 236, 240
Boeotia, 93, 123
Bradford, Ernle, 63 n.
Briseis, 47, 51
Bronze Age, Greek, 13, 22–23, 84, 156
Bronze art objects, 162–65, 169–72
Bruni, Leonardo, 236
Brutus, 220
Bryant, William Cullen, 280
Bulgars, 233
Bury, J. B., 121
Butcher, S. H., 280, 282

Butler, Samuel, 32 n.
Byron, George Lord, 120, 249
Byzantine Church, 230
Byzantine Empire, 219–37, 238, 242
Byzantine Period, Greek, 86
Byzantium, 231

Cacoyannis, Michael, 256
Calendar, Greek, 199
Callas, Maria, 256
Callias, 203
Callicrates, 188
Calypso, 64, 74, 79, 80, 81
Cape Sounian, 184–85
Capital punishment, practice of, 207
Capodistrias, Count Ioannes, 250–51
Carthage, 110, 220
Cassandra, 15
Cassius, 220
Catherine II (the Great), 247
Center Union party, 263, 265–66
Cervantes, Miguel de, 75
Chalcondylas, Demetrius, 38
Chapman, George, 280
Charlemagne, 41
Charybdis, 79
Children in Greece, 208
Chios, xi, 34, 248
Christianity, 200, 214, 221, 222, 226, 227, 228–30
Church, Sir Richard, 249
Church Fathers, 135, 226
Churchill, Winston S., 261
Cicero, 103, 217
Circe, 59, 64, 74, 79
City-states, Greek, 86–88, 90–92, 97, 121, 129, 198; see also Athens; Sparta
Classical Period, Greek, 31, 37, 55, 85, 156, 157
Cleisthenes, 109
Clement, 226
Cleopatra, 85, 224
Climate of Greece, 3, 253
Clothing in Ancient Greece, 67
Clytemnestra, 15, 25, 61, 76
Cochrane, Thomas Lord, 249
Colonies, Greek, 96–97, 124
Colophon, 34
Constantine, 226, 228–29, 231, 235, 236
Constantine I, 259, 260
Constantine II, 259, 263, 266–67, 274

Constantine XI Palaeologus, 242
Constantinople, 38, 231–33, 238, 240, 241–42, 245, 260
Constantius, 228
Corfu, xi, 63, 185
Corinth and the Corinthians, 4, 87, 122, 128, 132, 184, 193, 220
Corsica, 63, 73, 81
Cortes, Hernando, 41
Cos, xi
Cowper, William, 280
Crete and the Cretans, 3, 4–11, 13, 20, 63, 79, 85, 162, 237, 246, 261
Critias, 211, 212
Croesus, 105–06
Crusades, the, 234, 235–36, 238, 242
Culture, Greek, 226–27
Cumae, 198
Cyclops, 74, 79
Cyrus the Great, 105, 106, 127
Cyprus, 260, 264, 272
Czechoslovakia, 275

Dante, Alighieri, 239, 240
Darius the Great, 118, 120, 121
Dark Age, Greek, 14, 85, 92, 96, 158, 162, 197
Da Vinci, Leonardo, 241
Delian League, 129–30, 187
Delos, xi, xii, 27, 129, 185–86
Delphi, 27–30, 193
Delphic oracle, 27–28, 30, 105
Demeter, 27, 45, 97
Demodokos, 78
Demos, Raphael, 256
Demosthenes, 39, 209, 215–16, 240
Diocletian, 228
Diogenes, 209, 217
Diomedes of Argos, 13, 39, 44–45, 48, 49, 51, 54
Dionysius I of Syracuse, 215
Dionysus, xi, 27, 28, 96, 98, 136–39, 143, 186, 252
Dogs in Ancient Greece, 65–66
Dorians, 14, 24, 26, 33, 40, 92, 96, 102, 110, 197
Doric mode, 111
Draco's laws, 104
Drama, Greek, 1, 20, 31 57, 71, 72, 88–89, 129, 134–55
Dromeus, 100

Dryden, John, 280, 282
Durrell, Lawrence, 257

Earth Mother, 9, 45, 92
Eastern Orthodox Church, 231, 237
Ecclesiastes, Book of, 223
Eden, Anthony, 261
Edrisi, 239
Education, Greek, 201, 202–06, 213
Egypt and the Egyptians, 63, 73, 86, 112, 198, 224–25
Eleazer, 225
Electra, 15, 88
Eleusinian Mysteries, 135–36, 221
Eleusis, 254
Elgin, Lord, 173, 191
El Greco, 243
Emigration from Greece, 255–56
Ephesus, 193
Epictetus, 222
Epicureanism, 223–24
Epicurus, 222–24; quoted, 238
Epidaurus, 27, 144, 145, 193
Eris, 46
Essay on Epic Poetry (Aristotle), 31
Ethos of Ancient Greece, 42–57
Etruscans, 5, 11, 161
Euclid, 87
Eumenides, The (Aeschylus), 153
Euripides, 1, 39, 47, 57 n., 71, 100, 138, 140, 146, 149, 154, 155, 208, 210, 282
Evans, Sir Arthur, 5–6, 14

Family life in Greece, 64, 89–90
Finley, M. I., 38, 110
Fitzgerald, Robert, 61, 64, 68, 74, 81, 280, 281, 282
Flaminius, 220
Florence, Council of (1439), 242
Florence and the Florentines, 236–37, 240–41
Food in Ancient Greece, 65, 253–54
France, 82, 233, 251, 270
Franks, 235, 236, 242
Frederick II, 239
French Revolution, 246, 247
Fresco painting, 7–8, 161–62
Freud, Sigmund, 72
Funeral games, 53–54
Furniture and furnishings, 66–67

Gela, 96
Gellius, Aulus, 34 n.
Genghis Khan, 241–42
Genoa, 237
Geography of Greece, 3, 63–64, 73, 253–54
George I of Greece, 251, 259
George II of Greece, 259, 261
George of Antioch, 239
Germanos, Archbishop, 248
Ghiberti, Lorenzo, 52
Glaucus, 49
Gods and goddesses, Greek, 8–10, 20, 26–30, 42, 44–47, 50, 51, 52, 55, 56, 58, 59–60, 61, 64, 69, 78, 90–91, 92–93, 95, 97–98, 134–39, 200, 221
Goethe, Johann Wolfgang von, 50
Grand Catalan Company, 236
Graves, Robert, 32 n., 257
Great Britain, 251, 260, 261, 262, 268, 270
Great Dionysia festival, 137, 138, 139, 140, 199, 221
Greek Civil War, 268
Greek life, realities of, 63–67, 73
Greek National Liberation Front, 261
Greek Orthodox Church, 231, 237, 243, 244
Greek War for Independence, 245, 247–50, 251
Gregory, St., 226
Grivas, General, 264
Gunther, John, 262

Hadas, Moses, 51, 141, 149
Hades, 50
Hadrian, 85, 183, 195, 225
Hagia Lavra monastery, 248
Halicarnassus, 125, 193
Hamilton, Edith, 222, 257, 282
Hannibal, 220
Harrison, Jane, 28
Hector, 47, 48, 49, 51, 52, 53, 55, 56, 57, 68, 69, 200
Helen, 42, 46–47, 49, 67, 71, 110, 114, 115
Heliaea, Athenian, 107
Hellas, 86, 96, 117, 128, 215
Hellenistic Period, Greek, 85, 156, 157
Hellespont, 121
Helots, 115–16
Hephaestus, 42, 47, 52, 78, 92, 95
Hera, 43, 44, 45, 46, 48
Heracleum, 5
Heraclitus, 200–01

Herculaneum, 161, 162
Hercules, 43
Hermes, 55, 59, 78
Herodotus, 15 n., 23, 37, 47, 87, 105, 109, 112, 118–21, 123, 125–28, 130, 149, 240
Heroic Age, Greek, 33
Hesiod, 39, 93–96, 103; quoted, 12
Hetairai, 208–09
Hippias, 99
Hippocrates, xi, 27
Historical Sketch of the Greek Revolution, 1828 (Howe), 249
History of Greece, chronology of, 84–86
Hitler, Adolf, 261
Holy Roman Empire, 239
Homer, xi, xv, 1, 3, 5, 7, 9, 10, 13, 15, 20, 23, 26, 28, 30, 42, 44, 48, 49, 50, 51, 52, 53, 54, 56, 63, 65, 72, 73, 74, 75, 78, 79, 82, 86, 93, 94, 102, 107, 110, 157, 198, 200, 201, 222, 225, 282; epics of, see Homeric epics, Iliad, Odyssey; history of, 39–41; texts of, 36–39
Homeric bards, 32–33, 34–36, 42
Homeric code, 82–83
Homeric epics, 31–41, 198, 225, 257; "authorized" version of, 68–72
Homosexuality, 52
Hooper, Finley, 47, 106
Hoplites, 124
Horace, 226; quoted, 219
Howe, Julia Ward, 249
Howe, Samuel Gridley, 249–50
Humanism, 197–218, 241
Huns, 232
Hunt, Leigh, 280

Ictinus, 188
Iliad (Homer), xv, 1, 4, 13, 15, 28, 31–41, 43, 44, 46, 47, 48, 49, 51, 52, 53, 55, 56, 57, 58, 59, 62, 63, 68, 69, 70, 71–72, 73, 77, 82, 109, 139, 159, 215, 280, 281; quoted, 10–11, 42, 199, 200
Industry in Greece, 254–55
Infanticide, practice of, 206–07
Inheritance from Greece, 1–2
Ionia and the Ionians, 26, 33, 73, 119, 120, 123, 210, 251
Ionian migration, 24–26
Iphigenia, 15, 72
Islam, 234, 243
Isocrates, 213, 215

Italy, 63, 73, 82, 86, 97, 219, 233
Ithaca, 4, 58, 59, 63, 76, 79

Janissaries, 243
Jason, 71, 159–60
Jerusalem, 236, 242
John, St., xii, xiii
Josephus, 224
Jowett, Benjamin, 282
Joyce, James, 75, 257
Julius Caesar, 220, 224
Justinian, 164 n., 213, 232–33

Kalamis, 179
Kallimachos, 179
Karamanlis, Constantine, 262
Kazan, Elia, 256
Kazantzakis, Nikos, 252, 256, 276–77
Keats, John, 159
Kemal (Atatürk), Mustafa, 260
Kennedy, Jacqueline, 256
Kings of Greece, chronological list of,
  258–59
Kitto, 199, 212
Knossos, 5–6, 10, 14, 22, 23, 31, 64
Kresilas, 179
Kublai Khan, 238

Laertes, 42, 59, 69
Lang, Andrew, 280, 282
Las Casas, Bartolomé de, 41
Lattimore, Richmond, 62, 77, 280, 281, 282
Lausanne Conference (1923), 260
Laws (Plato), 217
Leaf, Walter, 280
Leda, 42
Legal code of Solon, 103–05, 108
Leonidas, 121
Leontius, 231
Lesbos, 207
Libation Bearers, The (Aeschylus, 153
Libya, 63
Lindos, 185
Linear A script, 6–7
Linear B script, 6–7, 13, 14, 40, 197
Literature, Greek, xiii–xiv, 1, 31, 134–55,
  199, 232, 239
Logos, the, 202, 203, 212, 213, 227, 228
Lombards, 230, 233
Lotus Eaters, 74, 79

Louis of Bavaria, 251
Luctra, 116
Lyceum in Athens, the, 217
Lycurgus, 112–13, 114
Lyons, Sir Arthur, 268
Lysippus, 179

Macedonia, 15, 207
Magic, 58–59
Mahaffy, J. P., 205
Makarios, Archbishop, 237
Mallia, 10
Malta, 63
Marathon, 119, 120–21, 124
Marriage customs, 114–15, 207–08, 257
Mathematics, Greek, 198–99
Maxentius, 228
Medes, 119, 121
Medicine, Greek, 2, 27
Meditations (Aurelius), 225
Melos, 91
Menelaus, 13, 39, 42, 46, 47, 48, 71, 110
Mercouri, Melina, 256
Messina, straits of, xi
Metaxas, John, 261
Meteora area of Thessaly, 244
Michelangelo, 24, 180, 240–41
Middle class in Greece, 270–71
Milan, Edict of (313), 228
Miletus, 4, 26
Miller, Arthur, 141
Miller, Henry, 257
Minoans, 3, 4–11, 12, 13–14, 22, 24, 26, 84
Minos, 4, 6, 9, 22
Minotaur, the, 6, 9, 160
Mitropoulos, Dmitri, 256
Mohammed, 234
Mohammed II, 242
Mongols, 241
Monte Cassino monastery, 240
Montezuma, 41
Morosini, Francesco, 191
Morris, William, 280
Mosaics, Greek, 161
Moses, 135, 200
Moslems, 233–35, 239, 250
Mummius, Lucius, 220
Murray, A. T., 280
Music, Greek, 30, 146, 257
Mussolini, Benito, 261

Mycenae and the Mycenaeans, 4, 5, 6, 7, 12–22, 23, 24–26, 31, 39, 40, 41, 64, 73, 84, 85
Myers, Ernest, 280
Mykonos, xi, xii, 243
Myron, 179, 209
Mysticism, Oriental, xv

Naples, 96, 239
Napoleon I, 247
Napoleonic Wars, 246
Nationalism, 247
Nausicaa, 67, 74, 75, 76, 77
Nauplia, 237, 250
Neoplatonism, 227
Nero, 85, 165, 221
Nestor, 13, 39, 48, 51, 53
New Testament, 2, 226
New York Times, 275
Nicaea, Council of (318), 229–30
Nicene Creed, 229–30
Nicephorus II, 248 n.
Nicias, 132
Nikoas, 179 n.
Nikousios, Panayiotis, 246
Nobility, Greek, 43–44, 67
Normans, 233, 235, 236, 238, 239
North Atlantic Treaty Organization, 264

Octavian, *see* Augustus Caesar
Odyesseus (Ulysses), xi, 4, 13, 30, 36, 39, 42, 43–44, 45, 49, 50–51, 54, 73–82, 277; world of, 58–72
Odyssey (Homer), 1, 4, 5, 13, 15, 31–41, 42, 44, 46, 49, 50, 54, 58, 59, 60–65, 69, 70–72, 73–82, 109, 110, 122, 139, 159, 280, 281; *quoted,* 1, 73, 79, 80, 81, 82
Oedipus, 4, 20, 88
Oedipus at Colonus (Sophocles), 148
Oedipus trilogy (Sophocles), 149
Oedipus Tyrannus (Sophocles), 150
Old Testament, 225
Olympia, 99, 169, 191
Olympian Games, 2, 85, 99–101, 120, 199, 231
Olympus, Mount, 46, 62, 92, 253
Onassis, Aristotle, 256, 257
Oresteia (Aeschylus), 140, 150–54
Orestes, 15
Origen, 226

Orpheus, 27, 97, 200
Orphism, 200, 221
Ostrogoths, 232
Otho (Otto), 251, 259
Ottoman Empire, *see* Turks

Paestum, 96, 97
Page, Denys, 36
Painting, Greek, 160–62, 179 n.; *see also* Fresco painting
Paionios, 179
Palmer, George, 280
Palmer, Richard, 239
Pan, 51
Panathenaeic Festival, 69–70, 109
Pandora, 95
Pantahos, George, 256
Papadopoulos, George, 268
Papandreou, Andreas, 263–67, 269, 270, 273, 274–75
Papandreou, George, 261, 263–67, 269, 273–74
Papanicolaou, George, 256
Papas, Irene, 256
Papyrus, 198
Paris, 46–47, 48, 49, 56, 72, 114, 126
Parnassus, Mount, 30
Parrhasius, 162
Parry, Milman, 35
Patmos, xi–xii
Patroclus, 47, 51, 52, 53, 55, 56, 76
Paul, St., 222, 226
Paul I, 259, 262, 263
Pausanius, 14–15; 99, 145
Paxinou, Katina, 256
Peisistratus, 37, 38, 69, 108–09, 119, 139, 195
Pelasgians, 2–3, 12, 26
Peleus, 42
Peloponnesian League, 129
Peloponnesian War, 115, 130–33, 209–11
Penelope, 58, 59, 61, 64, 66–67, 69, 71, 74, 76, 77
Pentelicus, Mount, 194–95, 244
Pergamum, 194
Pericles, 130, 131–32, 177, 187, 207, 209; *quoted,* 118
Persephone, 27, 97
Persia and the Persians, 4, 80, 86, 105, 118–24, 125, 127–28, 133, 149, 169, 210, 233

Persians, The (Aeschylus), 149
Persian War, 118–28
Peter the Hermit, 235
Petrarch, Francesco, 236, 240
Phaecia and the Phaecians, 75, 79, 80, 122
Phaistos, 10
Phallic symbols, 9, 20
Phanariots, Greek, 245–46, 247
Phemios, 77
Phidias, 70, 129, 157, 164, 169, 173, 177, 188
Philip of Macedonia, 28, 86, 133, 215, 216, 221
Philip II of Spain, 243
Philip V of Macedonia, 220
Philo, 224
Philosophy, Greek, xvii, 2, 87, 199, 200–02, 214, 216–18, 221–24, 226, 227–28, 231
Phoenicians, 7, 64, 122–23, 197
Phryne of Athens, 209
Physical training, 98–101, 204–05
Piraeus, 171, 255
Pisa, 240
Pisano, Niccolò, 240
Plataea, 115, 116, 119, 121, 123, 124
Plato, xv, 4, 37, 38, 39, 68, 87, 92, 96, 112, 114, 117, 202, 203–04, 206, 207, 212, 213–14, 215, 216, 217–18, 221, 233, 234, 276; *quoted,* 84, 102, 203–04
Pliny, 180
Plotinus, 227–28
Plutarch, 99, 112, 115, 188; *quoted,* 113, 118
Poems from the Greek Anthology, xiii
Poetics (Aristotle), 148
Polo brothers, 238
Polybius, 206–07, 220, 240
Polycarp, 226
Polycleitus, 168, 179; *quoted,* 156
Polycleitus the Younger, 145
Polyphemus, 79, 81
Pompeii, 161
Pompey, 220
Pope, Alexander, 280
Population of Greece, 255
Poseidon, 61, 74, 82
Pottery, Greek, 157–60
Praxiteles, 137, 157, 171, 177–79, 183, 209, 231
Priam, 15, 55, 56, 57
Private property in Greece, 89

Prometheus, 95
Protagoras, 202; *quoted,* 197
Protagoras (Plato), 203
Proteus, 47
Ptolemy, 224
Ptolemy II, 225
Pylos, 6, 13, 14, 31, 48, 63, 84
Pyrrhus of Epirus, 219
Pythagoras, 179; *quoted,* 58
Pythian Games, 169
Python, 27

Racine, Jean Baptiste, 155
Ravenna, 233
Recent years in Greece, 258–77
Rees, Ennis, 44, 45, 47, 48, 49, 50, 53, 280, 281, 282
Religion, Greek, 8–10, 20, 26–30, 44–47, 88–89, 221–22, 231, 243
Renaissance, the, 2, 238–52
Republic (Plato), 213, 221
Rexroth, Kenneth, xiii, 30 n.
Rhodes, xi, 34, 165, 180, 185, 260
Ridgeway, Sir William, 40
Rieu, E. V., 280
Roche, Paul, 150, 151, 152, 282
Roland, 41
Roman Catholic Church, 230, 239
Roman Greece, 219–37
Roman Period, Greek, 85–86
Roman Way, The (Hamilton), 222
Rome and the Romans, 43, 97, 86, 109, 161, 165, 180, 183, 196, 198, 219–21, 223, 226, 231, 232, 233
Russia, 247, 251, 264, 275
Russian Orthodox Church, 247

Sacred League of Greek Officers, 266
Salamis, 34, 91, 121, 122, 123, 124
Salonika, 244
Santorini (Thera), xi, 13, 14
Sappho, xiv, 160
Saracens, 235
Schliemann, Heinrich, 5, 15, 18, 22, 31, 39
Scott, Michael, 239
Sculpture, Greek, 2, 24, 129, 137, 157, 162–83
Scylla, 74, 79
Seareach, 78
Second Macedonian War, 220

Seferis, George, 256
Senate, Athenian, 106
Septuagint, the, 225
Sex in Greece, 64–65, 114, 257
Shakespeare, William, 155
Sicily, 4, 63, 73, 82, 96, 128, 132, 210, 215, 219, 239
Simonides, 109, 121
Sirens, 74, 79
Skopas, 179
Skouras, Spyros, 256
Slavery in Ancient Greece, 67, 87, 103, 206, 207, 220
Slavs, 233
Smyrna, 34
Socrates, xv, 4, 202, 207, 209–10, 211–12, 216–17
Soldier, the Greek, 124–25
Solon, 103–06, 107, 109
Song of Roland, The, 41
Sophists, 202
Sophocles, 1, 92, 140, 144, 146, 148, 149, 154, 155, 210, 240, 282; quoted, 134
Spain, 5, 23, 73, 82, 230, 233, 234, 243
Sparta and the Spartans, 4, 26, 63, 86, 87, 107, 110–17, 119, 122, 123, 124, 126, 128, 129, 130–33, 204, 206, 209, 210
Stele or stone relief, 181, 182
Stoicism, 221, 222, 226, 227
Strongylion, 179
Sulla, 220
Sybaris, 96, 114
Symposium (Xenophon), 203
Syracuse, 4, 96, 210, 219

Taranto, 96
Telemachus, 58, 59, 60, 63, 64, 67, 68, 72, 77, 110
Tennyson, Alfred Lord, 76, 280
Terpander, 111
Thasos, xi, 185
Thebes, 4, 6, 13, 64, 69, 87, 128, 132, 133
Themistocles, 121, 122, 128
Theodosius, 231–32
Theogony (Hesiod), 12, 94
Thermopylae, 116, 121, 124
Thersites, 43–44
Theseus, 6, 160
Thespis, 139, 144
Thetis, 42

Third Macedonian War, 220
Thrace, 15 n., 138
Thucydides, 26, 102, 113, 115, 130, 132, 149, 207, 240
Tiryns, 13, 14, 18, 31, 84
Titian, 243
Translations, concerning, 279–82
Trelawney, E. J., 249
Trikoupes, Charilaos, 251
Trojan cycle, the, 34
Trojan War, 13, 23, 25, 31, 40–41, 43, 46–57, 72, 73, 78, 115
Troy and the Trojans, 4, 5, 13, 15, 31, 39, 40, 41, 43, 46, 47, 50, 56, 57, 59, 63, 71, 72
Truman, Harry S., 262, 275
Turkish occupation of Greece, 242–48
Turks, 235, 236, 237, 238, 240, 241, 242, 249, 260, 264, 272
Tyrtaeus, 111

United States of America, 262, 263, 268–69, 270, 275–76
Urban II, Pope, 235

Vandals, 230
Vaphio, 20, 21
Vassilikos, Vassilis, quoted, 253
Venice and the Venetians, 236, 237, 238, 243, 246
Venizelos, Eleutherios, 258, 260
Ventris, Michael, 7
Vergil, 43, 226
Villoison, Jean, 38
Visigoths, 230

Warner, Rex, 281, 282
Weil, Simone, 56
Wellington, Duke of, 248
William George of Denmark, 251
Wolfe, Thomas, 75
Women, status of, 207
Woodhouse, C. M., 257
Works and Days (Hesiod), 93, 94
World War I, 259, 260
World War II, 259

Xenophon, 15 n., 100, 203
Xerxes, 118, 121, 122, 123, 125, 126, 128

Yiaros, 267
Ypsilanti, Alexander, 247
Ypsilanti, Alexander (son of Constantine), 247–48
Ypsilanti, Constantine, 247
Ypsilanti, Demetrius, 247

Zeno, 221, 222
Zenodotus, 225
Zeus, 8, 9, 42, 43, 45, 55, 60, 62, 69, 74, 94, 95
Zeuxis, 161–62
Zonas, *quoted,* xi

70 71 72 73 10 9 8 7 6 5 4 3 2 1